Prosperity and Unemployment

Prosperity and Unemployment

Edited by **ROBERT AARON GORDON**

and **MARGARET S. GORDON**

One of a series of books from the
Research Program on Unemployment

Institute of Industrial Relations
University of California, Berkeley

JOHN WILEY & SONS, INC.

NEW YORK   LONDON   SYDNEY

Preface

In 1962 a four-year program of research and conferences on the subject of unemployment and the American economy was initiated at the University of California. The Ford Foundation made a generous grant to the Institute of Industrial Relations on the Berkeley campus to support this work. We have had the privilege of serving as co-directors of this research program since it was initiated.[1]

Our program grew out of widespread and deep concern over the persisting high level of unemployment in the United States, a concern that has not disappeared even with the gratifying acceleration in the growth of employment and output during the last four years or more. It was our hope to stimulate research on the underlying forces at work which were affecting both the demand for and the supply of American workers—not merely in the aggregate but also along all of the significant dimensions of what is perhaps the most heterogeneous labor force of any industrialized nation. Through such research and the convening of groups of specialists to exchange views on various facets of the unemployment problem we hoped to make some contribution to the formulation of policies, both public and private, that would help to move us closer to the goal of full employment.

To these ends we have been conducting a coordinated group of studies which we hope will help us to understand more fully

[1] Arthur M. Ross is now on leave from the University of California to serve as U. S. Commissioner of Labor Statistics.

what has been and is happening and at the same time will furnish new and better guidelines for the development of appropriate policies. The project also includes closely related studies designed to clarify our employment goals and to facilitate more accurate prediction of labor-market trends in the next decade or so. The studies are being conducted by economists and sociologists at Berkeley, by doctoral candidates, and by several economists in eastern universities who have become associated with the project.

An important element in our program is an annual conference on unemployment which brings together key people involved in research and in the formulation and administration of policy. The first of these conferences, in 1963, resulted in the book *Unemployment and the American Economy.* The second, a year later, led to the publication of a substantial collection of research papers under the title *Employment Policy and the Labor Market.* The present book contains the papers and formal comments presented at the third annual conference, held in New York in June 1965.

It seemed to us that a useful purpose would be served at this time if a group of experts were to gather to review in detail the behavior of aggregate demand, employment, unemployment, and the labor force during the last several years of uninterrupted expansion. This book is the result. We believe that it makes a significant contribution to our understanding of the forces which have been determining the course of employment and unemployment in the United States in recent years. Further, we believe the articles and comments included here offer valuable suggestions for the kinds of policies needed in the years ahead to achieve and maintain the goal of full employment.

We are glad to acknowledge our indebtedness to Mrs. Marcia Schramm, until recently Secretary of the Research Program on Unemployment, for her invaluable assistance in organizing the 1965 conference. Thanks are due also to Judy Cowman, Joan Lewis, Barbara Palmer, Ruth Parker, and Günter Wittich for their help in getting the manuscript ready for publication.

Berkeley California　　　　　　　　　　　　R. A. GORDON
February 1966　　　　　　　　　　　　　　ARTHUR M. ROSS

Contents

Chapter 1   **Introduction**   **1**
The Editors

PART I   **THE CURRENT BUSINESS EXPANSION**

Chapter 2   **The Current Business Expansion in Perspective**   **15**
R. A. Gordon, *University of California,*
Berkeley

Discussion
Otto Eckstein, Member, *Council of Economic*
Advisers   **48**
Martin R. Gainsbrugh, *National Industrial*
Conference Board   **57**
Joseph A. Pechman, *The Brookings Institution*   **64**

PART II   **THE RESPONSE OF LABOR SUPPLY TO THE**
DEMAND FOR LABOR

Chapter 3   **Labor-Force Participation and Unemployment:**
A Review of Recent Evidence   **73**
Jacob Mincer, *Columbia University and*
National Bureau of Economic Research

Discussion

W. G. Bowen, *Princeton University,* and
   T. A. Finegan, *Vanderbilt University*   **113**
Frank C. Pierson, *Swarthmore College*   **122**
Richard A. Easterlin, *University of
   Pennsylvania*   **126**

**PART III   THE CHANGING LEVEL AND PATTERN
            OF EMPLOYMENT**

Chapter 4   The Behavior of Employment, 1961–1965   137
            Margaret S. Gordon, *University of California,
            Berkeley*

            Discussion

            Solomon Fabricant, *New York University and
               National Bureau of Economic Research*   **177**
            Harold Goldstein, *U. S. Bureau of Labor
               Statistics*   **180**
            Stanley Lebergott, *Wesleyan University*   **184**

PART IV   THE PATTERN OF UNEMPLOYMENT

**Chapter 5   Lessons from the Pattern of Unemployment in
            the Last Five Years   191**
            Gertrude Bancroft, *U. S. Bureau of Labor
            Statistics*

**Chapter 6   The Composition of Unemployment and Public
            Policy   227**
            Edward D. Kalachek, *Washington University*

            Discussion

            Charles C. Killingsworth, *Michigan State
               University*   **246**
            Lester C. Thurow, *Council of Economic
               Advisors*   **256**

PART V   UNEMPLOYMENT AND THE STRUCTURE OF WAGES

Chapter 7   Wage Levels and Differentials   265
George H. Hildebrand, *Cornell University* and
George E. Delehanty, *Northwestern
University*

Discussion
H. M. Douty, *U. S. Bureau of Labor Statistics*   **302**
M. W. Reder, *Stanford University*   **308**
Lloyd Ulman, *University of California,
Berkeley*   **314**

PART VI   AN OVERVIEW

**Chapter 8   Economic Expansion and Persisting
Unemployment: An Overview   327**
Albert Rees, *University of Chicago*

Index   349

Prosperity and Unemployment

CHAPTER 1

Introduction

Excessive unemployment in the face of unprecedented prosperity: this is the troubling theme with which this book is concerned.

American aspirations to keep unemployment at a low level are less ambitious than those of the Western European countries. Since the adoption of the Employment Act of 1946, "full employment" has been interpreted in official circles as meaning a national unemployment rate of about 4 per cent,[1] although since 1962 this figure has been labeled only an "interim target" by the Council of Economic Advisers. Yet for most of a decade now we have failed by a wide margin to achieve this moderate goal. In terms of annual averages, the unemployment rate has not been below 5 per cent since 1957, although the annual average is virtually certain to fall below this figure in 1965. The seasonally adjusted rate of 4.8 per cent achieved in the first six months of 1965 was the lowest semiannual average since the second half of 1957.

During this time the American economy has been enjoying a period of unprecedented prosperity. The current business upswing is now approaching the end of its fifth year—a period of uninterrupted expansion longer than we have ever experienced in peacetime, certainly for more than a century. The rise in output and employment began with the end of the very mild recession of 1960–1961; this mildest of the postwar recessions meant that there was little lost ground to be recovered first. The expansion since then has been a vigorous one, with new vigor being added by the highly successful tax cut in 1964.

Yet the national unemployment rate has remained uncomfortably high. Moreover, unemployment is not merely uncomfortably but tragically high in some parts of the labor force, notably young people and nonwhites.

Why have we had so much difficulty in reducing unemployment to a satisfactorily low level; and why did unemployment rates of 5 per cent or more persist for so long?

These questions have generated a debate which is still going on. More important, these and related questions have led to a good deal of new, useful research which has added significantly to our understanding of the recent behavior of the American economy, including the various parts of the national labor market. It is fair to say that we have made considerable progress during the last five years in narrowing the area of disagreement on what has been happening—and why—and what needs to be done.

The papers and commentary in this book, the results of a conference held in New York in June 1965, provide a valuable, although incomplete, inventory of what we now think we know about the reasons for the continued high level of unemployment in the United States in the last five years.

The Needed Rate of Growth

One thing that stands out immediately is how fast we must run today just to stand still. Apparently the national output will have to grow during the rest of the 1960's at an average annual rate of 4 per cent or better just to prevent unemployment from rising further. The needed rate of growth in the 1950's, the result of a less rapid increase in the labor force than is now occurring, was probably only around 3.5 per cent. However, from 1953 to 1960 Gross National Product in constant prices grew only at a rate of about 2.5 per cent—and the unemployment rate climbed from a low of 2.9 per cent in 1953 to 5.6 per cent in 1960. (The peak of the cyclical upswing out of the 1957–1958 recession occurred in June 1960.)

R. A. Gordon's chapter seeks to explain why the economy grew so slowly during the period 1953–1960. Thus, when the present expansion began, what the economy had to recover from was not the mild cyclical dip of 1960–1961 but more than half a decade of retarded growth dating back to the end of the Korean War.

The American economy expanded rapidly enough after 1961 to permit some reduction in the over–all unemployment rate. But, as we have seen, the expansion in output and employment left us for too long a time short of our goal of full employment. The uneven course of the rise in employment and decline in unemployment is traced out in the chapters by Mrs. Gordon and Miss Bancroft and is also discussed by Eckstein.

Could we have expanded more rapidly after 1960 without untoward consequences in the form of unacceptable price increases or other maladjustments that might by now have brought on another recession? And what are the chances of bringing the unemployment rate down to 4 per cent or less during the next two or three years? To do so implies further acceleration in the expansion of aggregate demand and continued success in avoiding another recession.

Gordon gives somewhat pessimistic answers to these questions. This pessimism is obviously not shared by Eckstein or Gainsbrugh in their discussions of his chapter. Pechman argues that we could have had full employment before this—and could achieve it in the next few years—if we were prepared to make sufficiently vigorous use of fiscal policy and avoid the monetary restraints that have been imposed on some previous cyclical expansions.

Deficiency of Aggregate Demand or Structural Changes?

Is the high level of unemployment since the late fifties to be attributed primarily to a deficiency of aggregate demand or to "structural" changes which make a growing fraction of the labor force unsuited for the jobs available? The "structural" argument emphasizes technological change (particularly of the sort implied by the term "automation"), the increasing emphasis on education and training in industrial and commercial employment, and the decline in the importance of blue-collar jobs. An implication of the structural argument is that expanding aggregate demand will not bring about a significant reduction in unemployment; that it is likely merely to create bottlenecks in occupations and industries in which qualified workers are already in short supply without significantly reducing unemployment among the poorly educated and relatively unskilled workers who have the highest unemployment rates. This general position is stated by Killingsworth in his discussion in this book.

The chapters presented here suggest that this debate on the relative importance of deficient aggregate demand and of structural changes in the composition of the demand for labor is on its way to being resolved. The chapters and discussions in this book as well as the general discussion at the conference give substantial confirmation to the position that the chief problem has been the failure of aggregate demand to rise rapidly enough. There is almost complete agreement that what we call automation has not been a significant factor in keeping unemployment at a high level. This theme runs through the chapters by Mrs. Gordon, Miss Bancroft, and Kalachek. It is stated strongly by Rees, who comes to the conclusion that "one can say with confidence that automation and the structure of demand have not been major forces in the unemployment experience of the last four years." The same theme runs through the comments of many of the discussants, with the important exception of Charles Killingsworth.

To say that structural changes in the composition of the demand for labor are not an important reason for the high level of unemployment in recent years is not to deny that we now have, and always have had, structural imbalances in the relation between demand and supply for particular kinds of labor. The differential unemployment rates cited by Miss Bancroft are eloquent testimony to the difficulties experienced by teenagers, those in their early twenties, nonwhites, and the least skilled in finding jobs. But with one important exception there is little evidence that changes in the composition of the demand for labor have played an important role in explaining the rise in unemployment rates for these groups relative to the national rate. The exception results from the marked decline in agricultural employment. For a detailed analysis of the changing volume and pattern of employment during the current and earlier postwar upswings, the reader is referred to the chapter by Mrs. Gordon and to the discussion by Fabricant, Goldstein, and Lebergott.

However, as Miss Bancroft's chapter brings out, there have been significant structural changes on the *supply* side of the labor market. This theme is repeated by Eckstein and is taken up again in Rees' concluding essay. The changes in the composition of supply have been of several kinds. First, there is the sharp increase in the supply of teenagers entering the labor market. Second, the share of the labor force composed of women is continuing to increase. And third, the particularly sharp decline in agricultural employment in the early stages of the present upswing was an important factor not only in holding back the over-all increase in employment but in releasing supplies of workers from agriculture. In an environment of declining employment opportunities in agriculture and of improving urban job opportunities, both push and pull factors encouraged accelerated migration from farm to city and the resulting augmentation of the urban labor supply. This has been particularly true of the nonwhite labor force. Nonwhite migrants tend to have little education or marketable skills, and, as Rees points out in his concluding paper, "hidden" unemployment on the farm is converted into open unemployment in the city.

Lester Thurow, in his prepared discussion, takes a more optimistic view of the problem of youth unemployment than Miss Bancroft does. He points out that (a) the growth in the teenage labor supply will decelerate sharply after 1966, (b) youth employment is highly sensitive to increases in total employment, and (c) a significant part of the high unemployment rates among young people reflects the high mobility which is part of the process of "getting ahead" and contributes to the flexibility of adjustment which a dynamic world requires of the labor force.

As Miss Bancroft and Mincer both point out, the fact that the national unemployment rate is higher today than in the mid-1950's results almost entirely from higher unemployment rates among secondary workers—youth and women—who move

in and out of the labor force. The same general point is emphasized by other contributors. Kalachek argues, however, that even
this new "structural" element is largely explained by the failure
of aggregate demand to rise rapidly enough. He explains how
the composition of unemployment depends to a significant degree on the time–path of employment and unemployment in the
past. A 5.5 per cent unemployment rate reached at the bottom
of a short recession will reflect substantial layoffs of primary
workers during the period of declining output. But if roughly
the same unemployment rate is maintained for a relatively long
period of moderate expansion in output, which was substantially
the case during 1962–1965, the pool of unemployed will come
to be increasingly composed of youth and women—i.e., of those
who acquire the status of unemployed through voluntary quits
or new entry into the labor force. Kalachek is inclined to place
more weight on this set of factors than on changes in the composition of labor supply. In the remainder of his paper, Kalachek
not only argues for the strong use of monetary-fiscal policy, but
takes a skeptical view of the effectiveness of labor-market policy—a view not shared by the majority of conference participants.

Killingsworth, although badly outnumbered at the conference,
skillfully defends his version of the "structuralist" position. He
particularly emphasizes the plight of the poorly educated, especially when account is taken of the decline in their labor-force
participation rates.

The Sensitivity of Labor-Force Participation

A vigorous debate has gone on during the last few years as
to how sensitive the size of the labor force has become to
changes in employment conditions. If a rise in employment directly stimulates an increase in labor-force participation rates,
the increase in the demand for labor may be in good part offset
by an automatic increase in supply, so that unemployment declines relatively little.

A number of recent studies mentioned in Jacob Mincer's chapter have concluded that labor-force participation rates—except
those for men in the prime working-age groups—have become
very sensitive to changes in the level of unemployment. This

has generated considerable argument about two related aspects of the current situation. First, how much "hidden unemployment" exists among people who do not report themselves as looking for work but would actively enter the labor market if they thought jobs were available? Second, if attempts are made to speed up the increase in aggregate demand, how much of this increase will be absorbed by a rise in labor-force participation rates without consequent reduction in unemployment? Some fairly pessimistic answers to this second question have been offered in the last few years.

Mincer's chapter makes a significant contribution toward the clearing up of these issues. There *has* been a trend toward increased responsiveness of the labor supply to employment conditions, primarily because of the growth of the female labor force and the lessened attachment to the labor force of youth and older workers; but Mincer presents convincing evidence that labor-force participation is less sensitive cyclically than some recent studies seem to show. Easterlin adds some useful historical perspective on the sources of growth in the labor supply over the successive decades in this century, and suggests that during the remainder of the 1960's the labor force will grow less rapidly than is generally assumed.

Mincer concludes, as have a number of others, that there is a substantial amount of hidden unemployment today. His cautions regarding the undiscriminating addition of such hidden unemployment to reported unemployment are well taken, although, as Bowen and Finegan suggest in their discussion, he may be overemphasizing the differences, from the point of view of both policy and behavior, between these two groups. Pierson, more than the others, emphasizes the need for specific policies to deal with disguised unemployment.

Another striking aspect of Mincer's paper is his examination of the possible effects of changes in social-security benefits and in minimum wages. Liberalization of social-security provisions has contributed to the downward trend in participation rates among older people—and also to an increase in part-time and intermittent work at the expense of full-time work among men in the 65-and-over age group. At the other end of the age distribution, increases in minimum wages and extension of coverage seem to have exerted significant downward pressure on the labor-force participation of teenagers not in school. This is an aspect of the school dropout problem to which more attention clearly needs to be given.

Changes in the Structure of Wages

We still know far too little about the relation between the structure of wages, on one hand, and the pattern and level of unemployment, on the other. As Douty says in his discussion of the Hildebrand-Delehanty chapter, "it is indeed extraordinary that so little attention has been devoted to employment barriers that may exist in the structure of wages." The chapter by Hildebrand and Delehanty is a welcome contribution to this difficult subject. So are the additional evidence cited by Ulman and the findings by Mincer and Rees on the employment effects of the minimum wage.

Hildebrand and Delehanty begin with the relatively high unemployment rates among the unskilled and the inexperienced. These high unemployment rates imply that the supply of such workers is in excess of demand at prevailing wage rates. They then seek to determine if market forces have been tending to widen wage differentials between the skilled and unskilled, making the unskilled more attractive to employers. Their conclusion is that, generally, "relative spreads between high and low-wage occupations and high and low-wage industries have not been widening to the extent one might expect, given the persistence of excess supplies of unskilled and inexperienced labor in this period." On the whole, the discussants agreed with these findings, while raising questions regarding the underlying factors at work and the policy implications that should be drawn. Thus, Reder challenges the authors on the extent to which strong unions have in fact influenced these wage differentials.

One of the policy implications raised by Hildebrand and Delehanty is the possible need for a multiple federal minimum wage. We have already noted that Mincer and Rees offer evidence that past increases in the federal minimum wage unfavorably affected employment opportunities in the low-wage sectors of the economy that were covered. In the general discussion at the conference considerable support was expressed for a differential minimum-wage structure that might stimulate the employment of young entrants into the labor force, and thus possibly contribute to a reduction in the very high unemployment rates among teenagers. A thoughtful demurrer is offered by Ulman, who proposes, instead of differential minimum wages, "a policy of public spending where projects can be tailored to the capabilities of the unemployed."

Policy Implications

What are the major policy implications that emerge from these chapters? The most important is the most obvious one: the need to maintain an adequate level of aggregate demand. In his emphasis on this need, Rees reflects the views of the other authors and discussants as well as of economists generally. At the same time, it is well to remember Fabricant's warning (fully documented in Mrs. Gordon's paper) that it is not an easy matter to predict precisely the employment effects of policies aimed at stimulating aggregate demand.

The crucial role of fiscal policy in maintaining the level of demand is emphasized by various contributors. The success of the 1964 tax cut is generally recognized. As Rees puts it, "it is clear that if the amount of the tax reduction was not correct, it erred on the side of being too small rather than too large."

Several of the authors express the hope that further use of fiscal policy will be weighted more heavily in the direction of increased government expenditures than it has been under the Johnson Administration. Needs for increased expenditure programs are suggested: job creation programs for youth and for the unskilled, the liberalization of income-maintenance programs, further efforts to improve the quality of education available to the underprivileged, the improvement of urban transportation to increase the local mobility of workers, and other measures. One of the strongest statements on the need for large increases in expenditure to expand job creation and rehabilitation programs is made by Killingsworth. (As this is being written, it appears that in the near future the largest increase in federal spending on goods and services is likely to come in the defense sector.)

On the side of taxes, Rees recommends raising the tax base

for unemployment insurance and possibly also for OASDI. He urges no further increases in the already high withholding rates on the first $3,000 or $5,000 of annual earnings on the ground that they discourage hiring additional workers to meet augmented labor demands and encourage employers to resort, instead, to increasing hours of work.

In the field of manpower policy, Rees cautions against too rapid expansion of our burgeoning training programs. "A major contribution of the manpower program has been not its contribution to employment in the present expansion, but the establishment of machinery that will be valuable in the long run." Several of the other contributors—for example, Harold Goldstein—also caution against expecting too much in the short-run from our manpower training programs. But few would quarrel with Rees when he says: "Probably the most important manpower policy of all is one whose effect on employment still lies entirely in the future: the recently enacted federal aid to elementary and secondary education in low-income areas."

Among other policy suggestions to be found in these chapters and in the discussion at the Conference are tax incentives to business to stimulate special training programs for young entrants into the labor force; reforms in vocational education, including more effective linking of high school education with part-time on-the-job training; and some form of general income-supplementation for low-wage workers.

Prospects for Further Progress

It has not been easy, but progress has been made in the last two years in bringing down the national rate of unemployment. For men 25 and over, including blue-collar workers and the semi-skilled, unemployment rates in mid–1965 were back to about the level of 1957. However, compared to 1957, the relative position of youth and of women had deteriorated. As we noted earlier, there have been "structural" changes in the pattern of unemployment, but they have originated primarily on the supply rather than the demand side of the labor market.

It is still our national objective to bring the over-all unemployment rate down to 4 per cent or less and at the same time improve the position particularly of those groups with the highest unemployment rates—nonwhites, youth, and generally those with the least skill and education. What are the prospects in the months ahead, and can we succeed without undue cost in terms of other economic goals such as reasonable price stability and improvement in our balance-of-payments situation?

Here, it seems to us, a note of caution emerges. The change in the age-sex composition of the labor force that has been occurring means that the specific age-sex unemployment rates that would have yielded an over-all rate of 4 per cent a decade ago would give a national figure of about 4.2 per cent today. And, given the sensitivity of their labor-force participation rates that has been demonstrated, it will not be easy to drive down unemployment rates for the younger age groups and for women. Thus far, we have had only limited success in reducing the tragic differential between nonwhite and white unemployment rates, although certainly the national effort now being made will have some success in the years ahead.

At this point we are reminded that, under the pressure of a *sufficiently rapid* expansion in aggregate demand, these persisting differentials in unemployment rates can be reduced, and large additions to the labor supply can be absorbed. This is true, as the war and early postwar years—including the Korean period—demonstrated. But to say this is to raise other troublesome questions.

If, through appropriate government policies and with adequate incentives to private spending, we raise aggregate demand enough to bring the differentially high unemployment rates sufficiently down so that the over-all rate is 4 per cent or less, what price may we have to pay in wage and price inflation, and what will be the effects on the balance-of-payments?

It is clear that various participants in the conference were quite prepared to incur some cost, in terms of accelerated increases in prices and wages, to bring the over-all unemployment rate down to 4 per cent or less; and some of them clearly also feel that an unchanging gold value of the dollar is too high a price to pay for excessive unemployment. The debate on how we are to reconcile our partially conflicting goals will not end soon.

Coming back to an issue that arose at the first session of the conference, what dangers may lie ahead in the form of another recession if we press too hard on aggregate demand—and possibly even if we do not?

The goal of full employment clearly carries more meaning to Americans today than it did 20 years ago when the Employment Act became law. Because of this increased sensitivity, we have made encouraging progress in recovering from the setback we experienced after 1957. But the encouraging progress of the last two years should not blind us to the problems that still lie ahead. To the participants in this conference, full employment in terms of a national unemployment rate of 4 per cent or less is still a goal toward which we should strive. To be aware of the difficulties that may lie in the way of achieving it is to increase the chances that the goal will be reached, without too long a delay or excessive cost.

NOTES

1. As early as 1947, one can find official statements suggesting that the goal of full employment, taken by itself, should be interpreted as implying a national unemployment rate within a moderate range around 4 per cent. But when other goals were also taken into account, the attempt to reconcile partially conflicting objectives did not always yield the same unemployment rate as an immediate policy goal. Cf. R. A. Gordon, "Full Employment as a Policy Goal," in A. M. Ross, editor, *Employment Policy and the Labor Market* (Berkeley: University of California Press, 1965), pp. 45–47.

PART I

THE CURRENT BUSINESS EXPANSION

CHAPTER 2

The Current Business Expansion in Perspective[1]

BY R. A. GORDON

Economic activity in the United States has been expanding virtually without interruption since February 1961. As has been widely advertised, this expansion has become the longest peacetime cyclical upswing in more than a century.[2] In addition to its unusual duration, the present business upswing has been notable for at least two other features.

1. Although output has been expanding for more than four years and the preceding recession was both brief and mild, unemployment has remained at an unsatisfactorily high level. The unemployment rate did not fall below 5 per cent until November 1964, and it remained in the range of 4.6 to 5 per cent during the first six months of 1965.[3]

2. The upswing has been unusually steady and moderate. Although the rate of expansion compares favorably with that of past increases, prices have been exceptionally stable, inventory accumulation has been kept at a minimum, profit margins have

been well maintained, few supply bottlenecks have developed, the supply of money and credit has continued to expand at a steady rate, and, with perhaps a few exceptions, there has been little evidence of the exaggerated short-term expectations a prolonged boom usually engenders.

These features of the current upswing raise two questions. First, why have we not been able to achieve a closer approximation to full employment after four and a half years of steady expansion? Second, would an upswing rapid enough to have brought the unemployment rate down to 4 per cent have been undesirable for other reasons—either because it would have brought about an unacceptable rise in prices or because it would have set in motion forces that by now would have led to another recession? This last question is not asked as often as it should be.

In reviewing the course of the present rise, I shall, among other things, try to marshal the evidence I think is most relevant in seeking to arrive at answers to these questions. This is not to suggest, however, that clear and unambiguous answers will emerge from this evidence.

An Over-all View

Let us gain some perspective by looking first at Table 1, which compares the present business cycle with the several that preceded it. We have already noted that the pace of the current upswing has been relatively moderate. Table 1 suggests that the rate of advance has been slower than during the 1949–1953 or 1958–1960 expansion, although more rapid than that during 1954–1957. However, the 1960–1961 recession was one of the mildest on record, whereas the total amount and average rate of decline in 1957–1958 were the most severe of any of the postwar recessions. If we compare average rates of change in GNP between cyclical peaks, thus combining each cyclical expansion with the preceding recession, we see that the most recent period, 1960–1965, gives a very good account of itself. The average annual rate of growth in GNP since the 1960 cyclical peak is 4 per cent, much more than during the interpeak intervals 1953–1957 or 1957–1960, although considerably less than during

TABLE 1. Real GNP and Its Cyclical Changes

Quarter of Peak or Trough[a]	GNP[c] (1954 prices)	Number of Quarters	Per Cent Change in Real GNP		
			Total	Average Per Quarter[b]	Annual Rate[b]
			Peak to Peak		
P 1948-IV	297.3	18	25.5	1.3	5.2
P 1953-II	373.2	17	10.1	0.6	2.3
P 1957-III	411.0	11	7.6	0.7	2.7
P 1960-II	442.1	19	20.4	1.0	4.0
1965-I	532.2				
			Trough to Peak		
T 1949-II	290.3	16	28.6	1.6	6.5
P 1953-II	373.2				
T 1954-II	359.5	13	14.3	1.0	4.2
P 1957-III	411.0				
T 1958-I	393.0	9	12.5	1.3	5.4
P 1960-II	442.1				
T 1961-I	434.2	16	22.6	1.3	5.2
1965-I	532.2				
			Peak to Trough		
P 1948-IV	297.3	2	−2.4	−1.2	
T 1949-II	290.3				
P 1953-II	373.2	4	−3.7	−0.9	
T 1954-II	359.5				
P 1957-III	411.0	2	−4.4	−2.2	
T 1958-I	393.0				
P 1960-II	442.1	3	−1.8	−0.6	
T 1961-I	434.2				
			Entire Period		
P 1948-IV	297.3	65	79.0	0.9	3.7
1965-I	532.2				

Source: Adapted from *Survey of Current Business*, January 1965, p. 5, and May 1965, p. 5.
[a] P = GNP peak quarter; T = GNP trough quarter.
[b] Based on rates compounded quarterly.
[c] In billions.

TABLE 2. Annual Percentage Rates of Change in
Components of GNP, in 1954 Prices, Selected
Intervals, 1948–1964

	1948–1953	1953–1957	1957–1960	1960–1964
Total GNP	4.7	2.6	2.5	4.1
Personal consumption				
expenditures	3.4	3.6	3.2	3.9
Durable goods	6.1	3.9	3.1	6.5
Nondurable goods	2.4	2.9	2.2	2.9
Services	3.8	4.6	4.6	4.1
Gross private domestic				
investmentᵃ	0.3	3.5	1.2	4.2
Residential nonfarm				
construction	3.6	3.0	6.0	4.0
Other construction	4.6	4.2	−0.6	2.1
Producers' durable				
equipment	−0.3	2.3	−2.7	6.1
Net exports of goods				
and services				
Exports	2.2	10.4	0.7	7.6
Imports	6.2	4.5	4.0	5.5
Government purchases				
of goods and services	14.9	−2.7	1.9	3.8
Federal	20.8	−7.4	−0.7	3.3
State and local	5.8	6.0	5.3	4.4

Sources: Calculated on the basis of data in *Economic Report of the President*, January 1965, pp. 192–193, and *Survey of Current Business*, May 1965, p. 4.
ᵃ Total gross investment includes net change in inventories, but percentage changes in the latter are not shown here separately.

1948–1953. The relatively slow growth in GNP between 1953 and 1960 deserves particular attention. This is a subject to which we shall return at a later point.

Let us now move on to Table 2. Here we compare average rates of change between consecutive cyclical peaks, but now using annual rather than quarterly data. Table 2 permits us to examine the pattern of growth of all the major components of aggregate demand: consumers' expenditures, private investment, the net export surplus (of minor importance directly, although its indirect effect through the balance of payments is of considerable significance), and federal and state and local government expenditures on goods and services.

Again the retardation in growth between 1953 and 1960 stands out, as does the acceleration which has occurred during the last four years. The reasons for the retardation in 1953–1957 are different from those that explain the slow growth between 1957 and 1960. This contrast is of considerable significance in understanding the reasons for the high level of unemployment after 1957.

The period 1953–1957 was a period of retarded growth which culminated in the investment boom and inflation of 1955–1957. The drag on the economy during these years came chiefly from the federal government, whose expenditures on goods and services declined sharply between 1953 and 1957. The rate of growth in private investment during this period was a moderate 3.1 per cent per year excluding inventory investment.[4] But the increase in investment (excluding inventory change) between 1953 and 1955 was at the rate of no less than 6.1 per cent per year. Gross capital formation then remained virtually constant at this high level through 1956 and 1957. This horizontal movement during the prolonged investment boom of 1955–1957 reduces the average rate of increase for the whole period 1953–1957, and the moderate average rate of increase for the entire four-year period does not fully reflect the magnitude of the investment boom during the mid-1950's.

The effect of the decline in government expenditures was to hold back the expansion in total output, and the unemployment rate rose from 2.9 per cent in 1953 to 4.3 per cent in 1957. Paradoxically, wholesale prices were relatively stable in 1953, a year presumably of overfull employment, but rose sharply in 1956–1957, when unemployment was a bit over 4 per cent.

At the sacrifice of some increase in unemployment, though not to a level generally considered unsatisfactory, the federal government was able to cut back its expenditures sharply after the Korean War. The slack created was partly offset by the continued rapid increase in state and local government expenditures, by a slight acceleration in the expansion of consumers' expenditures (aided both by the automatic tax reduction at the end of 1953 and a slight decline in the rate of saving out of disposable income), and by the investment boom of 1955–1957. Then came the end of the investment boom and the sharp business contraction of 1957–1958. Recovery from the recession was sluggish. The explanation for this sluggishness clearly lies in the combined behavior of federal spending and private nonresidential investment. Although total output continued to grow at a modest pace between 1957 and 1960, a rate not much different from that during 1953–1957, nonresidential construction and expenditures on producers' durables showed net declines between 1957 and 1960. (The newly revised GNP data, which became available only after this chapter was completed, show a slight increase for producers' durables between 1957 and 1960 rather than the decrease in Table 2. But the retardation compared to 1953–1957 is still quite marked.)

The federal government sharply decelerated the rate of decline in its expenditures after 1957, but there was some further net decrease between 1957 and 1960. The one type of nonconsumption expenditure that showed marked acceleration in growth between 1957 and 1960 was residential building: the average rate of its increase jumped from 3 per cent during 1953–1957 to 6 per cent during 1957–1960. This was sufficient to bring the average rate of increase in total gross private domestic investment up to only 1.2 per cent—0.4 per cent if we exclude inventory change. With total government expenditures rising at a rate of less than 2 per cent it is not surprising that the growth in total output averaged only 2.5 per cent between 1957 and 1960, about one percentage point less than the rate needed to maintain full employment. As a result, the unemployment rate rose from 4.3 per cent in 1957 to 5.6 per cent in 1960.

As we have noted, the 1960–1961 recession was very mild—the mildest of the postwar period. Further, it was brief, in all lasting only nine months. It was enough, however, to push the unemployment rate up to an annual average of 6.7 per cent for 1961. Yet, as we have just stated, the rate in the peak year 1960 was already at 5.6 per cent.

It is not putting matters too strongly to say that what the American economy had to recover from, when expansion began in 1961, was not the mild recession of 1960–1961 but the relative stagnation of the late 1950's, particularly of the period 1957–1960.[5] This stagnation was associated with an absolute decline in private nonresidential investment which the federal government made no attempt to offset, either by increased spending or a cut in taxes. It has been increasingly recognized in the last few years that the tax reduction eventually made in 1964 should have been made in 1958.

The net rate of growth in real GNP since the 1960 peak has been much higher than during the two preceding peak-to-peak periods. Indeed, the growth rate of 4.1 per cent achieved during 1960–1964 is one on which we would ordinarily congratulate ourselves. It has, however, had only a modest effect in lowering the unemployment rate from 5.6 per cent in 1960 to 5.2 per cent in 1964. (The accelerated expansion in the first three months of 1965 brought the seasonally adjusted quarterly average below 5 per cent for the first time since the last quarter of 1957.)

Accelerated growth since 1960 has been particularly stimulated by the marked and widespread revival in private capital formation. The 1960–1964 rate of increase in gross private domestic investment, inclusive and exclusive of inventory change, has been by a considerable margin the largest of any peak-to-peak period since the revival of private investment immediately following the war. The acceleration since 1957–1960 is particularly notable. So, too, is the striking turnabout in the behavior of producers' durables from a net decline of 2.7 per cent per year during 1957–1960 to a net growth during 1960–1964 at the unusually rapid rate of 6.1 per cent per year. The acceleration in other construction more than offsets the retarded expansion in residential building.

There was also a marked change in the trend of federal expenditures. For the first time since 1953 federal spending ceased to be a net deflationary force during the interpeak intervals we are examining. The acceleration considerably more than offset the moderate retardation in the rate of growth of state and local government expenditures.

I shall save until later most of what I want to say about the expansion in consumer expenditures. The unusually high rate of growth for the entire 1960–1964 period owes a good deal to the

1964 tax cut. Even so, the rate of increase was less than in GNP, unlike the relationship that prevailed from 1953 to 1960. If we take only the period 1960–1963, to exclude the effects of the tax cut, we get a slower rate of increase in both consumption and GNP, 3.5 and 3.8 per cent, respectively, than over the four years 1960–1964.

Growth of Potential Output

So far we have been tracing the changing rate of expansion in aggregate demand during the postwar period. It is now time to look at the supply side of the picture. This can be done most conveniently by examining the course of potential output (GNP) at full employment, which boils down to assessing the combined effect of the growth in the labor force and the net increase in labor productivity. The increase in labor productivity, which is difficult to measure, represents the net effect of a variety of forces—the growth of the capital stock *in toto*, the change in the composition of the capital stock, shifts in the industrial and occupational pattern of employment, changes in the intensity with which the factors of production are being used, net changes in the quality of the labor force (primarily by education and training), and a residual set of influences loosely referred to as the course of technological change.

Under Walter Heller the Council of Economic Advisers from 1961 through 1964 continued to estimate that potential output at full employment was growing at the rate of 3.5 per cent per year. This 3.5 per cent rate represented approximately a 1 per cent rate of growth of the labor force and a net increase in labor productivity of 2.5 per cent.

Some economists have been urging that this estimate was too low, even for the period before 1964, and that it is considerably too low for the rest of the 1960's.[6] There is some evidence that the upward trend in productivity in the early 1960's has been higher than the Council has estimated, and we know that for the rest of the 1960's a sharp acceleration in the growth of the labor force is already under way.

This acceleration in the rate of growth of potential output is recognized, albeit somewhat belatedly, in the January, 1965

Economic Report of the President. In this *Report*, the Council first states:[7]

> In its past three Annual Reports, the growth of potential GNP since mid-1955 has been approximated by a trend line rising at a rate of 3½ per cent a year. It now appears that the growth of potential has recently stepped up: a real growth rate of actual GNP somewhat greater than 3½ per cent has been required to prevent a rise in the unemployment rate.

The *Report* goes on to state that "the best estimate of recent potential growth must be placed somewhat above 3½ per cent and below 4 per cent," and it then proceeds to portray "the growth rate of potential GNP at 3½ per cent from 1955 through 1962 and 3¾ per cent thereafter."[8]

Having made this concession and recognizing the sharp acceleration in the rate of growth of the labor force that is now occurring, the Council then goes a step further:[9]

> The prospects for growth of the labor force and productivity suggest that the increase of potential GNP in 1965–70 will exceed the 3½ per cent annual rate of the 1955–1962 period and even the 3¾ per cent rate estimated currently. *Indeed, over the next five years it is likely to average about 4 per cent a year,* a rate approaching that of the early postwar period.

The Secretary of Labor, in the latest *Manpower Report of the President,* goes still further:

> If we assume no more than a continuation of the long-term productivity trend, and no significant changes in the workweek or workyear, the combined requirements for additional real gross national product . . . imply the need for an average annual increase *well above* 4 per cent between now and 1970. . . . taking into consideration the need to create jobs to reduce the unemployment rate from the current level of 5 per cent to a more acceptable level, it will be necessary to sustain an annual average rate of increase in real gross national product about equal to this year's high rate of growth for the next half dozen years.[10]

This implies the need for a growth rate of 4.5 per cent a year or better for the remainder of the 1960's.

Let us accept for the moment the Council's estimate that potential GNP in 1964 was about 27 billions higher than the GNP actually achieved. This is the level that would have been required to bring the unemployment rate in 1964 down to 4 per cent. For this level of GNP to have been achieved by 1964, starting from the actual level of output in 1961, there would have been required an annual rate of increase in GNP between 1961 and 1964 of more than 6 per cent a year—and an annual rate of growth since the cyclical peak year of 1960 of about 5.1 per cent. This would not have been an unprecedented performance; the economy expanded almost this rapidly in 1949–1953. However, it took the stimulus of the Korean War to do it. Various European countries have been able in the postwar period to maintain such high rates of growth for considerable periods without being interrupted by a serious recession. I have doubts, though, that the American economy could have maintained such a rate of expansion during 1961–1964 without, by 1965, running into some combination of the following difficulties. Prices certainly would have risen faster than they did during the last year and a half. In the absence of earlier and stronger measures to curb the outflow of capital than were taken in 1964, the balance-of-payments situation would have been worse than it was. Such balance-of-payments deterioration, combined with the speed of the expansion, rising prices, and the approach to full employment, almost certainly would have led the Federal Reserve authorities to adopt a moderately tight monetary policy in 1964. And very probably the rapidity of the expansion and the faster rise in prices would have generated considerably more inventory accumulation and led to the other stresses and strains that in the past have typically developed in the late stages of a prolonged boom. As a result, I think it likely that if we had achieved a 4 per cent unemployment rate by 1964 a cyclical contraction would today be imminent (if it had not already occurred).

Obviously, this is all unverifiable conjecture, but it is conjecture that at least to me has the ring of plausibility.

To achieve an average unemployment rate of 4 per cent in, say, 1967, the rise in real GNP between 1964 and 1967 would have to be at an average annual rate of virtually 5.5 per cent, considerably higher than the rate achieved during 1961–1964.[11] To achieve this goal, not only must the recent rate of expansion in aggregate output be accelerated but we must also, of course, avoid a recession for another three years. Even with the new sophistication now being shown in Washington, one does not have to be a pessimist to express some doubt that unemployment can be brought down to 4 per cent by 1967 (unless we have another Korean type boom). And, as for Senator Clark's goal of 3 per cent by 1968,[12] more than mild skepticism would, regretfully, seem to be in order. This is apart from the structural problems involved in achieving and maintaining an unemployment rate as low as 3 per cent in the United States.[13]

Behavior of Private Investment

I turn now to examine in greater detail the behavior of each of the main components of aggregate demand during the current expansion and the years immediately preceding it. Let us begin with private investment and look at Table 3.

We have already commented on the stagnation in private investment that occurred after 1957. Total fixed investment (in constant prices) remained below the peak reached in 1956 until 1962.[14] Thus we went through a five-year period with no net expansion at all in private capital formation. In the absence of more aggressive action by the federal government, it is no wonder that growth was slow and unemployment rose.

Let us look particularly at the period 1956–1960, the interval between two successive cyclical peaks in gross capital formation (excluding inventory change). Gross investment in constant prices, including change in inventories, showed a small net decline; total fixed investment, excluding inventory change, was virtually the same in 1956 and 1960 (Table 3). Plant and equipment expenditures by business showed a net decline of nearly 3 billion dollars between 1956 and 1960. This is equivalent to an average annual rate of decrease of 2.4 per cent. In real terms, plant and equipment expenditures remained significantly below the peak reached in 1956–1957 until 1964, and even after the leap in such expenditures between 1963 and 1964 (a year-to-year increase exceeded only by that between 1955 and 1956), the net increase in plant and equipment expenditures between 1956 and 1964 averages at an annual rate of not quite 1 per cent. Given this behavior of a segment of nonconsumption expenditures making up approximately half of total gross capital formation, it is

TABLE 3. COMPONENTS OF PRIVATE GROSS CAPITAL FORMATION, SELECTED YEARS, 1948–1965

	Annual Amount (billions of 1954 dollars)						Annual Rate of Change (per cent)				
	1948	1953	1956	1960	1963	1964	1948–1953	1953–1956	1956–1960	1960–1963	1960–1964
Business expenditures on new plant and equipment											
Manufacturing	11.4	12.1	13.5	11.7	12.3	14.3	1.3	3.8	−3.5	1.7	5.1
Durables	4.3	5.7	6.8	5.8	6.1	7.2	5.7	6.2	−4.3	2.2	5.7
Nondurables	7.0	6.4	6.7	6.0	6.2	7.1	−2.0	1.4	−2.7	1.3	4.6
Mining	1.1	1.0	1.1	0.8	0.8	0.9	−1.3	3.8	−8.0	0.4	3.2
Railroad	1.5	1.3	1.1	0.9	0.9	1.2	−3.0	−5.6	−6.5	2.3	9.2
Other transportation	1.5	1.6	1.6	1.6	1.6	1.9	0.5	−0.4	0.5	−0.4	4.0
Public utilities	3.5	4.7	4.4	4.5	4.4	4.8	6.4	−2.6	0.7	−0.5	1.6
Commercial and other	8.3	8.2	10.3	9.6	10.7	11.4	−0.5	8.0	−1.8	3.8	4.6
Total new plant and equipment	27.4	28.9	31.9	29.0	30.8	34.5	1.1	3.4	−2.4	1.9	4.4
Residential nonfarm construction	11.4	13.6	16.2	18.2	21.2	21.3	3.6	6.0	3.0	5.2	4.0
Farm construction and equipment	4.9	4.5	3.6	3.3	3.8	4.0	−1.6	−7.0	−1.9	4.7	4.7
Other fixed investment[a]	1.8	3.1	5.5	6.5	7.8	7.8	11.5	21.1	4.3	6.3	4.7
Total fixed investment	45.4	50.1	57.2	57.1	63.6	67.6	2.0	4.5	0.0	3.7	4.3
Inventory investment	4.4	0.5	4.5	3.1	4.1	3.4	—	—	—	—	—
Gross capital formation	49.8	50.6	61.7	60.2	67.7	71.0	0.3	6.8	−0.6	4.0	4.2

Source: See text and tables in the appendix to this paper.

[a] "Other fixed investment" is a residual.

hardly surprising that aggregate demand has not risen rapidly enough since 1956–1957 to keep the unemployment rate down to 4 per cent. (The newly revised GNP data, published since Table 3 was prepared, suggest that the retardation in business investment may have been somewhat less marked after 1956 than Table 3 suggests. But the broad picture remains unchanged.)

The slump in business investment after 1956 or 1957 was widespread, occurring not only in manufacturing but in mining, railroads, public utilities, and the "commercial and other" categories.[15] The largest absolute declines between 1956 and 1960 were in manufacturing (particularly in durables) and in the "commercial and other" sector. Also, after 1957 a significant decline in public-utility investment occurred.[16] If we measure from 1957 to 1960, about 90 per cent of the net decline in total plant and equipment expenditures occurred in manufacturing and public utilities. It is worth noting that even in 1964 public utility investment was still below the level reached in 1957.

At least three sets of forces were at work by the mid-1950's to bring about a marked retardation and an absolute decline in private business investment.

1. Underlying forces reduced the over-all marginal capital-output ratio and therefore the ratio of gross investment to GNP at any given rate of growth in total output.[17]

2. The investment boom of 1955–1957 rested in part on the satisfaction of pent-up demands: the construction of capacity to meet the pent-up demands for consumers' durables and, more generally, accumulated demands for the expansion and modernization of capacity which had been held back by the Korean War.[18]

3. Expectations were too optimistic in 1955–1957. Investment in some lines generated a larger capital stock than was warranted, given the level and underlying trend in demand, and considerable excess capacity resulted. The capacity-utilization rates achieved in manufacturing in 1955–1956 have not been matched since, even in 1964.[19] According to a recent McGraw-Hill survey, the rate of operation in manufacturing in December 1964 was still below the preferred rate (though considerably closer to the latter than a year earlier). It is worth noting that

a moderate amount of excess capacity in the last year has not prevented the sharp rise in plant and equipment expenditures shown in Table 3.

The expansion in plant and equipment expenditures accelerated markedly in 1964. In terms of 1954 prices, the rate of increase in such expenditures between 1963 and 1964 was a little more than 12 per cent. (For manufacturing alone it was about 16 per cent.) A comparable rate of increase now seems likely for 1965, with a larger fraction than in recent years going for capacity expansion rather than replacement and modernization. Similar acceleration, however, is not evident in the other types of fixed investment, which add up to about half of gross capital formation exclusive of inventory investment. Indeed, this other half of fixed investment (of which residential building alone constitutes two thirds) showed little change between 1963 and 1964. As a result, total fixed investment rose by 6.3 per cent in 1964 or at about half the rate of increase for plant and equipment alone. This is still quite a respectable figure. Along with the tax cut, it helped to generate a 4.75 per cent increase in GNP between 1963 and 1964. As we have seen, however, it appears that this rate of increase in GNP would hardly be enough to bring the unemployment rate down to 4 per cent in the next two or three years. The probability that a rate of expansion in total fixed investment of better than 6 per cent can be maintained for many years strikes me as being rather low, even with good economic management in Washington. The outlook for much expansion in residential building in the next few years is not promising, and this increases the need for very rapid expansion in plant and equipment expenditures—at a rate that may not be sustainable for long.[20] This remains to be seen.[21]

The Role of Fiscal Policy

We have already referred to the shifting trend in federal government expenditures during the postwar period. In fact, it is not unfair to say that, at least until recently, the federal government has been one of the major sources of instability in the American economy.

In real terms, federal government expenditures on goods and

services expanded rapidly between 1960 and 1962, rose very little in 1963, and showed a modest net decline in 1964. Thus on the side of expenditures on goods and services the federal government has been a drag on the economy during the last two years. This has come about, of course, through the moderate cutback in defense expenditures, which in 1964 still accounted for more than 80 per cent of total federal spending on goods and services. State and local government expenditures, however, increased more rapidly during the last two years than between 1960 and 1962, although the average rate of increase over the four years 1960–1964 was noticeably lower than during the preceding decade or more (Table 2).

To evaluate the federal government's total effect on aggregate demand, we must of course look at more than just its direct expenditures on goods and services. We must take into account not only the behavior of tax receipts but also the rapid expansion of transfer payments. Let us therefore turn next to Table 4, which summarizes the recent behavior of the main "leakages" from and additions to the income stream as we move from GNP to disposable personal income and consumers' expenditures on goods and services.

In current prices, GNP rose at an average rate of 5.1 per cent between 1960 and 1963, accelerating to 6.6 per cent in 1964. The rate of increase in disposable income between 1960 and 1963 (4.8 per cent) was slower than in GNP, suggesting that the net effect of leakages and transfer payments was to hold back moderately the rise in consumers' incomes after taxes. As a result of the tax cut, this relationship was reversed in 1964, even though the rise in GNP accelerated. In current prices, GNP rose by 6.6 per cent between 1963 and 1964. (On an annual basis the rise was at this same rate if we measure from the fourth quarter of 1963 to the first quarter of 1965). The rise in disposable income in 1964 was significantly larger—7.3 per cent (7.2 per cent if we measure from 1963-IV to 1965-I). This change is entirely accounted for by the substantial reduction in personal income taxes, which is the only item in Table 4 to show an absolute decrease between 1963 and 1964.

It is worth noting that the percentage rise in *personal income* in 1964 was less than that in GNP, as it had been in 1962 and

TABLE 4. RELATION OF GROSS NATIONAL PRODUCT TO DISPOSABLE INCOME AND CONSUMPTION EXPENDITURES, 1960-1964[a]

Item	Amount (billion dollars)					Annual Percentage Change				
	1960	1961	1962	1963	1964	1960–1961	1961–1962	1962–1963	1963–1964	1960–1963
GNP	502.6	518.7	556.2	583.9	622.6	3.2	7.2	5.0	6.6	5.1
Capital consumption	43.0	44.5	48.7	50.8	53.4	3.5	9.4	4.3	5.1	5.7
Indirect business taxes										
Federal	14.0	14.1	15.1	15.6	16.4	0.7	7.1	3.3	5.1	3.7
State and local	32.5	34.9	37.8	40.2	43.0	7.4	8.3	6.3	7.0	7.3
Corporate profits[b]	44.5	44.1	48.4	50.8	57.4	-0.9	9.8	5.0	13.0	4.5
Social security contributions	20.6	21.4	23.9	26.9	28.7	3.9	11.7	12.6	6.7	9.3
Government transfer payments	27.3	31.3	32.3	34.3	35.7	14.7	3.2	6.2	4.1	7.9
Government interest payments	7.8	7.4	8.0	8.6	9.2	-5.1	8.1	7.5	7.0	3.3
Dividends	14.5	15.2	16.5	18.0	19.8	4.8	8.6	9.1	10.0	7.5
Personal income	401.3	417.6	442.4	464.1	491.4	4.1	5.9	4.9	5.9	5.0
Personal taxes	51.4	52.9	57.9	61.6	59.5	2.9	9.5	6.4	-3.4	6.2
Disposable income	349.9	364.7	384.6	402.5	431.8	4.2	5.5	4.7	7.3	4.8
Consumption expenditures	328.2	337.3	356.8	375.0	399.3	2.8	5.8	5.1	6.5	4.5

Sources: Economic Report of the President, January 1965, pp. 204–205, 208; and Survey of Current Business, May 1965, pp. 5–6.

[a] Minor deductions and additions in going from GNP to disposable income are omitted.

[b] Including inventory valuation adjustment.

1963. The rise in corporate profits sharply accelerated in 1964. As a result, there was a marked acceleration in gross and net business savings, although the reduction in the rate of the corporate income tax did lead to modest retardation in the rise in corporate taxes.

We should not confine our attention only to the federal income tax. Much publicity has attended the substantial reduction in federal excise taxes recently enacted by Congress, but state and local indirect taxes are far more important than those of the federal government, and they have been increasing faster than GNP (Table 4). This continued to be the case in 1964, and the moderate acceleration in the rise in such tax revenues was another reason why personal income continued to grow less rapidly than GNP.

A further reason is to be found in the behavior of government transfer payments, which also decelerated their rate of increase in 1964. The rise in federal transfer payments to individuals in 1964 (Table 5) was only about 60 per cent as large as in 1963. On the other hand, there continues to be a strikingly rapid increase in federal grants-in-aid to state and local governments (Table 5), which permits the latter to continue to increase both their expenditures on goods and services and state and local transfer payments.

Let us now take a closer look at the 1964 tax cut. There is no question that this action had a strong expansionary effect on the economy. In the face of a continued rapid rise in personal income (Table 4) the federal government collected 5.6 per cent less in personal income taxes in 1964 than in 1963 (Table 5). Contrast the annual increases of 8.9 and 5.7 per cent in 1962 and 1963. If we take the five quarters from 1963-IV to 1965-I, we find that disposable income increased (on an annual basis) at the striking rate of 7.2 per cent, and, with a decline in the rate of personal saving during this five-quarter period, personal consumption expenditures expanded even more rapidly.

Further fiscal stimulus is scheduled for 1965. There is the second and smaller installment of the reduction in income taxes enacted in 1964. In addition, a liberalization of social security benefits, retroactive to the beginning of the year, and a substantial reduction in excise taxes were approved by Congress in

TABLE 5. RECEIPTS AND SELECTED EXPENDITURES OF THE FEDERAL GOVERNMENT, 1960–1964

Item	Amount (billion dollars)					Annual Percentage Change				
	1960	1961	1962	1963	1964	1960–1961	1961–1962	1962–1963	1963–1964	1960–1963
Receipts										
Personal tax and nontax receipts	44.0	45.1	49.1	51.9	49.0	2.5	8.9	5.7	−5.6	5.7
Corporate profits tax	21.0	20.9	21.8	23.0	24.2	−0.5	4.3	5.5	5.2	3.1
Indirect business tax	14.0	14.1	15.1	15.6	16.4	0.7	7.1	3.3	5.1	3.7
Social insurance contributions	17.6	18.2	20.5	23.0	24.4	3.4	12.6	12.2	6.1	9.3
Total receipts	96.6	98.3	106.4	113.6	114.1	1.8	8.2	6.8	0.4	5.6
Selected Expenditures										
On goods and services	53.1	57.4	62.9	64.7	65.5	8.1	9.6	2.9	1.2	6.8
Transfer payments to persons	22.2	25.8	26.7	28.3	29.3	16.2	3.5	6.0	3.5	8.4
Grants-in-aid[a]	6.3	7.2	8.0	9.1	10.4	14.3	11.1	13.8	14.3	13.0
Surplus or deficit on income and product account	3.5	−4.3	−4.1	−1.5	−5.1					

Sources: *Economic Report of the President*, January 1965, p. 263, and *Survey of Current Business*, May 1965, p. 6.
a To state and local governments.

mid-1965. A substantial offset, however, will be the sizeable increase in social security taxes beginning in January 1966. On balance, the net additional fiscal stimulus from these measures in the calendar year 1965 will be significantly less than that resulting from the tax reduction effective in 1964. As things now stand, some moderate deflationary pressure will be exerted in the first half of 1966, for the rise in social security taxes will be considerably greater than the second reduction in excise taxes scheduled to become effective in January 1966.

Fiscal policy should probably be given a good deal of credit for the rapid expansion in private investment that has occurred during the current upswing. The new depreciation guidelines and the investment tax credit in 1962 undoubtedly provided an additional stimulus to plant and equipment expenditures at the same time that particularly the more generous depreciation allowances, as well as the continued rise in profits, helped to generate additional cash flows available for such investment.[22] Then came the reduction in corporate income taxes in 1964.

It seems that, at least for the time being, Congress and the Administration have chosen to apply an expansionary fiscal policy (as needed) primarily through tax reduction rather than accelerated increases in federal spending, particularly on goods and services. Transfer payments to persons will continue to expand, especially in the near future as a result of liberalized social-security payments and Medicare; and the trend in grants-in-aid to state and local governments is still strongly upward, as Table 5 suggests. However, the tendency seems now to be toward reducing the federal government's share of the GNP, including the share that it diverts through cyclically sensitive income taxes. Continuation of this trend will weaken somewhat the effectiveness of the government's automatic stabilizers and place increased responsibility on private spending and the expenditures of state and local governments to maintain a satisfactory rate of growth and to avoid the cyclical instability to which private spending has been prone in the past.

Behavior of Consumer Spending

In its 1965 Annual Report the Council of Economic Advisers referred to "the dependable consumer" who could be counted on, year in and year out, to spend 92 to 94 per cent of his disposable income, after taxes, on goods and services.[23] In this respect, consumers have been behaving in this upswing as they have behaved in previous postwar expansions. Table 6 suggests, however, that there are a couple of differences that are worth pointing out.

TABLE 6. Relation of Expenditures on Consumers' Durables and on Automobiles and of Personal Saving to Disposable Personal Income, Quarterly, 1961–1965

| | As Percentage of Disposable Income | | |
| | Expenditures on | | |
Quarter	Durables	Automobiles and Parts	Personal Saving
1961-I	11.6	4.4	6.9
II	11.9	4.6	7.5
III	12.0	4.6	8.0
IV	12.4	5.1	7.9
1962-I	12.5	5.2	7.4
II	12.4	5.3	7.7
III	12.5	5.3	7.1
IV	12.9	5.6	6.8
1963-I	12.9	5.7	6.6
II	12.9	5.7	6.8
III	12.9	5.6	6.7
IV	13.0	5.6	7.3
1964-I	13.3	5.8	7.0
II	13.2	5.6	7.9
III	13.5	5.9	7.1
IV	12.7	5.2	8.0
1965-I	13.8	6.4	6.7

Sources: *Economic Reports of the President* and *Survey of Current Business*, May 1965.

In the first place consumers seem to have been even more "dependable"in this upswing than in the two preceding expansions. Over the 16 calendar quarters from 1961-II to 1965-I, consumers' expenditures varied between 92.0 and 93.4 per cent of disposable income. Their personal savings rate varied between 6.6 and 8 per cent (Table 6). This range was somewhat wider in both 1954–1957 and 1958–1960: between 91.9 and 94.5 per cent in the first case and between 91.6 and 94.4 per cent in the second.[24] Also, on the average, consumers have been saving a somewhat larger fraction of their disposable income in the current upswing: an average of 7.3 per cent since this expansion began compared to averages of 7.0 and 6.9 per cent during the two preceding upswings. Interestingly, the rate of personal saving averaged nearly the same for the period 1961-II to 1963-IV, before the 1964 tax cut, and for the period 1964-I through 1965-I, which includes a full year's effect of the tax cut as well as the effect of the automobile strikes in the last quarter of 1964 and the surge of pent-up demand for automobiles in the first quarter of 1965. It should be noted, however, that there was a fairly steady decline in the saving rate during the first two years of the upswing. For about a year, from 1962-IV through 1963-III, personal saving remained in a narrow range between 6.6 and 6.8 per cent of disposable income. The saving rate then moved to a higher level from 1963-IV through the year 1964 but fell to 6.7 per cent during the booming first quarter of 1965. It remains to be seen whether it will rise again. It is not likely to go much if any lower.

Table 7 provides additional material for judging the effects of the 1964 tax reduction, and, taken in conjunction with Table 6, provides some perspective on the continuing boom in automobile sales. In Table 7 we have divided the period since the beginning of 1962 into the subperiods shown in order to average some of the erratic fluctuations we get when we take quarter-to-quarter changes. We have computed average disposable income and average expenditures for each of the major categories of consumers' expenditures (including automobiles) for the following periods: the two halves of 1962 and 1963, the first three quarters of 1964, and the fourth quarter of 1964 combined with the first quarter of 1965. A combination of the first three quarters

TABLE 7. Ratios of Increments of Various Types of Consumer
Expenditures to Changes in Disposable Personal Income,
Selected Intervals, 1962–1965

Interval		Ratio of Change in Stated Type of Expenditure to Change in Disposable Income[a]				
				Automobiles	Non-	
From	To	Total[b]	Durables	Only	durables	Services
1962/I–II	1962/III–IV	1.250	.236	.167	.472	.542
1962/III–IV	1963/I–II	1.045	.225	.146	.292	.517
1963/I–II	1963/III–IV	0.822	.150	.037	.234	.439
1963/III–IV	1964/I–III	0.850	.209	.087	.345	.296
1964/I–III	1964/IV–1965/I	0.917	.119	.060	.411	.393

Sources: Original data are from *Economic Reports of the President* and *Survey of Current Business*, May 1965.

[a] In each case, the change in expenditures or income is that from the average of the quarterly figures (seasonally adjusted annual rates) in the first of the two periods to that in the second.

[b] Total consumer expenditures.

of 1964 picks up most of the effect of the first installment of the tax cut, in particular the substantial reduction in payroll-tax withholding. Combining the last two quarters permits us to allow for the effects of the automobile strikes. Table 7 presents the ratio of change in consumers' expenditures to change in disposable income as derived from the subperiod averages just described.

The rise in consumers' expenditures was greater than the increase in disposable income in the second half of 1962 and the first half of 1963. Relative to the continued rise in disposable income, the rate of expansion in consumers' expenditures tapered off after the first half of 1963. We have suggested that taking the first three quarters of 1964 together might help us assess the effects of the tax cut on consumers' expenditures. The rise in total expenditures relative to disposable income during this period, compared to the second half of 1963, was not much different from the ratio of increase in spending to increase in income which occurred during the preceding half year. It appears from Table 7 that the accelerated rise in disposable income associated with the tax cut went particularly into consumers' durables (especially automobiles) and, interestingly, into nondurables. The incremental ratio of spending to income fell off sharply in the case of services.

A further substantial rise in disposable income occurred during the next six-month period, covering the fourth quarter of 1964 and the first quarter of 1965. The incremental ratio of consumption to disposable income also rose from 0.85 in the first three quarters of 1964 to 0.92. The incremental ratio fell sharply for total durables and automobiles, with more than offsetting increases for nondurables and services. The decline in the incremental ratio for other durables was even sharper than that for automobiles.

If we turn to average rather than marginal propensities, we see that expenditures on durables constituted about 13.3 per cent and automobiles accounted for approximately 5.8 per cent of disposable income in the first three quarters of 1964 and during the half year that followed.[25] Durable goods had not accounted for this large a fraction of disposable income since the first quarter of 1957. The fraction was significantly higher, 14.5 per cent, in 1955, the height of the automobile boom of the 1950's. The fraction for automobiles, 5.8 per cent, was the largest for any six-month period since the half year spanning the fourth quarter of 1955 and the first quarter of 1956. The highest ratio of expenditures on automobiles to disposable income achieved in any quarter since the war was 7.1 per cent in the third quarter of 1955. The average for the year 1955 was about 6.7 per cent. This compares with 6.4 per cent achieved during the height of the automobile boom in the first quarter of 1965.

Can we say anything about the prospective relationship between consumers' expenditures and disposable income in the months ahead? Although prediction is no part of the purpose of this chapter, a few comments might help to put recent developments in perspective. The relatively high saving rate from 1963-IV through 1964-IV suggests that the saving rate may remain below 7 per cent for a while longer.[26] The incremental ratio of total consumers' expenditures to disposable income has shown a rising tendency since the beginning of 1964 (Table 7), but there is no assurance that this ratio will rise much further.

It also appears that expenditures for services have been responding somewhat sluggishly to the rise in income since the beginning of 1964, and a change toward a more rapid expansion may be in store here. The ratio of total expenditures on services to total disposable income since the tax cut has been lower than in either half of 1963. (The same has been true of nondurables.) It is possible that an accelerated rise in expenditures on services and nondurables would help to offset an absolute decline in expenditures on automobiles. (It is worth noting that a survey of consumer intentions taken early in 1965 indicated that more families planned to buy new cars during the ensuing 12 months than at the same time during any of the preceding four years of expansion.[27])

The "dependable consumer" has indeed done a good job in helping to support the current expansion; but he is by no means an automaton, responding in completely predictable fashion to every change in his after-tax income. His rate of personal saving has varied, and some of the changes in the *pattern* of his expenditures have been quite dramatic. It appears that he is likely to continue to give strong support to the expansion in the months ahead. This will be particularly true if he keeps his saving rate below 7 per cent.[28]

Other Characteristics of The Expansion

I should now like to offer a few observations about some other characteristics of the current business expansion, particularly those aspects of the behavior of the economy that have contributed to the duration and steadiness of the upswing. This has been a remarkable expansion in the degree to which excesses and maladjustments have been avoided.[29]

We can begin with the behavior of prices. As is generally known, wholesale prices have been remarkably steady, although there has been some inching up in recent months. The index of industrial materials prices was no higher in mid-1964 than at the beginning of the upswing, but there has been a significant rise in the last nine months. The rise in the consumer-price index has been quite moderate, with no clear tendency toward acceleration in its rate of increase.

The behavior of prices reflects in part the behavior of labor costs, which in turn depends on changes in hourly earnings and labor productivity. Labor cost per dollar of real corporate GNP declined during 1961, as is typical in the early stages of recovery, and has shown surprisingly little increase since then, much less than in the latter part of any previous postwar expansion. Labor cost per unit of output in manufacturing has actually drifted downward since mid-1962, and this tendency toward decline was still apparent in the early months of 1965.

It hardly needs to be added that the excess capacity carried over from the boom of the 1950's has contributed to the good behavior of prices and probably also to the continued rapid rise in labor productivity.

It has been typical of cyclical expansion that eventually, as the boom continues, costs begin to encroach on prices and profit margins fall.[30] This happened in each of the postwar expansions preceding the present one, but it has *not* happened during the current upswing. The ratio of price to unit labor cost in manufacturing was still rising in early 1965, and so was the ratio of profits to income originating in the corporate sector as a whole. The rise in total corporate profits (after taxes) accelerated in the second half of 1963 and, after a more or less horizontal movement during 1964, accelerated again in the first quarter of 1965.

Another feature of this expansion has been the close control of inventories and orders. Stock-sales ratios for manufacturing and trade have tended downward through the entire upswing and at the end of 1964 were at the lowest level in 10 years. As the Department of Commerce has pointed out, "the downward drift of the ratio in 1963 and 1964 has been quite different from the increases during the advanced stages of previous upturns."[31] There was a substantial increase in inventory investment in 1964-IV and 1965-I, but this was presumably temporary, associated with stockpiling in anticipation of a steel strike and restocking of cars after the automobile strikes.

Not only private business but the monetary authorities have behaved well. The rate of expansion in the money supply, excluding and including time deposits, has been unusually steady. Despite concern over the balance-of-payments the Federal Reserve authorities have carefully avoided putting monetary ob-

stacles in the way of the expansion. Although Treasury bill rates have been forced up to minimize the outflow of short-term capital, long-term interest rates have held remarkably steady during the entire upswing. Corporate and municipal bond yields, as well as mortgage yields, were generally no higher in the early months of 1965 than at the beginning of the upswing in 1961 and in some cases were even a bit lower. Corresponding to this behavior of interest rates has been a steady advance in the volume of bank and nonbank credit. If we have failed to achieve full employment after four years of rising output and employment, the blame can hardly be put on the monetary authorities.[32] This is in contrast to the monetary tightening that occurred in 1959–1960.

I shall make no attempt to deal at length with the balance-of-payments problems that have beset the United States in recent years. Except under the most skillful management, these difficulties can seriously interfere with the rate of domestic expansion we need to get closer to the full-employment goal. I shall limit my comments to the following points, which I shall not try to document fully.

1. During the current expansion exports have risen more rapidly than imports, with a consequent improvement in our balance of trade on goods-and-services account. The improvement was particularly marked in 1964. Domestic expansion has *not* led to a deterioration in our balance of trade in goods and services. This good performance is due to the rapid expansion of our exports, which more than offset the increase in imports induced by the continued expansion in domestic output and spending.

2. The most important reason for this improvement in the merchandise trade balance is undoubtedly the improved competitive position of the United States which resulted from the relative stability in the American price level, combined with the continued rapid growth of our principal customers.

3. Given the need to continue governmental aid abroad at something like the present level, our balance-of-payments problems have stemmed primarily from the large outflow of American capital. The net outflow of short-term and long-term capital increased significantly in 1963 and 1964 to a new record level.

The outflow was particularly heavy in the fourth quarter of 1964. So far, continued domestic expansion, higher profits at home, and rising domestic investment have not led to any decline in capital exports, as some economists predicted two or three years ago.

4. Against this background, and given the official assumption that the present gold value of the dollar must be preserved, the monetary and fiscal authorities have acted with skill and circumspection to achieve the goal of not interfering with the domestic expansion and at the same time seeking to reduce the balance-of-payments deficit. The chief measures have been tie-in arrangements to direct the proceeds of foreign aid toward the purchase of American goods, the Interest Equalization Tax passed in 1964, the new set of measures announced by the President in February 1965 (particularly but not exclusively aimed at securing voluntary restraints on the outflow of capital), and the "wage-price guideposts" (as far as they can be given credit for holding back the rise in wages and prices).

The answer to our balance-of-payments problem is not yet in sight, although it may be surmised that the deterioration in the latter part of 1964 was temporary. Fundamentally, and in the long run (assuming stable exchange rates at present levels), the answer must be found in two directions: (a) continued improvement in our competitive position resulting from a less rapid rise in American than foreign prices and (b) the development of more adequate sources of capital abroad. We can also count on a steady increase in the income on American investments already made abroad, and, of course, we must maintain profitable opportunities for a steadily expanding volume of domestic investment.

Concluding Comment

In the last *Economic Report* the Council of Economic Advisers predicted that GNP in 1965 would fall within a 10-billion-dollar range centering on 660 billions. The figure of 660 billions is widely accepted, both in and out of Washington, as a reasonable forecast for this year's GNP. If prices rise this year at the same moderate rate as in 1964, this implies an increase in real GNP between 1964 and 1965 of about 4.1 per cent. If potential output has now begun to grow at 4 per cent, the Council hardly did full justice to the problems still facing us when it said cautiously that "the increase in output is likely to exceed the growth of potential, reducing the gap moderately."[33] The reduction in the gap—and in unemployment—would be very moderate indeed.

GNP rose unusually rapidly in 1965-I, but the rate of increase for the remainder of the year will be lower. Expansion in real GNP during the final three quarters at an annual rate of not much more than 3 per cent, with prices continuing to rise at their recent rate, would yield a GNP for all of 1965 (in current prices) of just about the predicted 660 billions.[34]

The sharp rise in GNP in 1965-I brought the seasonally adjusted unemployment rate for the first quarter down to about 4.8 per cent. By July the seasonally adjusted monthly figure had fallen to 4.5 per cent. Unless the expansion in output for the rest of the year is more rapid than seems likely at midyear, unemployment in the fourth quarter will not be lower than 4.5 per cent.[35]

This brings us back to the dilemma suggested at the beginning of this chapter: we must run very fast these days just to stand still. Rapid growth, at the rate of 4 per cent or better, is needed to prevent unemployment (open and disguised) from rising. Yet to expand still faster in the next several years—fast enough to bring the unemployment rate down to 4 per cent or below—greatly increases the probability of accelerating price and wage inflation and eventually of another business recession. Constructive fiscal and monetary policies in the last four years have helped us to achieve substantial gains. Further advance toward the goal of full employment, while avoiding the conditions that might bring on another recession, will be increasingly difficult from here on. It will call for much wisdom and imagination in Washington and for cooperation and constructive long-range planning by business and labor.

TABLE A-1. Business Expenditures on New Plant and
Equipment, 1948–1964
(billions of 1954 dollars)

Year	Total (1)	Manufacturing			Rail-road (5)	Other Trans-porta-tion (6)	Public Utilities (7)	Commer-cial and Other (8)	Total (9)
		Dura-bles (2)	Non-durables (3)	Mining (4)					
1948	11.36	4.33	7.03	1.08	1.54	1.54	3.46	8.34	27.35
1949	8.64	3.09	5.53	.94	1.57	1.04	4.03	6.99	23.21
1950	8.78	3.67	5.14	.83	1.26	1.38	4.08	7.75	24.06
1951	11.62	5.49	6.12	.99	1.58	1.56	4.08	7.65	27.47
1952	12.13	5.80	6.31	1.02	1.46	1.54	4.23	7.37	27.73
1953	12.09	5.71	6.37	1.01	1.32	1.58	4.72	8.15	28.86
1954	11.04	5.09	5.95	.98	.85	1.51	4.22	8.23	26.83
1955	11.04	5.26	5.79	.93	.90	1.56	4.16	9.25	27.83
1956	13.50	6.84	6.65	1.13	1.11	1.56	4.36	10.26	31.93
1957	13.73	6.83	6.90	1.08	1.21	1.53	5.19	9.34	32.01
1958	9.61	4.54	5.06	0.80	0.63	1.26	4.96	8.44	25.72
1959	9.91	4.67	5.22	0.82	0.76	1.66	4.51	9.13	26.77
1960	11.73	5.75	5.97	0.81	0.85	1.59	4.48	9.56	29.03
1961	10.99	5.00	5.98	0.79	0.55	1.52	4.39	9.43	27.66
1962	11.66	5.54	6.11	0.86	0.70	1.69	4.33	10.35	29.60
1963	12.33	6.13	6.20	0.82	0.91	1.57	4.42	10.70	30.75
1964	14.32	7.18	7.12	0.92	1.21	1.86	4.77	11.44	34.52

Sources: See text following Table A-2.

TABLE A-2. Components of Gross Capital Formation, 1948–1964
(billions of 1954 dollars)

Year	Total New Plant and Equipment[b] (9)	Residen-tial Nonfarm Construc-tion (10)	Farm Construc-tion and Equip-ment (11)	Other Fixed Invest-ment[a] (12)	Total Fixed Invest-ment (13)	Inventory Investment (14)	Gross Capital Formation (15)
1948	27.35	11.4	4.9	1.8	45.4	4.4	49.8
1949	23.21	11.2	5.1	2.6	42.1	−3.6	38.5
1950	24.06	15.5	4.9	4.2	48.7	7.2	55.9
1951	27.47	12.9	4.9	2.7	48.0	9.7	57.7
1952	27.73	12.8	4.6	2.6	47.8	2.6	50.4
1953	28.86	13.6	4.5	3.1	50.1	0.5	50.6
1954	26.83	15.4	3.9	4.4	50.5	−1.6	48.9
1955	27.83	18.2	4.1	6.3	56.4	6.1	62.5
1956	31.93	16.2	3.6	5.5	57.2	4.5	61.7
1957	32.01	15.3	3.5	5.7	56.5	1.6	58.1
1958	25.72	16.2	3.8	4.8	50.5	−1.5	49.0
1959	26.77	19.5	3.9	5.7	55.8	5.9	61.7
1960	29.03	18.2	3.3	6.5	57.1	3.1	60.2
1961	27.66	18.2	3.5	6.3	55.7	1.7	57.4
1962	29.60	20.1	3.6	7.4	60.7	5.2	65.9
1963	30.75	21.2	3.8	7.8	63.6	4.1	67.7
1964	34.52	21.3	4.0	7.8	67.6	3.4	71.0

a "Other Fixed Investment" is a residual.
b Taken from Table A-1.

Sources for Tables A-1 and A-2. *Columns (1)–(9)* and *(11)*. The original undeflated data were taken from *Economic Report of the President*, January 1965, pp. 202, 236. These series are in current prices. Deflators used for 1948–1962 are those in Bert Hickman, *Investment Demand and U. S. Economic Growth* (Washington: Brookings Institution, 1965), pp. 236–237. We combined the price indices for Electric Utilities and Gas Utilities by weighting them according to Gross Investment in Plant and Equipment (*ibid.*, pp. 224–225) in the respective sectors. The indices for Telephone Communication and for Commercial and Other were analogously combined. We extended the deflators through 1964 by following Hickman's procedures as closely as possible.

Manufacturing. A weighted average of the Boeckh Construction Cost Index for Commercial and Factory Buildings (U. S. Dept. of Commerce, *Construction Review*) and Wholesale Price Index for Producers' Finished Goods for Manufacturing Industries (B.L.S., *Wholesale Prices and Price Indices*), the weights being 1:2.5, as suggested by the ratio of Structures to Equipment in Manufacturing Investment in 1957 (*Survey of Current Business*, November 1962, p. 10). The percentage of increase in the resulting index was then used to extrapolate Hickman's indices for total Manufacturing and Durables and Nondurables separately.

Mining. The implicit deflator for Total Gross Expenditures on Plant and Equipment.

Railroads. Extrapolation of Hickman's index by the percentage change of the Interstate Commerce Commission's Index of the Cost of Road and Equipment (*Schedule of Annual Indices for Carriers by Railroad*, mimeographed) to 1963, and assumed no change to 1964.

Other Transportation. Used Hickman's procedure (*loc. cit.*, p. 235).

Public Utilities. Assumed increase in Hickman's index by one percentage point per year, 1963–1964.

Commercial and Other. A weighted average of George Fuller Construction Cost Index (for Telephone Communication), Dept. of Commerce Composite Construction Cost Index (both in *Construction Review*), and Wholesale Price Index for Producers' Finished Goods for Nonmanufacturing Industries (B.L.S., *Wholesale Prices and Price Indices*). The weights used, so far as possible, were derived from the procedures used by Hickman.

Farm. Extrapolation of Hickman's index by percentage increase in Agricultural Machinery and Equipment Wholesale Prices (in *Survey of Current Business*).

Columns 10, 13–15. Derived from *Economic Report of the President*, January 1965, p. 192.

NOTES

1. The research on which this paper is based is part of the research program on Unemployment and the American Economy being carried on at the University of California, Berkeley, under a grant from the Ford Foundation. I should like to take this occasion to acknowledge the invaluable help of Mr. Günter Wittich. (A postscript: After this volume had gone to press, the Department of Commerce published its extensive revisions of the national income accounts. It has not been possible to incorporate these revisions into the tables presented here. I have, however, made a number of spot checks which suggest that the new revisions of the data on the GNP and its components do not alter the general patterns of behavior described or affect the conclusions I have drawn. In a few instances, in text or footnote, I have interpolated a brief reference to the revised figures.)

2. By June 1965, the current expansion had lasted 52 months. We have had one longer cyclical expansion in wartime—the 80-month expansion of 1938–1945. The National Bureau of Economic Research has carried its systematic dating of American business cycles back only to the 1850's. Hence, my qualification: "in more than a century."

3. Before 1960 and excluding the 1930's, the last cyclical expansion in this century that failed to push the annual unemployment rate below 5 per cent was that of 1908–1910.

4. If inventory investment is included, as it is in Table 2, the annual rate of increase between 1953 and 1957 was 3.5 per cent.

5. Cf. B. G. Hickman, "The Postwar Retardation: Another Long Swing in the Rate of Growth?" *American Economic Review: Papers and Proceedings*, LIII (May 1963), 490–507; also the ensuing discussion, *ibid.*, 530–540.

6. Cf. R. A. Gordon, *Some Thoughts on the Recent Slow Growth of the American Economy* (Athens: Athens Center of Economic Research Lecture Series, Nov. 11, 1964), p. 15.

7. *Economic Report of the President*, January 1965, p. 81.

8. *Ibid.*

9. *Ibid.*, p. 92. My italics. In a speech at the annual conference of the National Association of Mutual Savings Banks in May 1965, Gardner Ackley stated that growth of potential output "will accelerate to 4 per cent *or better* in the years immediately ahead." [My italics.]

10. Both quotations are from *Manpower Report of the President*, March 1965, p. 47. My italics.

11. This accepts the Council's estimate that actual GNP in 1964 was 4 per cent below potential output, and projects potential GNP at the rate of 4 per cent per year.

12. See Subcommittee on Employment and Manpower, Committee on Labor and Public Welfare, U. S. Senate, *Toward Full Employment: Proposals for a Comprehensive Employment and Manpower Policy in the United States* (Washington, D. C., 1964), p. 40.

13. Cf. R. A. Gordon, "Full Employment as a Policy Goal," in A. M. Ross, editor, *Employment Policy and the Labor Market* (Berkeley: University of California Press, 1965), pp. 49–55.

14. See Appendix Table A-2.

15. "Commercial and Other" includes trade, service, finance, communications, and construction.

16. See Appendix Table A-1.

17. The most important factor at work here was the effect of technological change in bringing about declines in desired capital-output ratios over a wide range of industry. See the stimulating new study by Bert G. Hickman, *Investment Demand and U. S. Economic Growth* (Washington, D. C.: The Brookings Institution, 1965).

18. It is possible, also, although this is not much more than a surmise, that 1957 marked the end of the first big wave of investment inspired by the so-called "automation revolution," particularly in durable-goods manufacturing, oil refining, and a few other lines. It is interesting that the kinds of shifts in unemployment that we associate with automation were more marked before 1957 than after. Cf. R. A. Gordon, "Has Structural Unemployment Worsened?" *Industrial Relations*, III (May 1964), especially 61–63, 72–75.

19. This statement is based on Federal Reserve estimates for capacity and output as reproduced in *Economic Report of the President*, January 1965, p. 231.

20. On a quarterly basis, residential nonfarm construction declined from the first to the fourth quarter of 1964 by about two billion (in 1954 prices) and then recovered about 40 per cent of this loss in the first quarter of 1965. A decline in residential building in the latter part of cyclical expansions has been a typical feature of postwar cycles, but the recent decline in residential building has a different origin from that of the two preceding expansions. In the earlier upswings, residential building fell off because of a scarcity of mortgage funds; in the present case, mortgage funds have remained plentiful.

21. In terms of conventional multiplier analysis, the expansionary stimulus of the trends in real investment observed in Table 3 has been somewhat stronger than is implied by the rates of increase actually shown. This is because capital-goods prices have been rising faster than the price level for consumers' goods and GNP as a whole. Cf. R. A. Gordon, "Differential Changes in the Prices of Consumers' and Capital Goods," *American Economic Review*, LI (December 1961), 937–957; Hickman, *op. cit.*, 202–207.

22. Note in Table 4 the sharp rise in capital consumption allowances from 1962 on.

23. *Economic Report of the President*, January 1965, pp. 41–42.

24. The relevant figures can be found in the *Economic Reports of the President* for the appropriate years. It should be noted that the revision of the GNP data published in August 1965 yields lower ratios of personal saving to disposable income than those shown in Table 6. The year-to-year

changes in the new series are quite similar to those in the old, but there is some difference in the longer-run movement. *Cf. Survey of Current Business,* August 1965, pp. 21, 22.

25. See the quarterly figures in Table 6.

26. The high saving rate from 1963-IV through 1964-IV may imply that there is still some backlog of demand to be satisfied. And it may imply an accelerated accumulation of liquid assets in the hands of consumers.

27. The same survey, however, suggests a possible weakening in the demand for used cars. See *The Outlook for Consumer Demand* (Ann Arbor: Survey Research Center, University of Michigan, 1965), especially Table 15 and p. 13. The survey of consumer intentions made by the Bureau of the Census in April 1965 again suggested that more families planned to buy new cars in the ensuing 12 months than was the case a year earlier. *Wall Street Journal,* May 26, 1965.

28. For further information on the recent behavior of consumer spending and saving see *Federal Reserve Bulletin,* April 1965, pp. 519–529.

29. The recent behavior of most of the variables mentioned in this section can be conveniently followed in the charts appearing in any recent issue of *Business Cycle Developments.* This source facilitates comparison of the current business expansion with earlier postwar upswings.

30. This is an aspect of the business-cycle self-generating mechanism that was much emphasized by W. C. Mitchell.

31. *Survey of Current Business,* January 1965, p. 9.

32. However, they have obviously been becoming more restive; witness the statement by Federal Reserve Board Chairman William Martin on June 1, 1965, warning against a "new era" psychology such as existed in the 1920's. Also, the rise in the Treasury bill rate accelerated in the closing months of 1964; and some additional pressure seems to have been put on member bank reserves in recent months.

33. *Economic Report of the President,* January 1965, p. 85.

34. Actually, the rise in real GNP in the second quarter of 1965 seems to have been close to an annual rate of 4 per cent. It now appears (September 1965) that the increase in real GNP in 1965 will be a bit greater than that implied in the original forecast of 660 billions (as estimated before the August 1965 revisions of the national income accounts.)

35. The lapse of six months between manuscript and proof suggests that this prediction was too pessimistic.

Discussion

BY OTTO ECKSTEIN

Since the first of the Berkeley conferences two years ago, our understanding of the behavior of unemployment under various economic conditions has advanced enormously. At that conference the main question was whether full employment could be restored by the general expansion of markets or whether the basic character of unemployment had changed. The papers at this conference indicate that a solid body of empirical knowledge about the relationship of employment and unemployment to the movements in the economy has been established. Differences have been narrowed, and, as with many other problems in macroeconomics, we are now able to evaluate the evidence in terms of the magnitudes of the key parameters of the equations. We no longer quarrel about signs.

Some Propositions

I think today most serious students of these problems would agree with the following propositions:

1. The movements of aggregate employment and unemployment are mainly determined by changes in aggregate production and the growth of the labor force.

The supply of labor is positively elastic with respect to the availability of jobs: when employment rises, additional workers are attracted into the labor force.

3. This elasticity is concentrated among female workers and among male workers less than 25 years or more than 54 years of age. Changes in the workweek augment this response as the workweek lengthens with improving economic conditions.

4. Output per manhour—hence the labor requirement per unit of output—is determined by long-run upward trends in education, technology, and capital per worker, by the operating rates of industries, and by a short-run adjustment mechanism in the response of employment to changes in output.

5. As a result of points two to four, the response of unemployment to changes in GNP is far less than proportionate. An extra 1 per cent of GNP results in a reduction of unemployment of only 0.3 per cent on the average, although some variation is introduced by the composition of the change in GNP, its rate of acceleration, and changes in the demography of the working-age population.

6. The trend advance in productivity and the normal growth of the labor force require an increase of production of 3.5 to 4 per cent a year to keep the unemployment rate from rising.

7. Unemployment rates vary among groups; rates for inexperienced workers, less educated nonwhites, and unskilled workers are higher than average.

8. The composition of unemployment varies systematically with its level. As unemployment increases, the relative rates for nonwhite workers, inexperienced workers, and the unskilled deteriorate more absolutely and possibly more than proportionately. Conversely, a reduction in the national unemployment rate results in a particularly large improvement for these groups.

9. The composition of unemployment for any given national unemployment rate changes over time because of (a) changes in the composition of the working-age population by age, sex, color, education, and skill, (b) trend changes in participation rates, particularly of women, teenagers, and older workers, and (c) changes in the composition of the demand for different types of labor.

10. Labor supplies in particular occupations and industries are affected by the general path of the economy. In an economy steadily close to full employment companies and unions maintain training programs and use hiring standards that produce the labor force necessary for the long-run expansion of the industry. Recessions and years of slack reduce the labor force of a cyclical industry through curtailed training programs, greater union emphasis on seniority in hiring and transfers, early retirements, and other withdrawals from the industry's labor force.

Similarly, there is shrinkage in the labor force of areas with high unemployment—mainly through retirement and movement to other areas.

11. In recent years the preponderant changes in the labor mar-

ket have been on the supply rather than the demand side. These supply changes have affected the composition of unemployment. (a) The relative decline in the number of male workers in the 25-54 age brackets has improved their position, giving them unemployment rates under today's conditions which they had previously enjoyed only when the national unemployment rate was down to 4 per cent. (b) The large influx of Negro workers into urban labor markets has raised their unemployment rates. (c) The great recent increase in the number of teen-age workers has hampered their position substantially. (d) The great increase in the participation rates of women has had some adverse effects on their unemployment rates. (e) Finally, the sharp increase of young college graduates has raised their (still low) unemployment rates.

Changes in Employment, Labor Force, and Unemployment in the Current Expansion

The employment and unemployment changes of the last five years can be understood in the light of these propositions. Five years ago, in May 1960, according to the chronology of the National Bureau of Economic Research, the last business cycle hit its peak. The unemployment rate in that month was 5.2 per cent. Four years later, in May 1964, the national unemployment rate was at the identical level. Real output over that four-year interval grew by 3.8 per cent, apparently the growth rate necessary to keep unemployment constant over that period. In the last 12 months, however, the rate of growth accelerated under the stimulus of the tax cut to a point in excess of 4.5 per cent, and this acceleration has accomplished a reduction in the unemployment rate to 4.9 per cent in April and 4.6 per cent in May 1965.

Even more striking are the changes in the composition of employment and unemployment. With the increase in the rate of growth in 1964, employment of semiskilled operatives and unskilled nonfarm laborers rose almost twice as fast as total employment. In the preceding four years the employment of nonfarm laborers actually fell, and the employment of operatives was rising only at the national average. The same phenomenon can be seen in durable goods employment. From May 1964 to

May 1965 employment rose more than twice as much as it had in the entire four-year period.

The most startling shifts occurred in the service occupations. With alternative employment opportunities, workers left these occupations for higher-paying alternatives. From 1960 to 1964 employment in the service occupations rose by 14.5 per cent, or almost three times as fast as the national average, but from 1964 to 1965 employment fell by 2.7 per cent. In private household employment, a large part of the service occupations, increases of the first four years were completely erased by the 1964–1965 changes. Thus a major part of the upward trend in service jobs seems to have been due to the lack of alternative job opportunities. This repeats a pattern found earlier in the postwar period.

Females, nonwhites, and especially teenagers, made large employment gains. Teenage employment rose rapidly over the five-year period, but with a higher rate of growth in 1964–1965 the number of employed teenagers rose almost four times as fast as the national average.

These employment gains, together with the changes in the working age population, led to significant labor-force changes. Because of greater participation by older women, the female labor force grew more than twice as fast as the male labor force over the five-year period. The magnitude of the job problem among young workers can be seen in the growth of their labor force. For the age-sex groups 14–19 and 20–24 the five-year period witnessed expansions ranging from 15 to 30 per cent.

Unemployment changes reflect these factors. From 1960 to 1964 there was no improvement in nonwhite unemployment, and unemployment among women workers rose by 0.6 percentage points. Unemployment fell slightly in the blue-collar occupations but rose in the service occupations. Given the large increases in their labor force, unemployment among teenagers and women rose, with an especially sharp rise of almost 5 percentage points among teenage girls.

However, in the most recent 12 months of accelerated expansion the pattern of unemployment changes differed from the years before. It was particularly favorable to unskilled workers, nonwhites, and women. Although the national unemployment

TABLE 1. PERCENTAGE CHANGES IN EMPLOYMENT, LABOR FORCE, AND UNEMPLOYMENT, 1960–1964, 1964–1965, AND 1960–1965 (MAY-TO-MAY)

	Employment (percentage change, May to May)		
Occupation	1960–1964	1964–1965	1960–1965
Total	5.79	1.84	7.74
White collar	8.24	2.75	11.21
Professional	14.63	2.16	17.10
Managers	6.69	0.90	7.65
Clerical	8.42	3.36	12.07
Sales	−0.61	5.57	4.93
Blue collar	4.70	2.22	7.02
Craftsmen	5.47	−0.10	5.37
Operatives	5.90	3.57	9.68
Nonfarm laborers	−0.68	3.13	2.43
Service	14.51	−2.74	11.37
Private household	7.23	−7.36	−0.66
Other service	17.20	−1.19	15.81
Farm workers	−15.27	3.06	−12.67
Farmers	−16.16	1.20	−15.15
Farm laborers	−14.30	5.04	−9.97
Age	1960–1964	1964–1965	1960–1965
14–19	11.88	7.23	19.98
20–24	17.25	6.17	24.48
25–34	−1.88	1.42	−0.48
35–44	4.38	−0.49	3.87
45–54	6.20	1.05	7.32
55–64	10.40	2.14	12.76
65 and over	−0.06	−0.47	−0.54
Sex	1960–1964	1964–1965	1960–1965
Males	4.09	1.73	5.89
Females	9.16	2.04	11.39
Color	1960–1964	1964–1965	1960–1965
White	5.70	1.73	7.53
Nonwhite	6.58	2.68	9.44
Industry	1960–1964	1964–1965	1960–1965
Total	6.65	3.70	10.60
Mining	−12.67	−0.63	−13.22
Contract construction	5.71	4.03	9.96
Manufacturing	1.92	3.88	5.88
Durables	2.49	5.35	7.97
Nondurables	1.17	1.92	3.12
Transportation and public utilities	−1.67	2.30	0.60
Trade	6.42	4.01	10.69
Finance	10.44	2.39	13.07
Service	14.95	3.60	19.10
Government	13.93	4.23	18.74
Federal	3.74	0.21	3.96
State and local	17.68	5.53	24.19

	Total Labor Force (percentage change, May to May)		
Males	1960–1964	1964–1965	1960–1965
Total	3.97	1.20	5.21
14–19	20.14	5.90	27.22
20–24	11.53	3.61	15.56
25–34	−2.92	0.57	−2.37
35–44	2.31	−0.51	1.79
45–54	4.33	0.69	5.05
55–64	5.99	1.24	7.31
65 and over	−4.47	0.00	−4.47
Females	1960–1964	1964–1965	1960–1965
Total	9.91	1.23	11.25
14–19	11.00	4.50	15.99
20–24	21.01	5.02	27.08
25–34	1.19	0.98	2.18
35–44	7.05	−0.33	6.70
45–54	8.28	0.07	8.36
55–64	19.08	1.40	20.74
65 and over	11.71	−2.74	8.65

TABLE 1 *(Continued)*

Civilian Labor Force
(percentage change, May to May)

Color	1960–1964	1964–1965	1960–1965
Whites	5.70	1.45	7.23
Nonwhites	6.33	0.43	6.79

Unemployment
(change in percentage points, May to May)

Occupation	1960–1964	1964–1965	1960–1965
Total	0.0	−0.5	−0.5
White collar	—	−0.2	—
Professional	0.2	0.0	0.2
Managers	−0.3	−0.1	−0.4
Clerical	0.2	−0.5	−0.3
Sales	0.0	−0.2	−0.2
Blue collar	—	−0.6	—
Craftsmen	−0.6	0.2	−0.4
Operatives	−1.3	−0.6	−1.9
Nonfarm laborers	−1.2	−2.6	−3.8
Service	—	−1.0	—
Private household	1.8	−3.0	−1.2
Other service	0.3	−0.3	0.0
Farm workers	—	−0.3	—
Farmers	0.4	−0.4	0.0
Farm laborers	−0.3	−0.1	−0.4

	1960–1964		1964–1965		1960–1965	
Age	Male	Female	Male	Female	Male	Female
14–19	1.7	4.7	−0.4	−1.7	1.3	3.0
20–24	−1.0	0.9	−0.7	−1.8	−1.7	−0.9
25–34	−0.7	−0.1	−0.5	−0.6	−1.2	−0.7
35–44	−0.9	0.1	0.3	−0.4	−0.6	−0.3
45–54	−0.9	−0.1	−0.5	−0.5	−1.4	−0.6
55–64	−0.5	0.7	−0.7	−1.0	−1.2	−0.3
65 and over	0.3	0.0	−0.6	0.1	−0.3	0.1
Total	−0.4	0.6	−0.4	−0.7	−0.8	−0.1

Color	1960–1964	1964–1965	1960–1965
White	0.0	−0.3	−0.3
Nonwhite	0.0	−2.0	−2.0

Industry	1960–1964	1964–1965	1960–1965
Experienced	−0.4	−0.6	−1.0
Agriculture	0.5	−1.4	−0.9
Nonagriculture	−0.4	−0.5	−0.9
Mining	1.9	−1.9	0.0
Contract construction	−2.3	−0.1	−2.4
Manufacturing	−1.1	−0.7	−1.8
Durables	−1.5	−1.0	−2.5
Nondurables	−0.6	−0.2	−0.8
Transportation and public			
utilities	−0.4	−0.6	−1.0
Trade	0.1	−0.6	−0.5
Finance	0.3	−0.4	−0.1
Services	0.5	−0.5	0.0
Public	−0.1	−0.1	−0.2

Duration	(Percentage change, May to May)		
0–4 weeks	2.01	1.02	3.05
5–14 weeks	−1.67	−4.86	−6.43
15–26 weeks	9.23	−20.50	−13.16
27 weeks and over	28.71	−31.38	−11.68
Total	5.23	−8.38	−3.59

rate was falling by 0.5 percentage points, the rate for nonfarm laborers fell by 2.6, for nonwhites by 2.0, and for women by 0.7.

The improvement in long-term unemployment in the last 12 months is also gratifying. In the four years from 1960 to 1964 the number of individuals out of work for 27 weeks or more rose by 28.7 per cent; but from 1964 to 1965 the number of individuals out of work for 27 weeks or more fell by 31.4 per cent, completely erasing the four-year upward trend.

Vacancy Data and Their Meaning

The progress in recent months is large and important. It verifies what we have been teaching our students for the last 20 years and sets to rest false fears about our economy that were raised in the years of slack and mounting unemployment. The Council of Economic Advisers believes that our economy can achieve full employment with an effective combination of job-creating fiscal and monetary policies and strengthened and improved programs of manpower policy.

At this time some people's concern about our ability to return to levels of unemployment of 4 per cent or less is based on the fear of a rising volume of job vacancies leading to inflationary labor bottlenecks even while some substantial slack persists. The Rochester pilot survey of the National Industrial Conference Board and the study plans of people inside and outside the government have focused great attention on the job vacancy concept. This work is one of the frontiers of research at this time.

We look forward to improved vacancy statistics for the United States, and I am sure they will provide a vital supplement to our elaborate system of unemployment statistics as a gauge of the supply and demand pressures in various labor markets. However, this work will take time. We should not expect to be able to interpret these vacancy statistics meaningfully until a considerable record is available. The concepts must be clearly defined in terms of specific wages and employee qualifications. Every employer experiences vacancies; he is unable to recruit the kind of employees he would wish to have at wage rates he would like to pay. It is important that we stay free of the fallacy that equality of vacancies and unemployment constitutes equilibrium

Adjusted for seasonal variations

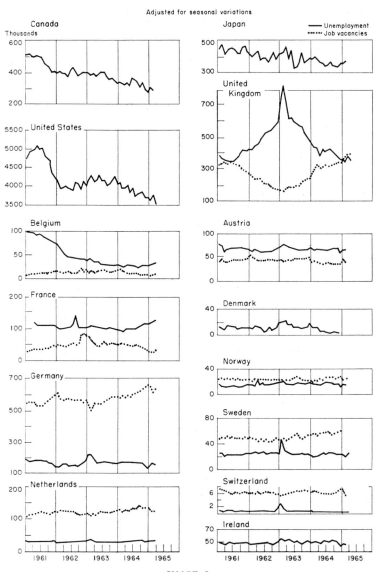

CHART 1

in the labor market—or full employment—in any meaningful sense.

The European experience is very useful in gaining understanding of vacancy statistics. In the four years from 1961 to 1965 vacancies have been consistently higher than unemployment in Germany, the Netherlands, Japan, Norway, Sweden, and Switzerland. Over the same period unemployment has been consistently higher than vacancies in France and Austria. (See Chart 1.) All of these countries have been at or near full employment by our standards.

Not only do the levels of the two series differ, from six times as many vacancies as unemployed in Germany to unemployment more than twice as high as vacancies in France, but the pattern of movement of the two series is not always consistent with the a priori expectations. From 1962 to 1964 the number of Japanese vacancies fell by 232,000, but the number of unemployed also fell by 30,000. In Belgium unemployment fell from near 100,000 to less than 40,000, but the number of vacancies was basically constant, between 10,000 and 20,000, over the entire period.

The United Kingdom comes the closest to exhibiting the expected pattern. Vacancies and unemployment move in opposite directions, with vacancies less than unemployment during recessions and the two series about equal during periods of full employment.

The problems of interpreting vacancy information can be seen in what little information we have for the United States. From 1963 to 1964 the help-wanted index rose, but the number of jobs in clearance with the employment service fell. Jobs in clearance for the skilled, semiskilled, and unskilled went up slightly, but these increases were more than offset by decreases in services, clerical, sales, and professional occupations. Yet from 1963 to 1964 employment rose by 1.5 million, and unemployment fell.

Discussion

BY MARTIN R. GAINSBRUGH

Once again the professional as well as the general public is in Dr. Gordon's debt, this time for his scholarly, dispassionate analysis of economic change in the second postwar decade, particularly as it has affected the course of national output, employment, and unemployment. Here is to be found a body of materials that first places the puzzling sequence of events since the mid-1950's, especially "sticky" unemployment, in balanced perspective and then raises penetrating and disturbing questions about the prospects of reducing the rate of unemployment in the years ahead.

Gordon's analysis is drawn largely from a common point of departure, the official national accounts in current and constant dollars (with the exception of a "new" series on deflated expenditures for new plant and equipment). This discussion thus centers on the interpretation of the evidence he assembles, particularly the degree of discount to be assigned to the improvement in employment that has accrued in the current expansion. My discussion is influenced by a recent similar examination of much the same period and data which came to somewhat more positive conclusions regarding the adequacy of the present and prospective rate of national economic growth.[1] My analysis suggests that the current improvement in job creation and the reduction in unemployment reflect the gratifying extent to which American industry has been restructured by the intensively competitive forces of the second postwar decade. Major industry after major industry has emerged from what, a decade ago, I identified as the "middle years," stripped of much postwar fat both organizationally and technologically. This, along with other factors such as intensification of R & D, tax relief, and tax reform, lead me to anticipate a more rapid rate of growth in real output in the third than in the second postwar decade. The major differences between Gordon's conclusions and mine arise from the following:

1. Economic Growth Rate High in Historic Perspective

In numerous instances it has been contended that "sticky un-employment" rose primarily because of inadequate growth in the late 1950's and the 1960's to date. This point is important because the prescription may be quite different for an economy suffering from a depressed growth rate than from an economy with a high growth rate but with an exceptionally high rate of entrance into its labor force.

Gordon examines national economic growth in this and the preceding three postwar expansions and finds the current rate to be "relatively moderate." This modest evaluation apparently stems from the fact that the rate for 1948–1953 was as high as 5.2 per cent. That period, however, benefited particularly from the Korean War. As he later shows, federal purchases rose by more

TABLE 1. ANNUAL PERCENTAGE RATES OF GROWTH FOR
SELECTED PERIODS, UNITED STATES, 1899–1964[a]

Period	Gross National Product (1963 prices)	Population[b]	Per Capita GNP (1963 prices)
1899–1964	2.9	1.5	1.6
1899–1929	2.9	1.6	1.3
1929–1964	3.9	1.4	2.5
1947–1964	3.4	1.7	1.7
1947–1950	3.7	1.7	2.0
1950–1955	3.8	1.7	2.1
1955–1960	2.2	1.8	0.4
1955–1964	3.1	1.7	1.4
1960–1964	4.3	1.5	2.7

Source: The Conference Board, based on data from U. S. Department of Commerce and National Bureau of Economic Research.

[a] Growth rates are computed from the least-squares trend of the logarithms of the data.

[b] Includes armed forces overseas. Data as of July 1.

than 20 per cent annually at that time. In contrast, personal consumption expenditures and private investment have advanced at a much more rapid rate in the 1960's than in 1948–1953.

On a per capita basis, using annual data, we find that the economic growth rate in the 1960's is as high as any preceding quinquennium in the postwar period. Population growth has slowed from 1.8 per cent per annum a decade ago to 1.5 per cent at present. Per capita GNP increased at an annual rate of 2.7 per cent during 1960–1964. As we can see from Table 1, this contrasts with about 2 per cent during the period 1947–1955.

Viewed over the long term, particularly for peacetime periods, the current rate of growth appears to deserve more positive emphasis than Gordon is inclined to give it. It may be that the "moderate" rating he assigns it underlies the barely passing grade he gives the process of job creation so far in the 1960's.

2. Record of Job Creation in the 1960's Impressive, Particularly in Private Sector

I am more impressed with the growth in employment than is Gordon, particularly because of the increase in the number of private payrolls. Gordon asks why we have not been able to achieve a closer approximation to full employment after more than four years of steady expansion. "It has," he indicates, "had only a modest effect in bringing the unemployment rate down from 5.6 per cent in 1960 to 5.2 per cent in 1964."

My reading is more positive. First, unemployment was cut from 5.7 per cent in 1963 to 5.2 per cent, with a rise of 4 per cent in real output. Gordon later suggests such a growth rate would have little impact on reducing the unemployment percentage. Second, and even more to the point, unemployment for the first half of 1965 has been cut to 4.8 per cent, compared with 5.4 per cent for the same period in 1964. The accompanying rate of increase in real output will apparently approximate 4 per cent. (The latter figure assumes a lower rate of growth in real output in the second quarter than in the initial quarter of 1965.)

The job creation rate has been particularly impressive in the private sector. The increase in private nonagricultural employment during the last year exceeded one and a half million. With the transition from an agricultural to an industrial society now virtually complete and with large-scale resource input exploiting the growth potential lying latent in the service industries, the setting for accelerated job creation may prove more favorable for the decade ahead than it did in the transitional years of the second postwar decade.

One might ask, in light of the job-creating performance of the mid-1960's, whether we are not close to, if not at, full employ-ment—at least in terms of adult, seasoned, habitual members of the labor force. The unemployment rate for married men, for example, is down to a decade low. Indeed, unemployment has in recent years changed in its character and causation for extra-ordinary social-demographic-economic reasons to which Gordon gives little attention in his present analysis. The unemployed of today are primarily the inexperienced young, nonwhites, and married women, many of whom seek part-time employment. The intent here is not to read these unemployed out of the labor force but rather to point up the significant change in the compo-sition of those now seeking employment. Unemployment differs sharply from what it was when the current business expansion began. The attack on it from now on could reflect this shift by emphasizing measures aimed at motivating, training, and placing these groups in productive employment, rather than relying as heavily on general fiscal and monetary stimulation of the econ-omy as in the opening half of this decade.

3. The "Middle Years" an Inheritance of World War II

Dr. Gordon advances the thesis that until recently the federal government has been one of the major sources of instability in the American economy. The evidence offered is largely the de-cline in federal purchase of goods and services after the Korean War without any accompanying significant cut in taxes. Ideologi-cally attractive as this argument may be to an observer, I find the basic source of the "middle years" in the imbalances stem-ming from World War II. The period Gordon describes as "rela-tive stagnation" is the traditional readjustment following great wars. In fact, such adjustments were far more devastating for

earlier postwar generations than the series of rolling readjust-
ments experienced by this postwar generation.

Gordon observes: "The drag on the economy during these
years came entirely from the federal government, whose expenditures on goods and services declined sharply between 1953 and
1957."

Those were years of widespread bottlenecks, particularly of
capital goods, with an accompanying sharp rise in prices. Would
not a still more rapid rate of increase in federal government expenditures have resulted in escalating prices still more without
adding significantly to real output? The ensuing recession might
then have been even longer and deeper.

At a later point Gordon places similar emphasis on two causa-
tive factors: "Recovery from the recession [1957–1958] was sluggish. The explanation for this sluggishness clearly lies in the combined behavior of federal spending and private nonresidential
investment."

Why was nonresidential investment so small? In my view, and
in Gordon's at a later point, this type of investment was low
because of the excess capacity created in the late stages of the
preceding expansion. In the broad sweep of time since World
War II the excesses touched off by the artificial stimuli of the
war—not the least of which was the rush to build capacity—
seem far more the root cause of the economic doldrums of the
middle years than does instability of federal purchases.

Job Vacancies, Unemployment, and Future Growth

In closing, I would like to offer a tentative conclusion derived
from The Conference Board's continuing job vacancy surveys in
Rochester and from those of the BES in 16 other labor markets.
These in combination suggest that the job vacancy rate in recent
months has hovered around 2 per cent of total labor demand.
Meanwhile unemployment has fallen to less than 5 per cent of
the labor force. This suggests a considerable excess of unemployed over unfilled jobs even after four years of expansion. Yet
this narrowing of the gap (not elimination) has apparently been
sufficient to trigger, or at least create a climate for, negotiated
wage bargains significantly in excess of those struck in recent

years, with concomitant pressure on producer prices. The steel negotiations still remain unresolved.

Offhand, one might theorize that the sizable excess of unemployed over job openings and the absence of bottlenecks would make possible a higher national economic growth rate without causing rising prices. But do not recent developments suggest the contrary?

The existence of this contradiction serves to underscore both the changing character of the unemployed and the serious immobilities existing in the unused labor supply. Many of the unemployed are in the wrong locations; sufficient numbers cannot be induced to relocate; a high proportion has inappropriate job qualifications—too old, too young, unskilled, or with obsolete skills. In the next decade, moreover, the greatly increased numbers and labor-force proportions of young workers will aggravate the existing imbalances.

The policy implications therefore appear to run strongly in the direction of mitigating imbalances in the unused labor supply by increasing the mobility and fluidity of the unemployed, thereby increasing aggregate demand. This would raise the probability of absorbing the unemployed, thereby raising the growth rate without overheating the economy. Given the combination of productive employment of otherwise submarginal labor coupled with the continuing new wave of massive capital investment, it might be necessary to have trade-offs between unemployment and inflation in the third postwar decade. By way of furthering fluidity and flexibility, special tax incentives might be offered for the training and employment of the young, similar to the 7 per cent tax incentive for investment. In addition, institutional barriers such as the minimum wage might be lowered temporarily for the young.

In summary, I return to the problem Dr. Gordon emphasizes of how best to reduce the unemployment rate without causing significant increases in prices. Further stimulation of aggregate demand alone may not succeed in substantially lowering unemployment without inducing significant price increases because of the prevailing composition of the unemployed. A combination of private and public labor-force policies designed to retrain, re-equip, and reallocate the presently unemployed, thereby increasing aggregate demand, holds far more promise. Much of the recent criticism of training and retraining programs arises from inadequate recognition that this may be an effective, if not the only, route toward further reduction of unemployment without concurrent inflation.

NOTES

1. Jules Backman and Martin R. Gainsbrugh, *The Forces Influencing the American Economy* (New York: New York University School of Commerce, 1965).

Discussion

BY JOSEPH A. PECHMAN

Professor Gordon's paper provides a systematic review of the factors that differentiate the present expansion from its three postwar predecessors. I find very little to quarrel with in his analysis, so my comments are largely in the nature of elaboration of some of the points he makes. Specifically, I should like to expand a bit on fiscal policy as it has developed in the last ten years and to discuss the outlook for continuation of the expansion in the year ahead.

Fiscal Policy

It is now clear that the major reasons for the slow rate of growth in the late 1950's were the disappointing performance of plant and equipment expenditures following the 1955–1957 private investment boom and the unfortunate fiscal policy that was pursued. (Monetary policy also contributed, and I shall have a word to say about that shortly.) In contrast, since early 1961, our fiscal authorities—though not sufficiently aggressive to achieve full employment—have been aware of the dangers of constraint and have supplied enough stimulation at strategic moments to keep the expansion going.

One indicator of the changed strategy is the balance in the federal income and product account. After each of the first three postwar recessions the federal deficit was sharply converted to a large unsustainable surplus. From the low point in the recession to the peak in the subsequent recovery the swing was $20.9 billion between 1949 and 1950, $19.5 billion between 1953 and 1956, and $19.3 billion between 1958 and 1960. In the current expansion the swing so far has been only $6.6 billion. (The particular quarters used in these calculations are shown in Table 1.) In fact, the federal government has run a continuous deficit on income and product account since the fourth quarter of 1960,

TABLE 1. Swing from Maximum Deficit to Maximum
Surplus in the Federal Income and Product
Account in the Four Postwar Expansions
(billions of dollars)

Quarter with Maximum Deficit	Deficit	Quarter with Maximum Surplus	Surplus	Swing from Maximum Deficit to Maximum Surplus
1949-II	− 3.9	1950-III	17.0	20.9
1953-IV	−11.8	1956-I	7.7	19.5
1958-II	−11.1	1960-I	8.2	19.3
1961-I	− 6.0	1963-IV	0.6	6.6

Source: Office of Business Economics, Department of Commerce.

with the exception of the third quarter of 1963 when there was
a small surplus of $0.6 billion (and this was quickly erased by
the 1964 tax cut).

Monetary policy also contributed to the disappointing performance of the economy in the late 1950's, as well as to the much
better performance between 1961 and 1964. The money supply
(demand deposits adjusted plus currency) rose at an annual rate
of only 0.9 per cent in the five years ending December 1960;
in the four years ending December 1964 it rose at the rate of
3.2 per cent per year. Thus, instead of offsetting the deficiency
in fiscal policy in the late 1950's, monetary policy aggravated
the situation. Happily, it has not been perverse so far in this
expansion, although the recent reduction in the rate of growth
of the money supply seems ominous.

In looking over the record of the last ten years, two major
policy errors stand out: one committed by the Eisenhower Administration, and the other by the Kennedy Administration. Had
these errors not been made, I feel reasonably sure that unemployment in the United States would long ago have been reduced to 4 per cent or less, and the nation's growth rate would
have been much higher.

The first error occurred in 1959–1960. The recovery from the 1957–1958 recession proceeded well in the first year. The full employment surplus was reduced from $7.4 billion in the last half of 1957 to $3.2 billion a year later (Table 2), and the federal government ran its largest peacetime deficit in history. Income and employment quickly exceeded their peak levels and rose at satisfactory rates as measured by the yardstick of previous recoveries. On the basis of experience, it was not unreasonable to assume that output would continue to improve and the economy would be back to an acceptable employment level in a short time. But fiscal and monetary policies were tightened drastically and prematurely. This aborted the recovery, and the next recession developed before full employment was reached.

The second error occurred in 1962. Again, the first year recovery from the 1960–1961 recession had proceeded at a satisfactory pace. Again, the federal deficit was enlarged through increased expenditures, and the economy responded well. And again it was reasonable to assume that the private economy would be strong enough—particularly with the additional investment incentives provided by the investment credit and the more liberalized depreciation allowances—to push through to a level satisfactory enough to warrant some reduction in the fiscal stimu-

TABLE 2. FULL EMPLOYMENT SURPLUS, BY
HALF-YEARS, 1957–1964
(BILLIONS OF DOLLARS)

Year	Amount	Year	Amount
1957-I	4.4	1961-I	11.7
II	7.4	II	9.4
1958-I	6.0	1962-I	5.6
II	3.2	II	7.6
1959-I	6.6	1963-I	9.7
II	7.0	II	11.1
1960-I	13.0	1964-I	4.3
II	13.6	II	3.2

Source: Council of Economic Advisers.

lus provided by the federal budget. The full employment surplus had been reduced from $13.6 billion in the last half of 1960 to $5.6 billion in the first half of 1962 (Table 2). Instead of continuing to ease up, however, the Administration reduced the growth of expenditures, and the decline in the full employment surplus was reversed. As we now know, the assumption that the recovery would be similar to those in 1948–1953 and 1955–1957 turned out to be erroneous, and the 1964 tax cut, officially proposed in January 1963 and publicly discussed by the President as early as August 1962, was needed to correct the error.

In short, I agree with what is implicit in Professor Gordon's paper, that the major errors in policy during the last decade can be traced to inadequate recognition in Washington of the drag on the economy resulting from the slow growth of investment. It is elementary that, with private investment lagging, either consumption or government expenditures must rise to fill the gap, and this requires the federal government to reduce taxes or to increase expenditures. The 1964 tax cut was required because it was recognized that the private economy cannot "go it alone" in present circumstances. There is no doubt that the prolongation of the expansion to record length can be attributed to the adoption of the tax cut.

The Outlook

My views on the outlook for the year ahead can perhaps be inferred from what I have already said. I agree with my colleague Bert Hickman and with Professor Gordon that private investment cannot be expected to grow sufficiently in the next few years to keep the economy moving upward without further fiscal stimulus. The rate of private saving is simply too high. In these circumstances economic policy should continue to chop away at the full employment surplus with federal expenditure increases and tax reductions.

Current estimates indicate that the full employment surplus ran at an annual rate of about $5 billion in the first half of 1965. The tax system generates at least $7 billion additional revenue each year, assuming growth in money GNP of about 5.5 per cent per year. My guess is that full employment in this country, under present and immediately prospective conditions, is not consistent with any surplus in the federal budget (on national income and product account). Our problem is therefore to increase expenditures or reduce taxes by much more than $7 billion per year if we are to prolong the expansion and achieve full employment in the not-too-distant future. Given the restraints imposed on policy by the political process, this will be no easy task.

The excise tax cut to be enacted by the end of this month will help. So will the increased social security and Medicare benefits that will soon be enacted. But these effects will be offset to a large extent by the $5 billion social security tax increase expected to become effective January 1, 1966. Thus present plans will not prevent a rise in unemployment later this year or next year.

It is still too early to judge the 1967 budget, but recent experience suggests that the concern about prices and the balance of payments will continue to exercise just enough influence to prevent the economy from reaching its full potential. As Professor Gordon has indicated, the performance of wages, unit labor costs, and prices have been noteworthy in the current expansion. Average compensation has not risen by more than the average increase in productivity, although some isolated settlements have exceeded the average productivity standard. Wholesale prices have crept up a bit in the last few months, but most of this rise is due to increases in farm prices. Wholesale prices of industrial products have inched up by less than 1.5 per cent in the last year and a half, a record which probably cannot be matched anywhere else in the world. Thus our competitive position in the world economy has improved. Although it is true that we have not completely solved our balance-of-payments problem, it is hard to see how it will be significantly improved if we continue to deny ourselves the benefit of an additional $25 or $30 billion of output (the gap between potential GNP at 4 per cent unemployment and actual GNP). Imports might rise a bit, but this would be more than offset by the effect of the increased productivity of firms operating at improved levels of capacity utilization and higher corporate profits on our competitive position and on the attractiveness of home as against foreign investment.

In brief, there is no *economic* reason why the current expansion need come to a halt in the foreseeable future. Nor is there any economic reason why we should not set our sights high enough to reduce unemployment below 4 per cent. The remedy is to continue to apply the same fiscal medicine—more federal expenditures and more tax cuts—that has worked so well in the last four and a half years.

PART II

THE RESPONSE OF LABOR SUPPLY

TO THE DEMAND FOR LABOR

CHAPTER 3

Labor-Force Participation and Unemployment

A Review of Recent Evidence

BY JACOB MINCER

Introduction

After three decades of research and occasionally animated controversy, the short-run behavior of the labor force is still not well understood.[1] We are not clear about the causes of monthly movements of as many as three million people in and out of the labor force, nor do we fully understand the huge seasonal swing in the labor force and the year-to-year variation in the seasonal. In the postwar years this variation amounted to a difference of two to four million people between the winter low and summer high. The net annual changes in the labor force were much milder, but these also varied from a quarter of a million to one and a half million during this period.

Relative to the size of the labor force and the population, these net annual fluctuations are small. Yet analytical interest has centered primarily on these nonseasonal net changes in the labor force rather than on the much bigger seasonal and gross (into and out of the labor force) movements. The reason is not hard to find. In the quest for diagnoses of unemployment and inflation problems it is important to know what are the labor-force responses, if any, to the short-run "cyclical" fluctuations in aggregate demand.

When the issue was first raised, after the Great Depression, the income and substitution effects of standard demand theory, as applied to the worker's allocation of time, were pitted against one another as separate and opposing theories under the labels "additional" and "discouraged" workers, respectively. It was soon realized, however, that these two effects may coexist in life, as they do in theory. Additional workers may enter the labor market to bolster declining family income in a recession, but at the same time some unemployed workers may give up the apparently hopeless job search and withdraw from the labor market, whereas potential labor-force entrants or re-entrants may be inhibited from even starting to look for jobs. Thus the question is not which of the tendencies is the true one but which is stronger.

This is an empirical question. Until recently the weight of evidence, emerging largely from the researches of Clarence Long [1], suggested that, except for periods of war mobilization when the labor force expands and severe depression during which it probably shrinks, the labor force neither receives clear-cut net gains nor suffers net losses under the pressure of cyclically high effective demand or cyclically high unemployment.

Recently, new studies have addressed themselves to the old question, attacking various bodies of data with modern analytical tools. Although the conclusions reached by some of these studies are best described as agnostic, a growing number give unqualified support to the notion that the labor force, as measured, responds positively even to the relatively mild fluctuations characteristic of the postwar period.

In what follows I shall examine (a) the recent empirical studies of the relation between labor-force participation and employment conditions, (b) the recent empirical record bearing on the question, (c) the concept of "disguised" unemployment, and (d) some relevant implications of recent labor-force trends.

Review of Recent Research

The studies under review fall into three distinct categories, determined by the kinds of data used. Each analysis specializes either in (a) monthly gross-flow data, (b) cross-section area comparisons of labor markets, or (c) time-series data.

Gross-change analyses. Gross-change data, derived from the monthly Current Population Survey, offer potentially the richest insights into labor-force behavior. The employment status of individuals—consisting of three categories, employed, unemployed, and out of the labor force—is presented in the current month with information on the employment status of the same individuals in the preceding month. This reveals the anatomy of any monthly net change in the labor force; a net increase (or reduction) in the size of a given labor force can be traced to its component flows into and out of employment. As mentioned before, these data show a huge amount of labor-force turnover even in periods of relative stability.

The major advantage of the data for our problem is that they permit the separate identification of the added-worker and discouraged-worker phenomena in the gross flows. The disadvantage of the data lies in the difficulty of reliably establishing inferences about net changes. This is because response errors, which in other data tend to be offsetting, are additive in the gross-change data, leading to large errors and biases.[2]

Hansen [2] examined the monthly gross-change data for the period 1948 through 1959. His focus was not, however, on labor-force changes but on the effects of labor-force flows on the observed level of unemployment.[3] He found that gross additions to unemployment by labor-force entrants and re-entrants increased in recession periods but that the same happened, and at about the same rate, to withdrawals of unemployed from the labor force. On balance, therefore, the observed increase in unemployment during recession periods was neither enlarged by the increased influx of additional workers nor reduced by the increased labor-force withdrawals of the unemployed.

These findings do not provide direct evidence on the total response of the labor force, since movements into and out of employment are not shown. It is likely, for example, that in recessions the flow from out of the labor force to employment diminishes. Of course, the opposite flow from employment to out of the labor force is also likely to decrease. But if the latter flow decreases less than the former, Hansen's results would imply a shrinking of the labor force during recessions.

In a more comprehensive analysis of gross-change data Altman [3] distinguishes the effects of gross flows on the size of the labor force from the effects on the observed size of unemployment. However, he restricts himself to an analysis of the labor force of married women for the period from 1955 to 1962. His findings on the cyclical flows between unemployment and out of the labor force are similar to Hansen's, but he establishes the reality of additional and discouraged workers a bit more clearly. There is a positive correlation between gross additions to the labor force of married women and the unemployment rate of married men. There is also a positive correlation between reductions in the labor force of married women and their own unemployment rate.

Concerning net effects, Altman suggests a slight dominance of the added worker in affecting the unemployment rate simultaneously with a small net discouragement effect on the size of the labor force during recessions. He also suggests possible differences in early and later stages of the cycle. These are interesting possibilities, but although the noise in the data is not fatal to the findings on gross changes it makes conclusions about net effects much less secure.[4]

Cross-section analyses. Comparisons during a given observation period of different family units in surveys, or of population groups in different areas, have also been utilized for exploring the determinants of labor-force participation. The empirical procedure now commonly used consists of estimating from these cross sections the parameters of a single equation relating labor-force rates of a given population group in the various areas to a set of independent variables. The major variables, based on price-theory considerations, are family income and the wage rate (or full-time earnings) of the individuals in the group. A simple statistical model is

$$(1) \qquad M = a + b_1 Y + b_2 W + e$$

where M is the labor-force rate, Y, the family income, W, the wage rate, and e, a set of other variables of possible interest, such as family size, education, or geographic area. In this model b_1 is an estimate of the income effect, expected to be negative, and b_2 is an estimate of the substitution effect,[5] expected to be positive. If Y and W are averages of groups in labor markets, they are likely to approximate "normal" or "long-run" levels of income and wage rate, and the coefficients, b_1 and b_2 measure long-run effects. Define variables y_t and w_t as short-run deviations of family income and personal wages, respectively, from their "normal," "full-employment" levels. Their inclusion in equation (1) makes possible a specific exploration of effects of short-term changes in economic conditions on participation rates. Equation (1) becomes:

$$(2) \qquad M = a + b_1 Y + b_2 W + c_1 y_t + c_2 w_t + e$$

The coefficient c_1 can be interpreted as the added-worker effect (per unit of cyclical income change) and c_2 as the discouraged-worker effect (per unit of wage change). Strictly speaking, this interpretation is valid only if Y and W, as measured, do not show any cyclical variations. If Y and W are affected by cyclical fluctuation, c_1 and c_2 do not tell the whole story. Parts of the cyclical effects are then contained in the b_1 and b_2 coefficients.

Separate estimates of c_1 and c_2 are difficult to obtain in the cross section.[6] However, an indirect estimate of the net cyclical effects on labor-force participation may be obtained under the additional assumption that the cyclical deviations y_t and w_t are negative functions of the relevant unemployment rate u in the area. Then equation (2) can be written as

$$(3) \qquad M = a + b_1 Y + b_2 W + b_3 u + e$$

If all these assumptions hold, the sign of b_3 represents the direction of the net response of the labor force to cyclical differentials in labor-market conditions among the areas.[7] Whether such an interpretation is valid depends on the nature of the inter-area differentials in unemployment rates. As we shall see, these need not reflect only, or even primarily, cyclical differences.

Two recent studies use model (1) in the form of equation (3), with a few variables added, for the specific purpose of explaining the net effects of employment conditions on participation rates. One is the study of Bowen and Finegan [6], the other of Cain, to which reference has already been made. Because the methodology, data, and results are very similar in the two studies, this discussion does not distinguish between them, except as indicated.

The results obtained by Bowen and Finegan and the comparable findings of Cain are impressive in that a strong net negative sensitivity of labor force to unemployment (a negative coefficient b_3) is apparent for all major population groups in the Census years 1940, 1950, and 1960.[8] For the whole labor force a combined estimate of the regression coefficient b_3 in 1960 was −0.68, suggesting that a 1-percentage-point increase in the unemployment rate is associated, on the average, with ⅔ of a percentage point decrease in the total labor-force participation rate.[9]

To anticipate later findings, the pattern of differential sensitivities, which they found in the age-sex cross sections, is qualitatively comparable with that found in time series. But the cross-section estimates of the net response of the labor force to unemployment are higher in total and in male subgroups than the corresponding estimates obtained from time series (see Table 1, next section). These high estimates also assert the existence of relationships in cross sections which are not visible in time series. For example, the significant effect of unemployment on the prime labor force of males (age 25–54) shown in the cross section is not detectable in time series.

The time-series parameters purport to measure short-run cyclical labor-force responses. Do the cross-section parameters represent incorrect estimates of the time-series relationship or do they provide somewhat different kinds of information than time-series estimates? The answer is both, to some degree.

A purely statistical exaggeration of the negative size and significance of the regression coefficients may result from spurious correlation. Recall that the independent variable U/L is the unemployment rate in the area (of the whole labor force in Bowen and Finegan, of the male labor force in Cain), and the dependent variable L_i/P_i is the labor-force rate of the particular population group i. Now, if job opportunities are the only variable, aside from those already included in the regression, which similarly affects the sizes of the total and component labor forces in the area, a smaller U in the numerator of the independent variable will be associated with a larger L in the denominator of the independent variable and with a larger numerator of the dependent variable, correctly showing a negative correlation. To the extent, however, that factors other than job opportunities and those listed in the regression create similar differences in (total and component) labor forces across areas they will again cause the numerator of the dependent and denominator of the independent variables to move in the same direction, creating some degree of "spurious" negative correlation and biasing the negative coefficients toward higher values.[10] It is possible, at this level of conjecture, to think of positive spuriousness as well. Autonomous shifts of labor supply of particular groups could create a positive correlation between U and L. It is unlikely, however, that such shifts would be random with respect to areas.

One factor amenable to investigation which might create a certain amount of negative spuriousness is the seasonal component of the unemployment rate. During the Census week, as at any other time, this component must vary from one area to another across the United States. Because the seasonal component of the labor force is inversely related, except in the summer months, to the seasonal component of unemployment,[11] this is a likely source of upward bias in the observed partial correlation and regression coefficients. An attempt to ascertain the magnitude of this bias suggests that it is likely to be small, though perhaps not negligible.[12]

The substantive question about the cross-section estimates relates to their interpretation. Do they represent responses to short-run (cyclical) variations in job opportunities or are they more appropriately recognized as long-run responses to long-run differences? Such responses are likely to be stronger in area cross sections than in aggregate time series. Migration to better job opportunities is an alternative to dropping out of the labor force, an alternative that is not available in the aggregate when conditions worsen.

If area differences in unemployment represent, in large part, short-run variations in job opportunities, the *levels* of unemployment in the various areas in, say, 1960, should be positively correlated with *changes* in these rates from 1959 or from 1958 to 1960. However, I found no correlation with changes from 1959 or from 1958.[13] At the same time, there was a strong correlation ($r = +.8$) between unemployment levels in 1957 and in 1964 in the same areas. The correlation between 1950 and 1960 was not much smaller. The conclusion must be that the unemployment rates in the areas do not reflect short-run, transitory components in Y and W of Model (1). Rather, they represent long-run structural differences among areas to which participation adjusts.

More evidence in favor of this interpretation is provided by the experience in the depressed areas. In 17 major depressed areas (as classified in 1961) the total labor force declined by 6.3 per cent between 1953 and 1960, whereas the national civilian labor force increased by 11.1 per cent.[14] Again, between 1957 and 1963, the aggregate work force in the 12 major depressed areas declined by about 6 per cent compared with an increase of nearly 8 per cent in all areas.[15]

How much of this response is migration and how much labor-force withdrawal is not clear. That migration may be important is readily apparent from the fact that there is a negative correlation between the relatively stable SMA levels of unemployment (1960 and 1957 were tried alternately) and the rates of population growth between 1950 and 1960 in these areas. To illustrate:[16] the 20 SMA's with slowest population growth (eight actually declined) were mainly depressed areas, with an average unemployment rate of 8.5 per cent in 1960, whereas almost all of the 20 fastest growing SMA's had unemployment rates below the national average. Migration, being selective, raises the labor-force rates in the receiving areas (and these have low unemployment rates) and lowers them in the areas of out-migration (which have high unemployment rates), even *within* age groups.

I conclude that the findings in the cross-section analyses constitute evidence largely in favor of a hypothesis that prolonged depressed employment conditions in an area tend to shrink the area's labor-force rates. If migration is relevant, this shrinking should be weaker when areas of potential immigration are also depressed. This may be the reason for the relatively low 1940 levels of the partial correlation and regression coefficients in the Bowen-Finegan regressions and for the dramatic increases in them afterward. If so, the parameters based on recent cross-section data may even overestimate the effects of a severe depression. Although the differential pattern of age-sex group labor-force behavior is qualitatively comparable in cross section and time series (see Table 1), I conclude that the application of cross-section sensitivity parameters to the fluctuations we have experienced in the postwar period may strongly overestimate the response.

Time-Series Analyses. Several recent studies undertake a direct attack on time series to explore the effects of short-run variations in employment demand on the size of the labor force.

Dernburg and Strand [7] apply multiple regression and simultaneous equations to the analysis of monthly data covering the period 1947 through 1962. Their basic equation is

$$\left(\frac{L}{P}\right)_t = a_m + a_1 \left(\frac{E}{P}\right)_t + a_2 \left(\frac{X}{P}\right)_{t+2} + a_3 \left(\frac{1}{P}\right)_t + e_{t1}$$

$(L/P)_t$ is the adult civilian labor-force participation ratio in month t, $(E/P)_t$ is the percentage of the adult civilian noninstitutional population employed in month t, and $(X/P)_{t+2}$ is the ratio of new unemployment-compensation exhaustions to the adult civilian noninstitutional population two months after t.

Variations in E/P are supposed to represent short-run variations in employment opportunities, and X/P the relevant variations in income prospects. The sign of a_1 is expected to be positive, reflecting the discouraged-worker effect. The sign of a_2 is also expected to be positive, reflecting the added-worker effect. The presumption is that the prospect of loss of income due to the exhaustion of unemployment compensation causes secondary workers in the family to enter the labor force.[17]

The following estimates were obtained (1) for the whole period and (2) for the shorter period 1953-1962:[18]

$$(1) \quad \left(\frac{L}{P}\right)_t = a_m + \underset{(.0308)}{.8715} \left(\frac{E}{P}\right)_t + \underset{(.641)}{12.347} \left(\frac{X}{P}\right)_{t+2}$$

$$- \underset{(419.4)}{3492.2} \left(\frac{1}{P}\right)_t + e_{t1}$$

$$R^2 = 0.8138 \qquad S_u = 0.00227$$

$$(2) \quad \left(\frac{L}{P}\right)_t = a_m + \underset{(.0367)}{.9490} \left(\frac{E}{P}\right)_t + \underset{(.735)}{12.699} \left(\frac{X}{P}\right)_{t+2}$$

$$- \underset{(695.4)}{5326.1} \left(\frac{1}{P}\right)_t + e_{t1}$$

$$R^2 = 0.8766 \qquad S_u = 0.00206$$

The results appear to be a striking confirmation of both the discouraged- and added-worker effects. An auxiliary simultaneous equation, which relates the exhaustion ratio to the employment ratio, permits an estimate of the total, that is, the net effect of changes in the employment ratio on the labor-force ratio. The net coefficient is positive, showing a dominant discouragement effect, that is, a clear procyclical behavior of the labor force. The size of the net coefficient is interpreted to mean that over the period 1947-1962 a fall in employment of 100 was on balance associated with withdrawal from the labor force of 38 workers.

Although the substantive meaning of the results seems clear and reasonable, some of the statistical coefficients pose difficulties. Thus I read the coefficient of X/P as saying that, other things being equal, the prospect of one additional exhaustion of unemployment-compensation benefits (say, by a family head) pushes as many as 12(!) wives or relatives into, or deters them from leaving, the labor force. If X/P does not mean what it says, it must be a proxy for some other variable which is at work.

Another doubt is raised by the over-all amazingly good predictability of labor-force size, even on a monthly basis, as shown by the remarkably small standard error of estimate (S_u). Translated into numbers of people, this standard error amounts to about 140,000–160,000, a figure that is *smaller* than the average sampling standard error of month-to-month changes in the labor force.[19]

These doubts are further increased by the following consideration: Suppose that X/P is indeed a proxy, namely for the unemployment-population ratio U/P. A multiple regression of $(L/P)_t$ on $(E/P)_t$ and $(U/P)_t$ would produce a perfect fit in which each partial regression coefficient is equal to unity. But U/P is not the same as X/P. Moreover, X/P has a lead of two months, whereas the tautological regression requires a concurrent figure. To check on these reasonable objections, I correlated U/P with X/P on a concurrent basis and then with X/P leading one quarter.[20] The lead boosted the correlation from $+.8$ to over $+.9!$ This comes dangerously close to fulfilling the requirements of the tautological model. Admittedly, neither the multiple correlation nor the regression coefficients are literally equal to unity in the empirical regressions. But the coefficient at E/P is close, whereas the coefficient at X/P is about half the value that would be obtained if X/P were a strict fraction of U/P.[21] However, this does not dispel the doubts: the random component in X/P differs from that in U/P, and creates "errors in variables" effects that bias the regression coefficients downward.

Having confessed to all these doubts, I do not propose to reject the Dernburg-Strand findings. Their message may be a correct one, but I do not see how one can reliably extract that message from their equations.[22] It might be argued that because it is the inclusion of the income variable X/P into the equation that creates most of the insecurity in interpreting the multiple regressions perhaps restriction of the equation to E/P would be a safer though cruder approach. It foregoes the ambition of detecting each of the separate income and substitution effects, but it would, at least descriptively,[23] indicate the net outcome.

Dernburg and Strand show the result of doing this in equation (1b):

$$\left(\frac{L}{P}\right)_t = a_m' + \underset{(.0373)}{.3902} \left(\frac{E}{P}\right)_t - \underset{(740.2)}{2341.0} \left(\frac{1}{P}\right)_t + e_{t1}'$$

$$R^2 + 0.405 \qquad S_u = 0.0041$$

Once again the triumph of the discouraged worker seems to be established for the period 1947–1962, on a monthly basis.[24]

This descriptive "net outcome" approach was followed by Tella [9, 10] and by Cooper and Johnston [11]. Tella relates trend-adjusted labor-force-population ratios to employment-population ratios of the same population group, first for men and women separately on an annual basis from 1948–1962 [9]. In a second paper [10] he extends this analysis to 14 age-sex groups, on a quarterly basis, from the end of 1947 to the middle of 1964. In the quarterly analysis the employment variable is lagged one quarter in order to avoid bias due to the presence of the same sampling error in the two variables. In each case the military is included in the labor force, employment, and population figures. Cooper and Johnston [11] used the same quarterly data to relate trend-adjusted unemployment-population ratios $(U/P)_t$ to employment-population ratios $(E/P)_t$. The (U, E) regressions can be translated into (L, E) regressions, and conversely, by means of the following identities:

$$b_{ue} \equiv b_{le} - 1 \quad \text{and} \quad \frac{b_{ue}{}^2}{r_{ue}{}^2} \equiv \frac{b_{le}{}^2}{r_{le}{}^2} - (1 + 2b_{ue})$$

where b_{ue} is the relevant (partial or simple) regression coefficient of U/P on E/P, b_{le} is the relevant (partial or simple) regression coefficient of L/P on E/P, and r^2 with corresponding subscripts is the relevant coefficient of determination.

Table 1 brings together the regression estimates of the net effect of employment variation on the size of the total labor force and its age-sex subgroups. Additional statistics of interest are shown in Table 2. It is important to note that in each case labor force of a group was related to its own employment. Columns 1, 5, 7, and 8 are conceptually comparable estimates of the net effect b_{le}. They differ, of course, in terms of data and of methodology, as already described and as noted in the table, but nevertheless there is a fair amount of agreement in the results. There is a net positive sensitivity to employment conditions in totals and in all groups with the exception of the primary male labor force, age 25–55, but even this group is positively sensitive in the cross section, as mentioned. There is further agreement on the greater sensitivity of females as a group compared with males as a group. Finally, the extreme age groups are more sensitive than the middle-age groups. The single most important conclusion is that, in time-series, *labor-force sensitivity to employment conditions is a characteristic of the secondary labor force.*

It is true, of course, that most of the males 20–24 and many of the other workers in the "secondary" labor force are not secondary in any sense. The results, however, suggest that differences in behavior among age-sex groups are likely to be attributable to the differential proportions of secondary workers in the groups. The rank correlations between the average labor-force participation rates in the groups (Column 9, Table 1) and the "employment-sensitivity" coefficients were +.85, +.80, and +.65, when compared with columns 8, 5, and 1, respectively.

Proceeding to the differences among the results of the studies, there are several noteworthy features:

1. The cross-section sensitivity estimates exceed the corresponding time-series estimates in the male group and therefore in total, but not in the female groups. As noted, the cross-section sensitivity also extends to the primary labor force of males. These differences from the time-series estimates again suggest the role of migration in the inter-area labor-force adjustments. Employment-connected migration is likely to be a family decision based largely on the employment situation of the primary worker.[25]

2. The estimates in Columns 1 and 5 are based on the same quarterly data. However, Tella (Column 1) lagged the employment variable one quarter, which reduced the sizes of his coefficients in all groups, except males 55–64.[26] Indeed, the coefficients in Column 5 are those that Tella would have obtained, if he had run a coincident rather than lagged regression.

3. The regression coefficients in the Cooper–Johnston (U, E) regression (Column 3) do not convey any different information from those obtained by an (L, E) regression of the same data. Strength of the net discouragement effect is measured by the extent to which the absolute size of the negative b_{ue} coefficient is less than unity. This difference is precisely equal to the coefficient b_{le}, by definition.[27]

TABLE 1. LABOR FORCE-EMPLOYMENT REGRESSION STATISTICS, TOTAL AND SUBGROUPS, 1947–1964

	Quarterly, 1947–1964 (Tella)		Quarterly, 1947–1963 (Cooper and Johnston)			Cross Section 78 SMSA's, 1960 (Bowen and Finegan)		Monthly, 1947–1962 (Dernburg and Strand)	Labor-Force Participation Rate, 1955
	b_{le} (1)	r_{le}^2 (2)	b_{ue} (3)	r_{ue}^2 (4)	b_{le} (5)	b_{lu} (6)	b_{le}' (7)	b_{le} (8)	(9)
Males									
14–19	+.36	.36	−.42	.09	+.58	−1.94	+.80	+.70	49.5
20–24	+.46	.67	−.54	.55	+.46	—	—	+.26	90.8
25–34	+.20	.40	−.77	.81	+.23	−.24	+.20	—	97.7
35–44	+.07	.06	−1.00	.82	.00			+.07	98.1
45–54	+.14	.16	−.82	.65	+.18	−.66	+.45	−.31	96.5
55–64	+.46	.60	−.76	.08	+.24	−1.62	+.83	+.74	87.9
65 and over	+.74	.60	−.12	.00	+.88			+.36	39.6
All Males	+.40[a]	.64[a]	−.65	.39	+.35	−.73[b]	+.75[b]		83.6
Females									
14–19	+.40	.20	−.26	.05	+.74			+.93	29.9
20–24	+.44	.20	−.41	.03	+.59			+.42	46.0
25–34	+.52	.36	—	—	—	−.57[b]	+.52[b]	+.46	34.9
35–44	+.51	.44	−.29	.00	+.71			+.57	41.6
45–54	+.69	.45	−.06	.00	+.94			+.68	43.8
55–64	+.63	.43	−.26	.00	+.74			+.83	32.5
65 and over	+.70	.50	−.01	.00	+.99			+.86	10.6
All Females	+.62[a]	.66[a]	−.28	.08	+.72	−.76[c]	+.67[c]	+.70	34.8
All	+.39[d]	.43[d]	−.62	.50	+.38	−.68	+.53	+.45	58.7

[a] Based on annual data, 1948–1962, Tella [10].

[b] Single women only.

[c] Married women only.

[d] Monthly data, 1947–1962, Dernburg and Strand [7], equation (1b).

Column

1   Partial regression coefficient of L/P on E/P shown in Tella [10], Table 1, p. 74.

2   Partial coefficient of determination of L/P on E/P, calculated by formula:

$$r^2 = \frac{t^2}{t^2 + \text{d.f.}}$$

where t is the ratio of the regression coefficient to its standard error, and d.f. is the number of degrees of freedom.

3   Partial regression coefficient of U/P on E/P, Cooper and Johnston [11], Table 5, p. 138.

4   Partial coefficient of determination, calculated as in Column 2.

5   Implicit partial regression coefficient of L/P on E/P, calculated.

6   Statistically significant partial regression coefficients of L/P on U/L as shown in Bowen and Finegan [6], Table 4–10, p. 154.

7   Rough estimate of implicit partial regression coefficient of L/P on E/P, calculated by formula:

$$b_{le}' = 1 + \frac{1}{b_{lu} \cdot (P/L) - 1}$$

8   Net effect of employment calculated by Dernburg and Strand [8] from simultaneous equations.

9   *Manpower Report of the President*, March 1964, Table A-2, p. 196.

TABLE 2. Labor-Force Attachment, Variation, and
Sensitivity to Employment, 1947–1964, Quarterly

	Labor-Force Participation Rate, 1955 (1)	Total Variation (2)	Residual Variation (3)	Labor-Force Turnover (4)	"Uncorrected" Sensitivity Coefficient (5)	"Corrected" Sensitivity Coefficient (6)	
						(a)	(b)
Males							
14–19	49.5	3.83	1.15	1.45	+.58	+.28	+.32
20–24	90.8	1.93	1.06	1.09	+.46	+.37	+.25
25–34	97.7	.64	.38	1.00	+.23	+.17	0
35–44	98.1	.31	.30	1.01	0	0	0
45–54	96.5	.43	.39	1.02	+.18	+.14	0
55–64	87.9	.97	.62	1.03	+.24	−.16	0
65 and over	39.6	5.64	.79	1.23	+.88	+.40	+.30
All Males					+.35	+.17	+.25
Females							
14–19	29.9	1.54	.91	1.60	+.74	+.41	+.30
20–24	46.0	1.31	.97	1.38	+.59	−.15	−.06
25–34	34.9	1.28	.58	1.34	—	0	0
35–44	41.6	2.40	.48	1.27	+.71	0	+.35
45–54	43.8	5.07	.71	1.23	+.94	+.72	+.68
55–64	32.5	4.64	.65	1.28	+.74	+.26	+.38
65 and over	10.6	.78	.47	1.52	+.99	+.60	+.80
All Females					+.72	+.33	+.50
All					+.38	+.19	+.29

Column
1   See Column 9 in Table 1.
2   Quarterly standard deviation of labor-force participation rates, uncorrected for trend, derived from Tella [10], Table 1, p. 74.
3   Standard error of estimate from regression of labor-force participation rates on employment ratio and time, Tella, *ibid.*
4   Ratio of number working some time during 1955 to average weekly size of labor force. G. Bancroft, *The American Labor Force*, Table 10, p. 16.
5   Regression coefficients in Column 5, Table 1.
6   Same coefficients adjusted by procedure described in text.
     6(a) utilizes the employment-population ratio of males (age 25–64) as the cyclical index of demand.
     6(b) utilizes the (BLS) employment-population ratio as the cyclical index.

This approach, however, produces low correlation coefficients in contrast to the high ones produced by (L, E) regressions.

The (L, E) partial correlation coefficients (Column 2) move together with the regression coefficients in column 1, suggesting that labor-force behavior is most predictable in those groups in which sensitivity to employment is highest. This seems puzzling, for the groups with highest sensitivity are groups with the lowest degree of labor-force attachment (Column 9) and with greatest degree of instability, as measured by their variances (Table 2, Column 2). These groups have much greater scope for labor-force decisions than the primary labor force. Many of these decisions are subject to factors other than and additional to the current general state of the labor market. We would therefore expect these parts of the labor force to be the least predictable *in the sense that even after the regression larger unexplained variation remains in these groups compared with the others.* This is shown by the residual variances from Tella's regressions in Column 3, Table 2.

The differences between the squared correlation coefficients in the (L, E) and the equivalent (U, E) regressions arise from the fact that fluctuations in the labor force exceed the fluctuations in unemployment in the secondary-worker groups, whereas the converse is true in the primary labor-force group.[28]

An error model. There remains the likelihood of upward biases in the sensitivity estimate, the b_{le} regression coefficients. Tella's lag procedure is designed to reduce biases, and it does reduce the b_{le} coefficients (Column 1 compared with Column 5 in Table 1) by a sizable amount in many of the groups. It is not clear, however, how effective such a makeshift is.

The general problem is posed by the procedure of correlating the labor force of a group with *its own* employment. First, since E_i is a part of L_i, any sampling response and other measurement errors in E_i will be duplicated in L_i, spuriously biasing the regression coefficients toward unity.[29] Second, specific groups may experience (a) employment-demand fluctuations independent of the over-all state of the market and (b) specific labor-supply fluctuations which result in employment fluctuations of the group.[30] If our purpose is to estimate the response of the group to the general cyclical state of demand, both phenomena create upward biases in the estimated coefficients b_{le}.

Formally, let E_i, the employment of a particular group i, consists of components

$$E_i = E_c + E_{sd} + E_{ss} + e$$

and

$$U_i = U_c + U_{sd} + U_{ss} + u$$

so that

$$L_i = L_c + L_{sd} + L_{ss} + (e + u)$$

Subscript c indicates the general cyclical component, sd the component resulting from specific demand fluctuation, ss the specific supply fluctuations, and e, u the measurement errors.

For simplicity, assume that (1) all components of E and U, except those with the same subscripts, are independent, and

(2) $\text{Cov } (E_c, U_c) < 0$
(3) $\text{Cov } (E_{sd}, U_{sd}) < 0$
(4) $\text{Cov } (E_{ss}, U_{ss}) > 0$[31]
(5) $\text{Cov } (e, u) = 0$

Then

$$b_{le} = \frac{\text{Cov } (L_c, E_c) + \text{Cov } (L_{sd}, E_{sd}) + \text{Cov } (L_{ss}, E_{ss}) + \text{Cov } (e + u, e)}{\text{Var } (E)}$$

Call the "true" cyclical regression coefficient $b(L_c, E_c) = b_c$, and the ratio $\text{Var } (E_c)/\text{Var. } (E) = k$. Then

$$b_{le} = kb_c + \frac{\text{Cov } (L_{sd}, E_{sd}) + \text{Cov } (L_{ss}, E_{ss})}{\text{Var } (E)} + \frac{\text{Var } (e)}{\text{Var } (E)}$$

Now, by lagging E one quarter, we are likely to eliminate most of the "error of measurement bias" $\text{Var } (e)/\text{Var}(E)$, since in the lagged regression this term becomes $[\text{Cov } (e_t, e_{t-1})]/\text{Var }(E.)$ The lag probably also reduces the remaining terms. But it does not provide the desired estimate b_c, though it probably comes close to it.

The equation can be further rewritten

$$b_{le} = kb_c + (1 - k) + \frac{\text{Cov } (U_{sd}, E_{sd}) + \text{Cov } (U_{ss}, E_{ss})}{\text{Var } (E)}$$

By assumptions (3) and (4), the two terms in the numerator on the right-hand side have opposing signs. Which predominates is not clear, but the fraction is likely to be small. Let us neglect it for the purpose of a rough estimating procedure. Hence

$$b_{le} = kb_c + (1 - k)$$

Note that k is the proportion of the variance of employment in a group E_i attributable to the general demand situation. It follows that a correlation of E_i with an appropriate aggregate employment demand index C will produce an estimate of k. The coefficient of determination r^2 (E_i, C) measures the proportion of variance E_i accounted for by C.

In view of the findings that labor-force behavior of the primary labor force is not cyclically sensitive, its employment fluctuations can serve as a good cyclical index of employment demand. Using the quarterly data to correlate the total employment ratio with the employment ratio of the "core" group of males (25–64), I obtained an $r^2 = .77$. Applying this estimate of k to the appropriate regression coefficient in Column 5, Table 1, which is $b_{le} = .38$, the corrected coefficient b_c is calculated from:

$$.38 = .77\, b_c + .23, \text{ so } b_c = .19$$

Similar correlations of the core group employment ratio with employment ratios of age-sex subgroups provided the means for a downward adjustment of all the coefficients of Column 5, Table 1. The corrected estimates are shown in Table 2, Column 6 (a), next to the uncorrected ones (Table 2, Column 5). An alternative set of corrected estimates was obtained by the same procedure, using the nonagricultural BLS employment series as the numerator of the cyclical index. Results are shown in Column 6 (b).

It seems clear that net labor-force sensitivity to employment demand in time series has been, perhaps quite strongly, overestimated by the regression procedures or the application of cross-section parameter estimates.

The Annual Record: Preliminary Findings

Considerations of errors and biases, analyzed in the preceding section, suggest a direct approach in which labor-force behavior of a group should be related to some index of the demand for labor which is statistically independent of the particular labor-force measurements. In this section I report such a preliminary survey of year-to-year movements, a subject to which previous studies gave only brief attention.[32] The description that follows raises many questions but provides some insights into the major cyclical and other responses of the labor force during the postwar experience.

Chart 1 shows the contrasting labor-force behavior of primary (males 25–65) and secondary (all other) labor-force groups, and provides a comparison of variation in the latter group's labor-force rate with that of several cyclical labor-market indicators. These include: the primary group employment-population ratio, the nonagricultural employment-population ratio, the workweek of production workers in manufacturing, the quit rate in manufacturing (adjusted for trend), first differences in hourly earnings in manufacturing, and the NICB help-wanted advertising index.

The general conformity of movement is positive and is best described by noting that, of the 17 year-to-year movements, the direction of change in the secondary labor force differs only four times from the quit rate, the primary employment-population ratio, and the nonagricultural employment-population ratio. Aside from the 1947–1948 difference in the quit rate, the periods with divergent movements were: 1951–1953, 1956–1957, and 1961–1962.

The differences are as instructive as the similarities. The 1948 peak and the 1949 trough are repeated in the labor-force rate. The differences in 1951–1953 are affected by the Korean War. There was a substantial influx of secondary workers in 1950 and 1951 during the early phase of the war. With the reduction of war effort and truce in 1953, there was an increasing outflow of secondary workers from the labor force, while the primary civilian labor force increased in size. This substitution repeats the post-World War II pattern between 1945 and 1947.[33]

The cycle troughs of 1954 and 1958 are duplicated in the secondary labor force. From 1956 to 1957 the labor-force rate declines sharply while demand indicators are level or decline. From 1961 to 1962 the labor force continues to decline, while demand

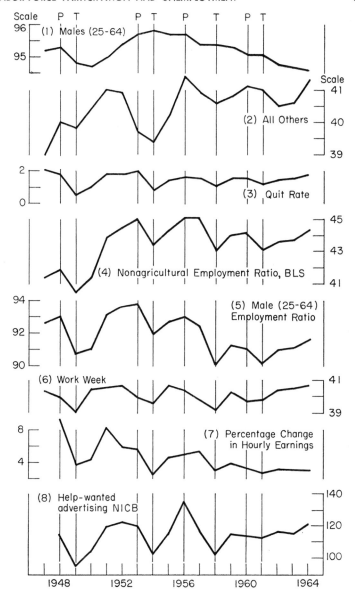

CHART 1. *Labor-force rates and cycle indexes.*

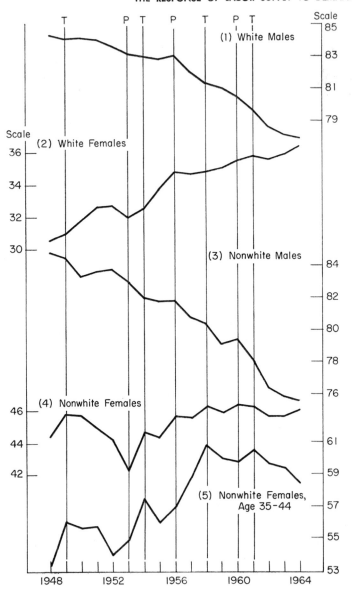

CHART 2. *Labor-force rates by color and sex.*

indicators are moving up. Thereafter, the labor force resumes conformity, though at a lower level.

Perhaps significantly, both of these differential episodes follow federal increases in minimum wages,[34] coupled with the 1961 extension of coverage to retail trade, an important employer of many secondary workers.[35]

Proceeding to a disaggregation of the labor force, Chart 2 presents five sex-color groups and Chart 3 portrays the behavior of the older labor force (65 and over) and the young group (14–24). The young group is shown for males and classified by school enrollment status.

Several features of the annual variation portrayed in these charts call for comment.

1. The cyclical conformity of the disaggregated groups is not as clear as in the aggregate of secondary workers. Evidently, disaggregation brings to the fore the "autonomous" labor-force components (L_{sd} and L_{ss} in the error model) and magnifies the importance of the measurement errors ($e + u$). However, the differential behavior of subgroups is interesting and suggestive.

2. Nonwhite females (Chart 2) exhibit peaks of participation *inverse* to the business cycle. It would seem that in this group the additional-worker effect dominates. This is clear in the case of adult women, as in the example of the 35–44 age group. This finding is important on theoretical grounds and in conjunction with other evidence. In my study of labor-force participation of women I interpreted the additional-worker effect as an alternative to dissaving, asset decumulation, or increasing debt in family attempts to maintain consumption in the face of unemployment and other income losses.[36] I argued, consequently, that such behavior should be particularly discernible in families at low levels of wealth, particularly in view of capital market imperfections. Supporting evidence in that study and in the work of Cain strengthens this inference.[37] In the present context this means *the "additional worker" is more likely to be a low-income person than the "'discouraged worker."*

3. Secular declines in participation dominate the pattern of labor-force behavior of older men. The declines are perhaps, on average, steeper in bad than in good times (Chart 3), but the

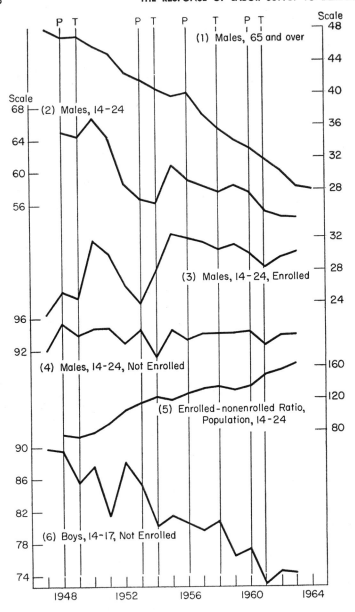

CHART 3. *Labor-force rates of the old and the young.*

particularly strong drop from 1951 to 1952 and the continued strong decline *after* the 1958 recession are not in consonance with general short-run demand fluctuations. The decline since 1958 may reflect a more-than-cyclical erosion of job opportunities, and the 1961 minimum wage increase and extension may have played a part in it.

All such factors were reinforced and possibly dominated by the changing retirement provisions of OASDI. The Social Security Act of 1935 made receipt of pension conditional on cessation of work. Subsequent amendments enabled beneficiaries to earn up to a certain minimum a month without reduction in pensions, or above the minimum with certain fractional reductions. These provisions were liberalized in the postwar period. The monthly minimum was raised to $50 in 1950, to $75 in 1952, and to $100 in 1958. These changes were followed by declines in participation of older males (Chart 3) at times when demand indexes (Chart 1) show upward movements.

Presumably, the result of such changes is that wage earners are allowed to take intermittent or part-time work without loss of benefits or with only small losses. This may bring some people back from complete retirement into intermittent participation, but it also strengthens the incentives of others to retire. The opposing effects, illustrated by data on work experience of men 65 and over, indicate a steep drop in their proportion of full-time job holding and increase in part-time and part-period work.[38] Evidently the net effect was to reduce the average weekly participation rate, and by more than participation on an annual basis: the participation rate dropped from 45.8 in 1950 to 28.4 in 1963, and the proportion working some time during the year dropped from 49.3 in 1950 to 37.6 in 1963.[39]

Of course, the downward trend in labor-force rates of older people has been influenced by increasing levels of benefit payments. The important point about the liberalization of penalty provisions is that it affects both the trend and the short-run flexibility of the older labor force.

Recent studies of the Social Security Administration[40] show that OASDI benefits may also have reduced the labor force of the 62–64 year group when in 1961 these benefits were made available to retired persons in this age range. The total number availing themselves has grown to 600,000 in 1963, so that 28 per cent of men in this age group now receive benefits.

In view of these figures, it would seem that the accelerated drop in the labor-force rate of men in the age group 55–64 since 1961 (from 87.3 in 1961 to 85.6 in 1964) is in part attributable to these provisions.[41]

The studies referred to show further effects of OASDI incentives. In the over-65 age group larger proportions of beneficiaries than nonbeneficiaries among those well enough to work are not working or not planning to work. Among those working, a majority of beneficiaries work intermittently or part-time, but most nonbeneficiaries work full time.

Most interesting, in conjunction with the unemployment situation, is the finding that although in 1951 22 per cent of the retired claimed layoffs as a cause of retirement only 8 per cent made this claim in 1963.[42]

The latter finding is, *prima facie,* not consistent with the view that high unemployment was the major cause of continued and perhaps accelerated labor-force withdrawal of older men. However, an isolated pair of survey responses is not a sufficient statistic; more evidence is needed. One could argue that although a clear response to expansion and liberalization of OASDI (and private) pension provisions is demonstrated, such responses are stronger in periods of depressed employment. It is probably true that the real-wage differential has changed from *both* directions. Developments on each side need to be explored further.

4. Labor-force participation of teenagers and young people (14–24) continued its secular decline during the postwar period. Changing employment conditions seem to be reflected in the behavior of the labor force of enrolled and not-enrolled youth, shown separately in Chart 3. The labor-force fluctuations are more pronounced in the enrolled group, whose average participation rate is lower.[43]

The data indicate not only labor-force withdrawals in recession periods but also relative increases in school enrollment at such times (Chart 3), an interesting reflection of changing opportunity costs during the business cycle.[44]

The downward trend in the labor-force rate of youngsters does not seem to accelerate. However, throughout the period, the subgroup whose participation continuously and most sharply declined is the 14-17-year-old not-enrolled. Its participation rate fell from 88 per cent in 1952 to 74 per cent in 1963. This group had severe declines during three cyclical downturns, as well as from 1950 to 1951, 1955 through 1957, and 1960 to 1961. The latter (also a cyclical decline) and two former declines coincided with federal increases in minimum wages and the extension of coverage. This group experienced a sharp increase in unemployment at the end of the 1950's, but there has been no further marked change since 1960.[45]

Supporting evidence for the probable role of minimum wages in the labor-market experience of this group is provided in a regression analysis of teenage unemployment by Arnold Katz, in which he finds that the employment-population ratio of boys age 14–19 who are out of school has been adversely affected by increases in minimum wages and the increased size of the teenage population group.[46]

The factor of population size has been receiving increased attention, particularly in connection with the growth of the teenage group. However, the population explosion has been blamed for sins it does not perpetrate without accomplices. The population factor, *by itself*, need not increase unemployment or decrease labor-force participation. In the absence of strong barriers to downward wage flexibility, an increased population group of teenagers will exert a downward pressure on their wages only to the extent of the inelasticity of substitution between less experienced and more experienced workers. Some and perhaps even a sizeable degree of wage decline is unlikely to produce labor-force withdrawal, *without going to school,* at this stage in life. Minimum wages, however, can effectively block entry to jobs for many of these youngsters. If their way back to school is blocked for reasons of low productivity (or "ability" or any other term indicating disadvantages), all these factors *interact* to lock a growing number of them out of the labor market and out of school as well.

5. Labor-force behavior of the primary labor force, particularly of males 25-54, is quite insensitive to demand fluctuations. A very gentle decline, however, has been perceptible since the

midfifties. It appears that this decline primarily involves non-white males. On further inspection the development is narrowed down to unmarried nonwhite males in this age group. In both color groups unmarried men had lower and decreasing participation rates as well as higher and increasing unemployment rates during the last decade. However, the proportion of married men in this age group is much higher among whites than among non-whites. Marital status is not unresponsive to economic conditions. The proportion of married white males in this group increased somewhat between 1950 and 1960, but the opposite is true of nonwhites. Slight as they have been, these trends suggest a more-than-cyclical deterioration in the low-income "marginal" groups.

To sum up: positive cycle sensitivity (net "discouragement" effect) is readily discernible in the annual behavior of the secondary labor force. So is the added-worker response in some of the low-income subgroups. But powerful trend factors and institutional changes continue to dominate the behavior of labor-force groups. Much more attention should be paid to these factors and changes.[47]

Disguised Unemployment

Because the recorded size of the labor force is lower in times of slack than it would have been under conditions of full employment, it follows that the observed unemployment count understates the magnitude of manpower loss created by the recession.

Calculation of this deficit, called "hidden" or "disguised" unemployment, utilizes the regression equations which relate labor-force ratios to employment or unemployment ratios. Full-employment levels are fixed for the independent variables in some conventionally arbitrary way, such as a 4 per cent rate of unemployment, and the hypothetical size of the labor force that would be obtained under these conditions is estimated from the equation. The difference between the estimated full-employment labor force and the actually reported labor force constitutes hidden unemployment. Addition of hidden to observed unemployment yields the "manpower gap," or "adjusted" unemployment.

Now, if this addition is to measure the total "manpower loss," the assumed level of "full-employment unemployment" should be subtracted from reported unemployment; that is, the manpower loss in reported unemployment is its *cyclical* component, not total unemployment. Otherwise, full employment must be defined by a zero unemployment level. The relative importance of disguised unemployment in this corrected manpower gap would, of course, loom much larger.

Estimates of hidden unemployment, without this correction, were calculated in several of the studies quoted earlier. The resulting estimates do, of course, differ from one equation to another, and they depend on the definition of full employment. The numbers are not small: by way of illustration, the numbers quoted run as high as three million in 1962 (under the prevailing 4 per cent assumption).[48] This is several times larger than the cyclical component of reported unemployment (a little over one million above a 4 per cent rate in 1962).

What are we to make of these numbers? Do they mean, for instance, that recession-caused "waste" in 1962 was a much bigger problem in its disguised than in its undisguised components? In what sense are the two components comparable and additive, as the calculation of the manpower gap implies?

To answer these questions, we must take account of two important aspects of disguised unemployment: (a) the method of its calculation and (b) the fact that it is almost exclusively *concentrated in the secondary labor force.*

It is clear from the method of calculation that, in a cyclical context, the importance of hidden unemployment in a population group is a direct function of the degree of labor-force responsiveness to short-run variations in employment conditions.[49] It is a reflection of short-run supply elasticity with respect to the real-wage differentials, in a broad sense, between labor-market and nonmarket activities. In addition to pecuniary conditions involved in the market alternative are the ease of finding a job, its locational and other conveniences, and attractiveness of the job content. All these dimensions of the real market-wage rate improve as the market tightens. Thus disguised unemployment indicates potential availability at higher than currently prevailing real-wage conditions. But reported unemployment is, implicitly,

and presumably behaviorally, defined in terms of currently prevailing real-wage conditions. The difference is real, though in
practice the boundary in attitudes and in survey responses is
fuzzy enough to create errors of misclassification. But these work
in either direction.

It might be argued that this distinction is not really relevant
to the manpower loss concept. If employment (wage) conditions
improved to normal levels, the million cyclically unemployed
who reported themselves as such would be absorbed into employment and so would the three million previously disguised
unemployed. Additivity of reported and disguised unemployment must mean that production would increase proportionately from each source. More precisely, the assumption
is that the net marginal products in the two groups are equal
to one another when they are employed, and equal to zero when
unemployed (one visibly, the other invisibly).

I submit that this assumption must be questioned precisely
in view of the differences in supply elasticities. These differences,
practically by definition, arise from the greater scope for substitution between market and non-market activities (including
leisure) in the disguised group. It is no accident that the disguised unemployed are found mainly in the secondary labor
force. This fact simply illustrates the strong inverse correlation,
predictable from economic theory, between labor-force sensitivity
and degree of labor-force attachment shown in Table 1.

Consider a population group whose average participation rate
is 40 per cent. This does not mean that 40 per cent of the individuals are almost always in the labor force; the remaining 60
per cent almost never. It means rather that the same individuals
are sometimes in and sometimes out during a period of years.
Data on labor-force turnover certainly support this proposition
(see Column 4, Table 2). Assume then that, on the average,
an individual in such a group expects to spend 40 per cent of
his time in the labor force. The fact that 60 per cent of his time
is spent outside the labor force means that other than "gainful"
activities are important. This implies that the opportunity costs
of job-searching and job-holding are greater for secondary
workers than for primary ones, and that the payoff to job mobility is smaller, since the expected period of employment is shorter.

Hence the *net* gain from moving into the labor market and the *net* loss from leaving it due to adverse conditions in the market can be quite small, and certainly much smaller than for the primary groups.[50] Given some scope for timing of their activities, work in the labor market will be preferred at times when search costs are low and job conditions attractive. The fact that many other factors influence timing helps to explain not only the greater sensitivity with respect to employment conditions (higher regression coefficients in Tables 1 and 2) but also the greater instability (variance, residual variance, and turnover in Table 2) in groups within *lower levels* of participation.

It is paradoxical that the optimization of timing labor-force activities creates the illusion of disguised unemployment. The more economical the timing, the larger the number of disguised unemployed! The paradox reflects a myopic preoccupation with GNP. The focus on disguised unemployment as a component of the manpower loss not only misses the broader view of total productivity but also the important fact that a flexible labor force is a source of strength in potentially inflationary situations.

This reasoning seriously questions the comparability and additivity of the two kinds of unemployment from a *total production* and *welfare* point of view. However, it should not be interpreted as denying the existence of "involuntary" labor-force withdrawal. I am simply suggesting that the regression procedures are more likely to catch the kind of behavior I describe in the above model than the classic type of discouraged worker. The latter is perhaps best defined in the words of the *President's Manpower Report:* "Where opportunities are *chronically* limited, some persons give up a fruitless search for work and rely on charity or in other ways subsist without recourse to work . . ."[51] Such cases are most likely to arise as a result of structural displacements, personal adversity, or other barriers to jobs. The business-cycle downturn aggravates such problems, but its effect is unlikely to be an immediate withdrawal from the labor force.[52]

In a series of case studies of plant shutdowns, Wilcock and Franke found that the unemployed continued their labor-force attachment for years.[53] About 10 per cent withdrew from the labor force after two years of search. After three years, 10–20 per cent of them wound up on relief. The process of discourage-

TABLE 3. REPORTED AND "ADJUSTED" UNEMPLOYMENT RATES

Age Group	Male Rates, 1962		Female Rates, 1962		Male Rates, 1964-II		Female Rates, 1964-II	
	Reported (1)	"Adjusted" (2)	Reported (3)	"Adjusted" (4)	Reported (5)	"Adjusted" (6)	Reported (7)	"Adjusted" (8)
14–19	13.4	23.4	13.2	24.8	15.6	18.1	16.1	19.3
20–24	8.9	12.7	9.1	10.0	8.0	9.3	9.1	11.5
25–34	4.5	4.8	6.5	9.6	3.4	3.5	6.0	7.7
35–44	3.6	3.5	5.2	9.0	2.7	2.7	4.9	6.2
45–54	3.9	4.2	4.1	8.4	3.3	3.4	3.8	5.9
55–64	4.6	4.7	3.5	9.2	3.9	4.4	3.7	4.6
65 and over	4.6	12.5	4.1	18.5	4.0	5.6	3.1	5.0
All	5.3	7.0	6.2	11.3	4.7	5.3	6.3	8.0

Sources: Annual rates, 1962, from Dernburg and Strand [8], Tables 7 and 8.
Second-quarter rates, 1964, from Tella [10], Table 3, p. 77.

ment and "squeeze out" of the labor force where it exists is not a matter of quick response to mild business-cycle fluctuations as we have known them in the postwar period.

The disguised unemployment which appears in Table 3 is probably best described as a part of the "labor-force reserve." There are many reasons why we may want to know a great deal about its size and composition. The procedures which led to the estimates in Table 3 are not the most suitable for this purpose.

Some Implications

Trends in labor-force flexibility. Only a few years ago, the accepted view of short-run labor-force behavior could best be described in the formula: "zero net cycle elasticity plus small random variation." Recent studies amend this formula (a bit drastically) into: "strong net cycle elasticity plus very small random variation." On the basis of the review described in these pages, I propose as a tentative diagnosis: "some net cycle elasticity plus much residual variation due to other factors."

Because other factors, mainly World War II, demobilization, and the Korean War, dominated labor-market conditions since labor-force surveys were initiated, it is not surprising that labor-force responsiveness to the mild peace-time cycle could not be well discerned in the mid-fifties. The evolving record, as the history of our topic illustrates, does reduce the standard errors somewhat, but this record leads to a hypothesis that the labor force exhibits a *trend toward growing responsiveness,* which is another reason why it is easier to observe it now than in the past.

The result is produced by a combination of long standing trends, the most important of which are the growth of the female labor force and the decreasing degree of labor-force attachment of the young and of older males.

These basic trends are intimately connected with the processes of economic growth. For the present discussion we can take these for granted and look at the consequences. The results can be summarized as: (1) growth of discretionary labor-force participation and (2) weakening of the income effect, that is, of incentives for added-worker behavior.

1. The growing female labor-force participation, the increasing rate and length of schooling among the young, and the growing tendency to combine early retirement with reduced labor-force participation, create a growing class of intermittent or "multiple" job holders.

The manifestations of these developments are observed as increasing proportions of part-time and part-period workers, increased degree of labor-force turnover, and increased proportions of inexperienced workers among the employed and the unemployed—all these phenomena being almost equivalent by definition.[54]

2. The growing level of income, assets, and credit availability diminish the need for emergency help by other family members when main earners become unemployed.[55] Unemployment compensation probably weakens, or rather, creates a lag in both the discouragement and added-worker effects. However, the availability of unemployment compensation and of social security payments may be contributing to the growth of the intermittent labor force.

Unemployment. Labor-force flexibility carries several implications for the study of reported unemployment.

1. The greater the labor-force responsiveness of a group, the lower is the cyclical amplitude and conformity of its unemployment rate to the business cycle. This is because labor-force withdrawals (largely from unemployment) increase and labor-force entries decrease during the downswing, while labor-force entries increase during the upswing. The conformity is weaker because the flexible labor force is also responsive to factors other than business conditions. A comparison of Columns 3, 4, and 9 in Table 1 illustrates these facts.

2. Because labor-force entrants and re-entrants must spend some time in job search, unemployment rates are likely to be higher in groups with higher labor-force turnover. Higher labor-force turnover is, of course, characteristic of secondary labor-force groups. A comparison of turnover rates, participation rates, and sensitivity coefficients (Table 2) with unemployment rates (Table 3) illustrates this.

3. In view of (1), the unemployment rate of the primary labor

force is a better cyclical index than the rates of other sex-age components. It is therefore also likely to be superior, in this respect, to the aggregate unemployment rate.

4. If labor-force responsiveness is growing, we should observe over time an increasing size and inertness in the aggregate unemployment rate. This would be consistent with observed unemployment patterns during the last decade. And if this were the whole story, we could look at the unemployment rate of the primary labor force and, finding that it (mid-1965) is as low as it was before the 1957 recession, conclude that all is well and clear.

However, the growing importance of secondary labor-force groups in the total labor force does not, by itself, imply an increase in the unemployment rates of secondary workers, such as is recently observed among teenagers and, to a much lesser extent, among women. The analysis presented in this paper suggests that, in some proportion, these increases in unemployment rates within the particular groups may be due to growing flexibility within the groups as well as to increases in labor supplies superimposed on downward inflexible wages. If so, the unemployment rate of the primary groups may not be a good index of current conditions. If, as a result of minimum wages, employers tend to substitute experienced for inexperienced workers, the unemployment rate in the primary group may have decreased, in part, *at the expense* of higher rates in other groups.

REFERENCES

1. Clarence D. Long, *The Labor Force Under Changing Income and Employment* (Princeton: Princeton University Press for the National Bureau of Economic Research, 1958).
2. W. L. Hansen, "Cyclical Sensitivity of the Labor Force," *American Economic Review*, LI (June 1961), 299–309.
3. Stuart Altman, *Unemployment of Married Women*, unpublished Ph.D. Dissertation, University of California at Los Angeles, 1963.
4. Glen G. Cain, *Labor Force Participation of Married Women*, unpublished Ph.D. Dissertation, University of Chicago, 1963.
5. Glen G. Cain, "The Net Effect of Unemployment on Labor Force Participation of Secondary Workers," *Social Systems Research Institute Paper 6408*, University of Wisconsin, October 1964.

6. W. G. Bowen and T. A. Finegan, "Labor Force Participation and Unemployment," in A. M. Ross, ed., *Employment Policy and the Labor
Market* (Berkeley: University of California Press, 1965), pp. 115–161.
7. K. Strand and T. Dernburg, "Cyclical Variation in Labor Force Participation," *Review of Economics and Statistics*, XLVI (November 1964),
378–391.
8. T. Dernburg and K. Strand, "Hidden Unemployment," unpublished
manuscript, 1965.
9. A. Tella, "The Relations of Labor Force to Employment," *Industrial
and Labor Relations Review*, XVII (April 1964), 454–469.
10. A. Tella, "Labor Force Sensitivity to Employment by Age, Sex," *Industrial Relations*, IV (February 1965), 69–83.
11. S. Cooper and D. F. Johnston, "Labor Force Projections 1970–1980,"
Monthly Labor Review, LXXXVIII (February 1965), 129–140.
12. J. Mincer, "Labor Force Participation of Married Women," in Universities-National Bureau Committee for Economic Research, *Aspects
of Labor Economics* (Princeton: Princeton University Press for the National Bureau of Economic Research, 1962), pp. 63–97.

NOTES

1. The research reported in this paper is an outgrowth of a larger study
of unemployment differentials in the United States, supported in part by
a grant from the Ford Foundation.

2. For a discussion of these issues, see Robert B. Pearl, "Gross Change
in the Labor Force: A Problem in Statistical Measurement," *Employment
and Earnings*, April 1963.

3. This aspect was the major issue in the Woytinsky-Humphrey debate
in the late 1930's.

4. In his study Altman explores a number of other questions, not directly
relevant to the present review. His work illustrates the promise the gross-
change data hold out and the great need for improving their quality.

5. Provided the full-time earnings W have been included in family income Y. For a full discussion of the theoretical and econometric considerations see the author's "Labor Force Participation of Married Women" [12].

6. In my study (*op. cit.*), I was able to estimate the effects of transitory
family income (coefficient c_1) in addition to the long-run parameters b_1
and b_2. The negative sign of c_1 supported the existence of the additional-
worker effect. I was not concerned in that study with coefficient c_2. However, I did attempt a very indirect estimate of the net cyclical effect and
concluded that it seemed negligible. In his recent study of the subject,
Glen Cain [4] points out that in this attempt I used one of the several
estimates of c_1 which biased the test in favor of the additional-worker
hypothesis. After recomputing an average estimate of c_1, Cain concludes
that my test supports the net-discouragement hypothesis.

7. This formal argument is explicit in Cain [5]. Bowen and Finegan [6] leave the coefficient b_3 open to interpretation.

8. See their summary Table 4-7 and Table 4-10 in [6].

9. *Ibid.*, p. 154.

10. This suggests that a cleaner analysis would utilize U/P, rather than U/L as the unemployment variable. The correlation that was studied is: $r [L_i/P_i, (U/P)(P/L)]$. We are interested in $r (L_i/P_i, U/P)$, but even if this were zero, the correlation that was observed would be negative if extraneous factors create a covariation between L_i/P_i and L/P.

11. That net discouragement is a fact in seasonal movements has been overlooked. Seasonal behavior illustrates the ubiquity of the phenomenon, as well as the inappropriateness of the term.

12. The coefficient of determination between the 1960 Census week unemployment rates for the Non-Southern SMSA's and the annual average rates in the corresponding areas (as shown in Table D-5, pp. 243–245, of the 1965 *Manpower Report of the President*) was about 0.70, despite the many noncomparabilities in the two sets of data. If at least half the "unexplained variation" is due to these measurement errors, the proportion of the seasonal component in the variance of unemployment across areas could not have exceeded 15 per cent.

13. Data are from the source listed in the preceding footnote.

14. Statement by Walter Heller before the Joint Economic Committee, *Hearings on the Economic Report of the President,* 87th Congress (Washington, Government Printing Office, 1961).

15. *Manpower Report of the President,* March 1964, p. 33.

16. Data from Population Census, 1950, 1960.

17. No direct evidence is provided on the notion that the entry of secondary earners is more sensitive to this state of unemployment experience than to the initial job loss and income decline of the family. Longer-run trends are supposed to be captured by the variable $1/P$. Seasonals are eliminated by dummy variables in the regression.

18. Standard errors of regression coefficients are in parentheses. R^2 is the multiple coefficient of determination. $S_u{}^2$ is the residual variance.

19. BLS, *Monthly Report on the Labor Force,* January 1965, p. 47.

20. I used mid-quarterly months, that is, four months each year, for this test.

21. U/P is over 20 times the size of X/P.

22. In a subsequent, as yet unpublished paper, Dernburg and Strand [8] apply similar procedures to population age-sex subgroups. Their findings are largely consistent with those in the first paper, and less vulnerable to statistical doubts. This is because in the sequel they relate *particular* group labor-force ratios to the *aggregate* employment and exhaustion ratio. I am grateful to Professor Dernburg for making the manuscript available to me.

23. If the relation between cyclical movements of the income and substitution variables is stable over the period, this approach is not misleading, even in a structural sense. Thus a regression of the workweek on wage

rates yields a net structural relation so long as we are willing to assume that in the long run income (properly defined) is a constant multiple of wage rate.

24. Interestingly, the partial regression coefficient of (E/P) which measures the net outcome is very close to that obtained by the full analysis involving two simultaneous equations (.3902 versus .3715). (*Cf.* note 25).

25. According to *Manpower Report of the President*, March 1964, pp. 33–34, outmigration from areas of high unemployment during the 1950's occurred almost entirely among men in the 24–44 age group.

26. According to Tella, this group's labor-force rate shows an exceptionally good fit with the employment variable lagged one and two quarters.

27. $$\frac{\text{Cov } (L, E)}{\text{Var } (E)} = \frac{\text{Cov } (U, E)}{\text{Var } (E)} + 1$$

28. Since predicting L from E means no more than predicting U, the residual must be the same in both regressions. However, the squared correlation coefficients are different:

$$r_{le}^2 = 1 - \frac{S^2}{S_l^2} \qquad r_{ue}^2 = 1 - \frac{S^2}{S_u^2}$$

where S^2 is residual variance.
Hence

$$\frac{1 - r_{le}^2}{1 - r_{ue}^2} = \frac{S_u^2}{S_l^2}$$

Tests of statistical significance, keeping in mind that the null hypothesis is $\beta_{le} = 0$ and $\beta_{ue} = -1$, respectively, must yield the same results, even though the correlation coefficients look different.

The Cooper-Johnston and Tella procedures are not exactly equivalent, because of the lag in Tella's regression. Moreover, the implicit standard errors are much larger in the former, because of a rather strong correction for auto-correlation. Aside from this, it should be clear that the (U, E) regressions overestimate the standard errors, just as the (L, E) regressions underestimate them.

29. The (U, E) approach provides no escape, since its regression coefficient will be *lowered*, in absolute value, to the same extent: biased toward zero.

30. Also resulting in a positive correlation between employment and unemployment. The summer seasonal is the best example. However, the phenomenon need not be only seasonal.

31. Cf. note 39.

32. Tella [9].

33. See Long [1], Appendix Tables B-1 and B-2. A similar very interesting pattern is observable each year in the seasonal movements: married women decrease their labor-force participation each summer when children

return home from school, and many of the latter enter the labor market. See Altman [3], Table 3, p. 33.

34. From 40 to 75¢ in 1950, from 75¢ to $1.00 in 1956, and from $1.00 to $1.25 in 1961, to be increased in two steps.

35. Cf. the findings by Albert Rees in this volume on the employment effects of recent minimum wage increases.

36. Mincer [12], p. 75 ff.

37. Cain [5], pp. 13–14, reports that cross-section area multiple regressions relating labor-force rates of nonwhite married women show little net response to unemployment in 1950, and a negative, but very small, response in 1960. He argues that in the case of nonwhite wives, the income effect (inducing work in this context) appears stronger than the substitution effect (discouraging work) relative to the case of white wives.

Cain found a similar differential pattern in the parameters of long-run income and wage variables. These long-run income and wage parameter estimates from the cross section help to explain a long-standing puzzle, the much milder upward secular trend in labor-force participation of nonwhite compared to white women. See Cain [4] and Long's comments on Mincer [12].

38. *Monthly Labor Review*, LXXXVIII (January 1965), p. 10.

39. *Manpower Report of the President*, March 1965, and Special Labor Force Reports, Annual Work Experience Surveys, of the Bureau of Labor Statistics.

40. *Social Security Bulletins*, June 1964 and August 1964.

41. This illustrates why the term substitution effect is more appropriate than the so-called discouragement effect: labor supply responds not to one market-wage prospect but, in general, to a real-wage differential. The same effect can be produced on labor supply by raising or lowering the alternative real income or the market wage. The example illustrates the fact that encouragement in one sector helps to create or to strengthen discouragement from another.

Thus labor-supply elasticity is not zero even in the primary groups throughout the range of the wage (real-wage differential) variable. It may appear to be almost zero in the normally observed range of variation (such as the mild business cycle), but a bigger change in the wage differential, in either direction, tends to produce a visible response.

42. At the same time, compulsory retirement age was quoted by 22 per cent recently, compared to 11 per cent in 1951, poor health by 35 per cent compared to 41 per cent earlier, and preference for leisure by 17 per cent compared to 3 per cent in 1951. *Social Security Bulletin*, August 1964, Table 5, p. 6.

43. This abstracts from summer months, as the data by enrollment status are based on October figures. Inclusion of summer months would greatly augment the fluctuations in the enrolled group.

44. In a recent study of chronically depressed areas, it was found that virtually all boys of high school age (16 and 17) attend school, and most of the young men aged 14 to 24 who are not in the labor force are

at school. See Bureau of Labor Statistics, *The Structure of Unemployment in Areas of Substantial Labor Surplus,* Study Paper No. 23 in Joint Economic Committee, *Study of Employment, Growth, and Price Levels* (Washington: Government Printing Office, 1960), p. 16.

Similar countercyclical effects on enrollment were found in longer time series by Beverly Duncan, "Dropouts and the Unemployed," *Journal of Political Economy,* LXXIII (April 1965), 121–134.

45. *Manpower Report of the President,* March 1965, Table B-8.

46. The regression was run separately for the 14–17 and 18–19 age groups. The population coefficient was more reliable and the minimum wage coefficient less reliable in the second group.

47. An exploratory analysis of trends is presented in the author's "Economic Factors in Labor Force Participation," to be published in the *International Encyclopedia of the Social Sciences.*

48. See Tables 2 and 3 in Dernburg and Strand [7], pp. 387, 388.

49. The level is also affected by secular trends which the equations fit to the various population groups. No analysis has been applied to explain the trends.

50. This is not to say that non-market activities of primary workers are not productive. In addition to differences in search costs, the marginal rate of substitution between market and non-market activities is weaker for primary than secondary workers. Hence it takes a much greater diminution of the marginal value product of *primary* workers to squeeze them out of the labor market.

51. *Manpower Report of the President,* March 1964, p. 30. My italics.

52. According to Altman's study of gross flows, most secondary workers with high labor-force mobility drop out of the labor force before their unemployment extends past five weeks. In contrast, those with stronger attachments do not drop out long after the exhaustion of unemployment benefits.

53. Richard Wilcock and Walter Franke, *Unwanted Workers: Permanent Layoffs and Long-term Unemployment* (New York: Free Press, 1963).

54. In nonfarm jobs, the number of voluntary part-time workers more than doubled between 1950 and 1964, while the number of full-time workers increased only 20 per cent. Special Labor Force Report, in *Monthly Labor Review,* LXXXVII (September 1964), p. 1009.

55. The growing number of women with marketable skills may be producing some added workers on a non-cyclical basis, namely, working wives in depressed areas and wives supporting schooling of their husbands.

Discussion

BY W. G. BOWEN AND T. A. FINEGAN

All of us who share an interest in the labor-force field owe a large debt of gratitude to Professor Mincer for his wide-range, incisive, and provocative review of recent evidence on the relationship between labor-force participation and unemployment. On our copy of his paper we have written in the margin in a number of places, "right!", "good point!", and "why didn't we think of that?". Alongside other passages, however, less enthusiastic comments appear; and in keeping with the traditional (and proper) role of commentators, we shall focus on the latter.

Some Technical Points

First, with regard to the underlying model of labor-force behavior, we feel that Mincer tries too hard to force explanatory variables into a very limited number of traditional, price-theory boxes. It is certainly correct to state formally that "labor supply responds not to one market-wage prospect but, in general, to a real-wage differential" (Note 41). However, we see no reason to move from this proposition to the position that the unemployment rate (or the employment/population ratio) is best viewed as a proxy for the "transitory" components of family income and market wage rates. To our way of thinking, it is more helpful to regard the unemployment rate as an important variable in its own right, serving as a measure of the probability that an individual job-seeker who is prepared to invest a given amount in "search" will not be able to find employment within a given period of time. The wage that the worker will receive if he finds a job is, of course, also relevant to his decision whether or not to seek work. However, the wage rate and the unemployment rate do not always move together; furthermore, the calculus of different groups of potential workers may well assign different weights to the expected wage rate and to the expected probability of finding a job within a given period of time.

From both the theoretical and policy standpoints, it seems desirable to try to develop separate *ceteris-paribus* estimates of the sensitivity of labor-force participation rates to unemployment rates, wage rates, and other variables. Our own cross-section work suggests that within the relevant ranges variations in area unemployment rates tend to be more important than variations in market wage rates in explaining labor-force participation rates.

For similar reasons we think Mincer tries to encompass too much in his "net substitution effect" concept. If we interpret him correctly, he views estimates of the sensitivity of participation to unemployment as measures of the strength of the net substitution effect. If one grants the usefulness of making separate estimates of the responsiveness of participation to the probability of success in job seeking (such as the unemployment rate), the market wage rate, family income, and other variables (such as education and race), it does not seem that much is gained by trying to use the two-dimensional income-and-substitution effect schema in this context.

We wish to emphasize that we do not advocate labeling the coefficient of the unemployment variable an index of the so-called discouraged-worker effect. While high unemployment undoubtedly does discourage some workers from initiating or continuing the quest for work, Mincer is right in pointing out that other factors may also account for the observed negative relation between unemployment and labor-force participation.

We turn next to some statistical issues. Mincer argues that certain extraneous factors may cause a covariation between L_i/P_i and L/P, biasing our negative regression coefficient for U/L toward higher negative values and causing us to exaggerate the sensitivity of labor-force participation rate to unemployment rate. We agree that this possibility exists, but Mincer reaches this conclusion by assuming that extraneous factors do not change the absolute volume of unemployment, and in the real world this assumption seems unlikely to hold in many if not most cases; and when the level of unemployment also changes, our regression coefficients may well be biased toward lower rather than higher values.[1] The important point is that the bias may go in either direction, and we see no a priori reason to expect that an overestimate of the true relationship is any more likely than an underestimate.[2]

Substantive Issues

We turn now to more substantive issues. Mincer makes a real contribution by emphasizing the potential importance of migration as a determinant of inter-area differences in labor-force participation rates.[3] The open question is the quantitative impact of migration on the cross-section regression coefficients.

In an effort to assess this impact, we introduced a migration variable, the net gain or loss in civilian migration for each SMSA between 1950 and 1960 as a percentage of its civilian population in 1960, into some of our 1960 cross-section regressions. The results are presented in Table 1. For three of the four labor-force groups, introducing the migration variable reduces the net regression coefficient for the unemployment variable, as Mincer suggests; however, the amounts by which these coefficients are reduced are very small, from 3 to 13 per cent of their original values and less than .5 of the standard errors of the respective coefficients in the original runs, where migration was excluded. It is noteworthy that the simple correlation among cities between unemployment in 1960 and migration during the preceding decade was negative but weak ($r = -.21$, barely significant at the 5 per cent level).

Perhaps the main point to be stressed is that the introduction of the migration variable has very little effect on the regression coefficient for unemployment in the case of prime-age males. Therefore the differences between the cross-section and time-series results for this important group do not seem to be attributable solely (or even primarily) to migration, at least as defined here.[4]

The reader may also be interested to know that the net regression coefficient for our migration variable was significantly *negative* in the case of older males and positive but non-significant for the other three groups involved in this experiment (teenage males, prime-age males, and married women).

To be sure, our measure of migration may be far from ideal, as it covers the entire decade from 1950 to 1960 and includes

TABLE 1. Net Regression Coefficients for Unemployment
in Inter-city Labor-Force-Participation Regressions,
With and Without a Migration Variable:
Four Population Groups in April 1960[a]

| Population Group | Net Regression Coefficients for Unemployment[b] | | | |
| | Without Migration[c] | | With Migration[c] | |
	b	t	b	t
Males, 14–19	−1.84		−1.78	
	(0.28)	6.52	(0.30)	5.91
Males, 25–54	−0.23		−0.20	
	(0.06)	3.71	(0.06)	3.18
Males, 65 and over	−1.44		−1.52	
	(0.21)	6.78	(0.20)	7.61
Married women,	−0.74)		−0.70	
husbands present	(0.17)	4.42	(0.18)	3.87

[a] The dependent variable in each regression is the percentage of individuals in the civilian, noninstitutional population of the designated group who were in the labor force during the Census week of 1960. The independent variables comprise the unemployment rate plus certain "control variables," which are described in our paper on "Labor Force Participation and Unemployment" (Arthur M. Ross, editor, *Employment Policy and the Labor Market* [Berkeley: University of California Press, 1965], Chapter 4). Our migration variable is the net gain or loss in civilian migration by each city (SMSA) between 1950 and 1960, expressed as a percentage of the city's civilian population in 1960. The source of our migration data is the Dept. of Commerce, *County and City Data Book: 1962*, Table 3, item 33, pp. 433, 441, and 449.

Those readers who have studied the tables in our paper (cited above) may observe that there are certain discrepancies between the net regression coefficients for unemployment shown there and those for the "without-migration" runs shown here. These differences are due to certain improvements in the control variables made since the above paper was published. We will be happy to furnish our latest multiple-regression results to anyone desiring them.

[b] *Notation:*
    b = net (partial) regression coefficient
    t = t-value of the regression coefficient ($|b/s|$); all t-values in the table are significant at the 1% level.

[c] Numbers in parentheses in the b column give the standard error of the regression coefficient.

migrants seeking retirement homes as well as those seeking jobs. The question of how best to take account of the migration phenomenon needs to be given much more careful thought. Nevertheless, until other evidence leads us to question the findings reported here, the conclusion seems to be that the sensitivity of labor-force participation to labor-market conditions shown by our cross-sectional regressions is only in small measure attributable to inter-city migration.

In addition to raising the question of the effect of migration, Mincer has challenged the applicability of cross-sectional results "to the mild cyclical fluctuations we have experienced in the postwar period" on the ground that the cross-sectional parameters provide information regarding the effect of long-run "structural" differences among areas rather than information on the effect of short-run "cyclical" forces on participation rates for the economy as a whole. We are not sure how to form any very precise idea of the importance of short-run versus long-run phenomena in our cross-section results, and this troubles us. However, even if we accepted the contention that it is the effect of long-run factors which cross-sectional coefficients reveal (and in general, we agree with this view), we would not conclude that the results of such analysis are inapplicable to recent American experience. The most noteworthy characteristic of the period since 1957 is not that mild cyclical swings have occurred, but that for over seven years the unemployment rate never fell below 5 per cent. It seems to us that it is to this kind of prolonged period of relatively high unemployment, especially for some labor-force groups, that inferences drawn from cross-sectional analysis should apply.

Towards the end of his paper Mincer considers the impact of various institutional-legal factors (changes in the minimum wage, in school enrollment patterns, retirement benefits, etc.) on participation rates. We applaud this emphasis on the need to pay more attention to the effects of variables of this kind, and are glad to learn that research on these questions is under way.

With regard to the sharp drop during the last decade in the participation rate for teenagers not enrolled in school, we wish to call attention to another causal factor which may have been of considerable importance—the decrease in the average quality of this group has probably been associated with the sharp increase in the proportion of teenagers remaining in school. Between 1947 and 1963, the proportion of males from 14 to 19 years of age who were enrolled in school increased from 64 per cent to 83 per cent. It seems reasonable to suppose that in the shrinking pool of youngsters *not* enrolled in school there is a growing proportion not well suited for participation in the market sector.[5]

A very brief comment on Mincer's helpful discussion of the role played by increased retirement benefits in reducing the labor-force participation rate of older males seems fitting here—namely, that the level of retirement benefits is not a wholly independent variable. Pressures for increases in retirement benefits, both via government legislation and through collective bargaining agreements, are stronger when unemployment is high and participation low than in the converse circumstances. Thus to some extent causation flows in both directions, i.e., from unfavorable labor-market conditions to more generous retirement provisions and benefits as well as from the latter to lower participation rates.

Some Further Implications

What policy significance is to be attached to all of this analysis? Mincer discusses this question mainly in the context of "hidden unemployment" estimates, and our first observation is that the questions he raises about the meaningfulness of simply adding hidden unemployment to reported unemployment are very well taken. Too many of us (ourselves included) have tended to ignore this additivity problem in practice although recognizing it in principle. This is not to say, however, that we agree with all aspects of his discussion of hidden unemployment.

In discussing the "manpower gap," Mincer argues that "the 'manpower loss' in reported unemployment is its *cyclical* component, not total unemployment." As we noted earlier, the experience of the last seven years illustrates that inadequate demand may persist over a relatively long period of time and need not be a purely cyclical phenomenon (in the short-run sense of that term). Hence, if one wishes to define a manpower gap in terms of the difference between actual experience and some ideal state of the labor market, we would define the gap as the *non-frictional component* of total unemployment rather than as the cyclical component.

A more substantive and important issue has to do with the economic and social significance of hidden unemployment. Mincer stresses that hidden unemployment is concentrated almost entirely in the so-called secondary labor force and therefore is really not commensurable with primary labor-force unemployment, either in terms of GNP foregone or social welfare costs. We certainly agree with this general point, as does Tella.[6] Just as there are considerable differences among the reported unemployed with regard to potential productivity, and hardship attendant upon unemployment, so there are, no doubt, differences in these respects between the average of the reported group and the average of the hidden group.

Where we differ with Mincer is in our implied assessments of *how* different the two groups are in these respects. While Mincer does not deny the possibility of some involuntary withdrawals from the labor force, he suggests that regression analysis is likely to pick up labor-force flows affected in their *timing* but not in life-time *amount* by labor-market conditions. The optimization of the timing of labor-force participation will create the illusion of disguised or hidden unemployment, but how important is this phenomenon quantitatively? Mincer does not claim to have any hard evidence, and neither do we; we are all driven back to the realm of speculation.

It seems implausible to us that there are many people who, in effect, devote 40 per cent of their lives to labor-force participation and determine the timing of their participation on the basis of changes in net advantages brought about by shifts in labor-market conditions. Economic theory suggests that the total amount of life-time participation will be influenced by the strength of the relevant economic incentives as well as by their timing. Furthermore, it should be recognized that many secondary workers have little control over the timing of their labor-force participation. It is increasingly common for married women to work steadily, interrupting their careers only for the at least semi-fortuitous appearance of young children. And for many teenagers, the decision as to whether to remain in school or seek full-time work represents a once-and-for-all choice between further education and full-time jobseeking.

This observation about the irreversibility of the teenager decision leads to a more general point of considerable importance: it may be that labor-force participation on the part of a person in year "x" *increases* the probability that the person will also participate in years "y," "z," etc. Many women who started work during World War II continued in the labor force afterwards, for a variety of reasons, some of which are: (a) many had learned skills which increased the pay-off from market work, and (b) many became accustomed to the routine of market work and the higher living standards it makes possible. The same phenomenon is likely to occur in the opposite direction in the case of older males: once out of the labor force, deterioration of skills and inertia combine to make re-entry difficult.

With regard to the social hardship associated with involuntary labor-force withdrawals on the part of members of the secondary labor force, our only comment is that while the average hardship is surely less here than in the case of the average unemployed head-of-a-household, there is considerable dispersion around these means. Consider the not-unusual case of the married woman who wants to work to facilitate the education of her children, or the not-uncommon case of the older person who would prefer to work rather than be dependent on social agencies or his own children.

To end on a general note: Mincer is certainly right in pointing out how much is still unknown about labor-force behavior; but we are less impressed by the remaining gaps than the recent additions to the stock of knowledge in this field. Mincer's paper represents a very significant contribution to this growing stock and to our own understanding of labor-force behavior.

NOTES

1. We are estimating the following relationship: $L_i/P_i = a + b(U/L)$. Suppose that there is an autonomous increase in labor supply, unaccompanied in the short run by any increase in labor demand. If nothing else happens, both L_i/P_i and U/L will increase, producing a positive relation between them. If the "true" relation (i.e., the relation generated by auto-

nomous changes in the *demand* for labor) is negative, this spurious positive association would bias the observed regression coefficient toward smaller (absolute) negative values. Over time the autonomous increase in supply would presumably lead to some increase in the quantity of labor demanded as relative wages fell and employers moved along their labor demand schedules. However, it is hard to see why the quantity of labor demanded should increase so much as to produce a lower unemployment rate than that which prevailed in the initial situation. And so long as the new unemployment rate is higher than the initial rate, some amount of spurious *positive* correlation will be found. Other autonomous changes and various errors of measurement tend to produce spurious positive or negative associations, and we are unsure whether the positive or negative biases are likely to predominate.

2. Mincer goes on to suggest that a "cleaner" analysis would utilize U/P rather than U/L as the unemployment variable. As we see it, the difficulty with using U/P is that it makes less intuitive sense than U/L as a determinant of participation decisions. The purpose of the unemployment variable is to provide a measure of the probability of not finding a job. The numerator U is a measure of the relevant number of trials. The alternative of using P in the denominator is less satisfactory because it treats all members of the population as equally interested in labor-force participation. In the case of inter-city cross-section analysis, for example, two cities might well have the same U/P but differ significantly in the tightness of their respective labor markets. For example, if city A is a "retirement city" (one in which an unusually large fraction of the adult population is not interested in working) and city B is "normal" in this respect, the same U/P ratio in both cities would imply that jobs were actually harder to find in A than in B.

3. We are also indebted to W. Lee Hansen for making a similar point in an oral criticism of our work.

4. The difference between the cross-section and times-series results is exaggerated in Mincer's Table 1 because the coefficient from our study is attributed only to males 35–44, when in fact it applies to males 25 to 54. The time-series studies show some labor-force sensitivity in the 25–34 and 45–54 intervals, and if a weighted average of time-series coefficients for all three of these ten-year age groups was compared with our finding for the over-all 25–54 group, the actual difference would be seen to be smaller than the apparent difference reported in the table.

5. For additional figures and comments on trends in teenage unemployment and participation, see the recent paper by Bowen, "Unemployment in the United States: Quantitative Dimensions," to appear in W. G. Bowen and F. H. Harbison, eds., *Unemployment in a Prosperous Economy* (Princeton: Princeton University Press, 1965).

6. See our paper in *Employment Policy and the Labor Market*, pp. 156–157, and Tella's article in *Industrial Relations*, IV (February 1965), 75.

Discussion

BY FRANK C. PIERSON

It looked for a while as though the controversy over the cyclical variation in the labor-force participation rate would drag on like the debate between the structuralists and aggregationists over unemployment, with both engagements ending in a kind of muddled justification for each camp's point of view. On the cyclical participation-rate question, however, it seems to me that Jacob Mincer's paper has now set matters about as straight as the available statistics will permit. Since it appears that the next advance in tested knowledge about this subject will have to wait on the development of new kinds of information, perhaps a scholarly cease-fire in the interim would be in order.

Interpreting the Findings

Mincer joins with a number of other recent investigators in trying to demolish the traditional position that save in hyper-booms or severe depressions the country's labor force is cyclically insensitive. I am not as impressed by the record as he and they seem to be with the effects of cyclical employment expansions, as opposed to employment contractions, on the labor-force participation rate. Mincer himself notes that in three post-war expansions, 1951–1953, 1956–1957, and 1961–1962, labor-force participation rates fell rather than rose, due to special circumstances. Current reports also raise the question whether there have been smaller than projected increases in 1964–1965 in such categories as teenagers or female workers. These exceptions indicate that the expected cyclical pattern may be submerged in expansion periods, with the labor-force participation rate forming something approaching an asymmetrical shape over the course of the cycle. Subject to this tentative reservation, the conclusion that a substantial part of the country's working-age population edges in and out of the labor force in harmony with the cyclical tides of business seems unassailable.

When it comes to specific numerical estimates of these relationships, Mincer leans to a middle-zone position. Here he makes an important contribution in showing why the findings of some recent studies are quite exaggerated. His own computations indicate, for example, that a cyclical drop in employment demand of 100 workers is associated with a decline of only about 18–19 workers in the labor force, less than half the amount indicated by the other investigations he examined. Unless I overlooked an error in his analysis, his estimate strikes me as the most defensible one available.

But just what does his position add up to? And where do we go from here? As best as I can interpret Mincer's findings, he is saying that a number of groups in the working-age population have a precarious footing in the country's labor force; and these groups, epitomized by women workers generally and male workers in the under-25 and over-54 age category, have become so large that their decisions to seek or not seek work materially affect the over-all labor-force participation rate. But at this point Mincer's discussion becomes both more blurred and more interesting because he finds that the cyclical conformity of the disaggregations is not as clear as that of the aggregate of secondary workers. In part, this reflects the effect of inverse-cyclical factors, for example, the additional-worker influence which characterizes the participation rate of non-white women workers. More importantly, it reflects the antecedent effects of various institutional changes, e.g., the rise in the federal minimum wage in 1956 and 1961, and the liberalization of limitations on income from work of social-security pensioners in 1950, 1952, and 1958, as well as the rise in their level of benefits.

Such changes in the legislative and institutional environment are perhaps better thought of as exerting long-term rather than short-term influences on labor-force participation rates, but taken together, these environmental developments may also affect the short-term rate itself. On one hand, the record indicates that the cyclical sensitivity of the labor force becomes greater as secondary workers become a larger proportion of the working-age population, as social safeguards against loss of income become more complete, and as the general level of incomes rises. On the other hand, the factors bearing on cyclical participation rates become more complex as the economy becomes more affluent and society becomes more responsive to different group needs. Thus, to drop out of the labor force because further job hunting has become fruitless is one thing; to drop out in order to enter a training program or to qualify for social-security benefits or, as a result of various personal considerations, to substitute leisure for money income is quite a different thing. The discouraged worker is certainly still with us, but the encouraged-non-worker is part of the picture, too, and both deserve attention.

Some Research and Policy Suggestions

The next step is to develop data which will throw a more discriminating light on the cyclical participation rate of secondary workers. Essential information is now lacking on the family-income-skill profiles of individuals who move in and out of the labor force with unusual frequency over the course of the cycle. There is also a paucity of data on the relevant personal and attitudinal characteristics of such persons. Fact gathering which reaches beyond broad statistical categories to special groups and particular individuals is needed to fill these gaps.

Two groups deserve special attention in this connection: part-time workers and the discouraged workers already mentioned. The labor-force status of the first group, an increasingly important part of the country's labor force, is subject to a variety of influences. Does a drop in the labor-force participation of such workers reflect an increase or decrease in their families' income status? Does it reflect a rise in full-time job opportunities or a drop in part-time jobs? Does it reflect the pull of positive economic and noneconomic incentives or the push of adverse job conditions and prospects? More detailed data and intensive study are needed before these questions can be answered.

The discouraged worker group poses still more puzzling questions. To identify and describe the make-up of this group, attention must be given to such matters as family background, educational status, and even certain personal traits. When, for example, does a worker actually cross the line into the labor-force dropout category? What steps had he previously taken to find a job? What further steps in the way of a reduction in pay, movement to another city, and training in other job lines were open to him? What were the "subjective" and "objective" circumstances which lay behind his decision not to take these further steps? Again, this type of information points to investigations of a detailed, intensive nature. Emphasis on the behavior and motivation of specific groups and individuals is in accord with the view expressed by Jacob Mincer that the usual economic explanations of cyclical variations in labor-force participation rates are unduly narrow and that attention must be directed to a number of non-economic influences if this murky area is ever to be made clear.

The usual policy implication derived from recent participation-rate studies is that much more aggressive measures to lift employment are called for as long as "true" unemployment remains so far in excess of measured unemployment. While Mincer's strictures about current estimates of hidden unemployment seem well taken, they do not warrant complacency (as I am sure he would agree) about the importance of this aspect of the manpower utilization problem. With the development of more refined data about the behavior of particular secondary-worker groups, more policy findings should also emerge. If differences in participation-rate responses of worker groups are as great as they appear to be, policy remedies need to be fashioned accordingly. Where the line between aggregative and disaggregative policy measures should be drawn will remain debatable, but the case for forging closer links between policy actions and the circumstances of particular worker groups is especially strong in this varied and complex area of human behavior.

Discussion

BY RICHARD A. EASTERLIN

In the last few years a much needed reopening of the question of the sensitivity of labor-force participation rates to variations in unemployment conditions has occurred. As the unemployment rate is reduced, does labor-force participation tend, on the average, to rise or fall, and by how much? The results of this research suggest, contrary to the accepted view, that labor-force participation tends to rise, and to a fairly substantial extent. This has led to the conclusion that the slippage in the unemployment rate in recent years has depressed labor-force growth unduly and that there is, in consequence, a substantial volume of disguised unemployment.

It has been inferred from this that public policy attempts to reduce the unemployment rate would be seriously handicapped by the need to create jobs not only for those now reported as unemployed, but for members of this disguised unemployment group who would enter the labor force as job opportunities expanded. As noted by Mincer, estimates of the quantitative magnitudes involved have placed the size of the labor force corresponding to a 4 per cent unemployment rate as high as three million more than that of the last year or so when the unemployment rate was in the neighborhood of 5 or more per cent—and, for 1970, almost four million greater than the official BLS labor-force projection which is based on the assumption of a 4 per cent rate.[1]

After a searching theoretical and methodological review of this work and an independent examination of the data, Professor Mincer arrives at conclusions which run counter to the recent trend. True, he concludes that on balance there is some tendency for labor-force participation to rise as unemployment conditions improve, but he feels that the magnitude of this effect, has been vastly exaggerated. He further concludes from his examination of the evidence that too little attention has been paid to secular or irregular factors influencing labor-force participation.

Mincer is to be congratulated for a timely and valuable contribution. Reflections such as his on the conceptual aspects of the subject under discussion are long overdue, and his empirical findings seem to me reasonable. This, of course, is not to disparage earlier efforts, the findings of which made Mincer's chapter possible.

My agreement with the nature of Mincer's empirical findings stems not only from the persuasiveness of his own analysis, but from independent research. Since I find little of importance with which to take issue in his paper, perhaps the most useful contribution I can make as a discussant is to indicate briefly some additional considerations pointing to conclusions similar to his. The present comments complement Mincer's chapter.

The questions that constitute the focus of the discussion are the following:

1. Has labor force growth since 1960, which has been less than projected, been depressed by unemployment conditions, and if so, how seriously?

2. Would a reduction in the unemployment rate to 4 per cent in the remainder of this decade accelerate labor-force growth, and if so, how seriously?

The present approach attempts to look at these questions in the light of experience since the beginning of this century by drawing on the decennial census data on the labor force. It is disturbing that so much research involving questions relating in essence to economic growth is based on cross-section studies or time-series analyses confined to the short span since World War II. (Mincer himself is a notable exception in this regard, as is witnessed by his pioneering analysis of trends in labor-force participation of married females.)[2] While there are undoubted biases and deficiencies in historical data, it is not clear that these are necessarily more detrimental to the ultimate research results than those arising from undue reliance on short time series or cross-section studies. Clearly the ideal approach is to exploit all sources of potentially relevant data, yet too often research stops short of using historical material.

The analytical framework employed here differs from the usual one in that the role of participation rate change is considered in a form which reveals immediately its significance for the growth of the labor force as a whole. This has the advantage of directing attention at the same time to other components of labor-force growth, notably, changes in the working-age population. The latter could be subdivided into growth through migration (including internal migration in the case of a subnational study) versus more purely demographic processes of aging and mortality, but this is not attempted here.[3] In concept, the approach takes into account all the sources of labor-force growth in exactly the same manner as does disaggregation of population change into births, deaths, and migration, and provides similarly useful descriptive information.

The reasoning is illustrated in Table 1, Columns 1-4. As shown on Line 6, in 1940–1950 the total labor force increased by 15.3 per cent (Column 2). In the absence of participation rate change, growth of the working-age population during the decade would have increased the labor force by 10.4 per cent (Column 3). The participation rate changes which occurred, however, added on balance another 4.9 per cent (Column 4), yielding an actual growth rate almost one-and-one-half times that which population growth alone would have produced.[4] To facilitate comparisons between participation rate change and unemployment conditions, information has been added in Columns 5-7 on the average unemployment rate in the quinquennium prior to the date of observation of the participation rates used in the analysis. The choice of this period is based on the view, supported by Mincer, that the effect of unemployment on participation rates is more likely to appear after several years of persistently high or low unemployment than immediately. In other words, if participation rates in 1910 differ significantly from those of 1900 because of unemployment conditions, it is because these conditions were substantially different, not between 1900 and 1910 alone, but between, say, 1895–1900 and 1905–1910. The choice of quinquennial period is somewhat arbitrary, of course, and identification of the proper period is itself a matter calling for empirical investigation.

The discouraged-worker effect of unemployment conditions on

TABLE 1. Average Growth Rate of Labor Force by
Component of Change, Specified Periods, 1900–1964,
and Projections, 1964–1970; and Average
Unemployment Rate, Specified Periods,
1895–1963, and Assumed, 1965–1969

Line	Period (1)	Change in Labor Force Due to: (per cent)			Period (5)	Unemployment Rate	
		All sources (2)	Popu-lation growth (3)	Participa-tion rate change (4)		Average for period (per cent) (6)	Change from preceding period (percentage point) (7)
1					1895–1899	12.3	—
2	1900–1910	25.8	25.4	0.4	1905–1909	4.2	−8.1
3	1910–1920	15.3	14.6	0.7	1915–1919	4.0	−0.2
4	1920–1930	16.8	18.4	−1.6	1925–1929	4.0	0.0
5	1930–1940	8.6	12.2	−3.6	1935–1939	14.1	10.1
6	1940–1950	15.3	10.4	4.9	1945–1949	4.0	−10.1
7					1945–1949	4.0	—
8	1950–1955	13.2	8.2	5.0	1950–1954	4.0	0.0
9	1955–1960	11.6	10.3	1.4	1955–1959	5.0	1.0
10	1960–1964	14.0	14.2	−0.2	1959–1963	5.8	0.8
11	1964–1970:				1965–1969	4.0/5.0	−1.8/−0.8
12	Ref. 8	28.3	16.3	12.0			
13	Ref. 9	22.3	16.3	6.3			
14	BLS 1	20.2	16.3	3.7			

Sources: *Columns 2 to 4:* basic data for 1900–1940 are from decennial census data as adjusted
by Clarence D. Long in *The Labor Force under Changing Income and Employment* (Princeton:
Princeton University Press, 1958); and, from 1940 on, from the Current Population Survey,
U. S. Bureau of the Census. (Alaska and Hawaii are included only from 1960 on.) *Data in
Column 6:* from 1895–1899 to 1935–1939 are from Stanley Lebergott, *Manpower in Economic
Growth* (New York: McGraw-Hill, 1964); and, from 1945–1949 on, from the Current Popu-
lation Survey.

labor-force participation is clearly suggested by comparison of
the 1930–1940 decade with the others. As shown in Column 7,
Line 5, the deterioration in relevant unemployment conditions
in this period was by far the greatest of any covered here. And,
as Column 4 indicates, participation rates moved on balance in
a way tending to reduce the labor force and in an amount
greater than for any other period. Indeed, the resultant growth
of labor force in this decade (Column 2) seems clearly
depressed relative to that of other periods. However, observations for some other periods seem less consistent with a hypothe-

sis emphasizing the predominant role of unemployment conditions. For example, between 1920 and 1930 relevant unemployment conditions showed no change (Column 7, Line 4), but the contribution of participation rate change to labor-force growth was again negative, second in magnitude only to the 1930–1940 period (Column 4).

Another variable influencing the role of participation rate change, however, is suggested by Table 1. Column 4 shows that the highest positive contributions of participation rate change to labor-force growth occurred in 1940–1950 and 1950–1955, periods when the contribution of population growth was at its lowest (Column 3). This suggests that, other things remaining equal, labor shortages arising from a disproportionately low contribution of population change to labor-force growth might create pressures for labor-force additions via increased participation by "labor reserve" groups. Again, however, there are conflicting observations. In 1955–1960, when the contribution of population change to labor-force growth was as low as in 1940–1950, the role of participation rate change, though still positive, was less than one-third as great.

These conclusions point to the desirability of considering concurrently the influence on participation rate change of variations both in unemployment conditions and growth of the working-age population. To this end, the values for the contribution of participation rate change in Table 1 have been classified in Table 2 according to the associated values of unemployment conditions and population change. The latter "independent" variables show no apparent correlation themselves.

Reading Table 2 horizontally, that is, holding population growth conditions constant, one finds the expected form of association between unemployment conditions and the contribution of participation rate change. For example, the smaller contribution of participation rate change in 1955–1960 than in 1940–1950 now appears consistent with the less favorable unemployment conditions associated with the former period.

Reading Table 2 vertically, that is, holding unemployment conditions constant, one finds the inverse relation between the contribution of population growth and participation rate change suggested above. For example, the negative contribution of par-

TABLE 2. Contribution of Participation Rate Change to
Labor-Force Growth, Specified Periods, 1900–1964,
Cross-Classified by Associated Values of Change
in Unemployment Rate and Contribution of
Population Change to Labor-Force Growth

Contribution of population change to labor-force growth (per cent)	Change in unemployment rate (percentage points)				
	Over −8.0	−1.0 to −1.9	0 to −0.9	1.0 to 0.1	11.0 to 10.9
(1) 25–25.9	1900–1910 0.4				
(2) 18–18.9			1920–1930 −1.6		
(3) 17–17.9					
(4) 16–16.9		1964–1970			
(5) 15–15.9					
(6) 14–14.9			1910–1920 0.7	1960–1964 −0.2	
(7) 13–13.9					
(8) 12–12.9					1930–1940 −3.6
(9) 11–11.9					
(10) 10–10.9	1940–1950 4.9			1955–1960 1.4	
(11) 9– 9.9					
(12) 8– 8.9			1950–1955 5.0		

Source: Table 1, Columns 3, 4, and 7.

ticipation rate change in the 1920–1930 decade, apparently inex-
plicable on the basis of employment considerations, falls into
place when account is taken of the fact that this interval was
the one with the second highest contribution of population to
labor-force growth.

In sum, while the observations are limited in number, they
form a pattern consistent with the hypothesis that the contribution of participation rate change to labor-force growth tends to
vary directly with improvements in unemployment conditions

and inversely with the contribution of working-age population to labor-force growth.

If this analysis is valid, what does it imply regarding experience in the 1960's to data and the outlook for the remainder of the decade? The observations for the period 1960–1964 appear consistent with those relating to earlier periods (compare, for example, 1960–1964 with both 1910–1920 and 1955–1960). One would be led to infer from this that the observed contribution of participation rate change to labor-force growth during 1960–1964 was partly depressed by unemployment conditions, but also partly by the substantial rise in the growth rate of the working-age population. If a closer approach to 4 per cent unemployment had been achieved in this period than in 1955–1960 (placing the 1960–1964 observation in the same cell as that for 1910–1920 in Table 2), the contribution of participation rate change probably would have been positive and labor-force growth as a whole correspondingly higher. However, whether the contribution of participation rate change would have reached a level approaching 2 percentage points as implied by the BLS projections for this interval is perhaps dubious.

As for 1964–1970, if one assumes progress toward the 4 per cent unemployment goal, with an average rate for this period somewhere between 4 and 5 per cent, the relevant cell can be readily located in the matrix, since the prospective contribution of population change is already reasonably well-known. The location of the cell (Table 2, Row 4) suggests that while improved unemployment conditions might raise the contribution of participation rate change compared to the 1960–1964 period, this would be offset, at least in part, by the depressing effect on the contribution of participation rate change of a further rise in population change.

The partitioning technique used here for historical analysis can be applied to the 1970 projections, private[5] and official,[6] to determine the contribution of participation rate change to 1964–1970 labor-force growth implicit in each. The results of this procedure are summarized in Lines 12–14 of Table 1, and provide a basis for evaluating the projections in terms of the present framework. Comparison of the values in Column 4 suggests that the contributions for participation rate change implicit in the private projections (Lines 12, 13) are out of line with past experience, even without allowing for the prospective contribution of population change to labor-force growth in the remainder of this decade. When the latter is considered (by entering the projected contributions in the 1964–1970 cell in Table 2) they seem even more doubtful. The contribution of participation rate change projected by BLS is more reasonable in magnitude, but even it, when located in the 1964–1970 cell in Table 2, seems high. The suggestion offered with regard to the BLS projection for 1960–1964—that it might have proved high even under more favorable unemployment conditions—seems even more pertinent to the projection for the remainder of this decade. This may appear startling in view of the extant criticisms of the BLS projections as too low. It reflects at bottom the conclusion implied by this analysis that the projections, official and unofficial, are questionable because they rely exclusively on experience of the recent past, when the role of participation-rate change was unusually high due to the disproportionately low growth of working-age population, a condition now in the process of reversal. If correct, this implies that while labor-force growth may be higher in the remainder of this decade, the extent to which this would handicap efforts to reduce the unemployment rate is overstated even in the official projections.

NOTES

1. Thomas Dernburg and Kenneth Strand, "Manpower Gap," *Challenge,* December 1964, pp. 41–43, and "Cyclical Variation in Civilian Labor Force Participation," *Review of Economics and Statistics,* XLVI (November 1964), 378–391.

2. Jacob Mincer, "Labor Force Participation of Married Women," in Universities-National Bureau Committee for Economic Research, *Aspects of Labor Economics* (Princeton: Princeton University Press for NBER, 1962), pp. 63–105.

3. See Richard A. Easterlin, "Discussion," *1964 Proceedings of the Business and Economic Statistics Section of the American Statistical Association,* pp. 387–392.

4. The partitioning technique used here is a simple one and the present results, which are preliminary, involve some differences in method among the periods shown. Typically, the procedure was as follows: the population change over the period was weighted by the beginning-of-period participa-

tion rates to obtain the contribution of population growth; the change in rates over the period by the end-of-period population to obtain the contribution of participation rate change. The calculations were carried through at a minimum for individual age-sex groups and for some periods for individual color-nativity components as well. As in most index number techniques, some variation in results will arise from altering the procedure, but the broad inferences drawn here will be unaffected.

5. Alfred Tella, "Labor Force Sensitivity to Employment by Age, Sex," *Industrial Relations*, IV (February 1965), 69–83; "The Relation of Labor Force to Employment," *Industrial and Labor Relations Review*, XVII (April 1964), 454–469; and Dernburg and Strand, *op. cit.*

6. Sophia Cooper and Denis F. Johnston, "Labor Force Projections for 1970–1980," *Monthly Labor Review*, LXXXVIII February 1965), 129–140, and "The Outlook for the Labor Force at Mid-Decade," *1964 Proceedings of the Business and Economic Statistics Section of the American Statistical Association*, pp. 367–383.

PART III

THE CHANGING LEVEL AND PATTERN OF EMPLOYMENT

CHAPTER 4

The Behavior of Employment, 1961–1965

BY MARGARET S. GORDON

Introduction

The majority of American economists seem to have in recent
years supported the position of the Council of Economic Advisers in favor of emphasis on measures to stimulate aggregate
demand as the primary instrument of public policy in combatting
unemployment.[1] The effectiveness of this approach clearly depends on a complicated set of interactions involving GNP and
its components, the labor force, employment, unemployment,
hours of work, and productivity changes. More particularly, the
impact of any increase in real GNP on employment depends on
(a) the composition of the increase in GNP by economic sector,
and (b) the behavior of productivity changes by sector. It also
depends on the rapidity with which bottlenecks develop in the
supply of skilled manpower of particular types and the effectiveness with which these bottlenecks are attacked by private and
public labor-market adjustment measures. To the extent that

such bottlenecks result in an acceleration of inflationary pressures, the expansion of employment will be slowed down.

Much of recent literature has been concerned with the conflict between the goals of full employment and price and wage stability, and relatively little attention has been paid to the impact on employment of differences in the composition of increases in GNP and their relation to differential increases in productivity. I shall devote most of my attention to the latter set of relationships, partly because it seems to have played an important role in explaining the sluggish behavior of employment in the early stages of the present upswing and the subsequent accelerated increase of employment, and partly because analysis of inflationary pressures involves a study of changes in wage relationships, which are considered in the paper by Hildebrand and Delehanty.

GNP and Employment—Relative Behavior in Postwar Upswings

Throughout the analysis which follows, comparisons of increases in GNP and employment during four postwar upswings, beginning with the 1949–1953 upswing, will be made. Whenever possible, seasonally adjusted quarterly data will be used, and to facilitate comparisons between upswings of varying length we shall measure the performance of the economy during each year of the upswing, beginning with the quarter in which the trough occurred. In Table 1, for example, the percentage increase in GNP during the first year of the first upswing represents the increase between the last quarter of 1949 (the trough, according to the National Bureau of Economic Research, occurred in November 1949) and the last quarter of 1950. Although the use of annual average increases is advantageous for some purposes, I have refrained from it in this analysis, because it would conceal the phenomenon which is of special interest in connection with the present upswing—the unusually sluggish response of employment in the early stages of the upswing and the accelerated response of employment later on. The first quarter of 1965 is treated as the peak of the present upswing *merely* because that was the last quarter for which data were available when the tables were prepared.

TABLE 1. Percentage Increases in Real GNP and
Employment, During Postwar Upswings
(Quarterly, seasonally adjusted data)

Variable and Dates of Upswing	Cumulative Increase				Noncumulative Increase			
	1st Year	2nd Year	3rd Year	4th Year	1st Year	2nd Year	3rd Year	4th Year
GNP (in 1954 dollars)								
1949-IV to 1953-III	13.2	18.4	23.7	[26.3]ᵃ	13.2	4.6	4.4	[2.2]ᵃ
1954-III to 1957-III	9.8	10.5	13.5		9.8	0.7	2.7	
1958-II to 1960-II	9.8	11.9			9.8	1.9		
1961-I to —	8.0	11.8	17.0	22.6	8.0	3.5	4.6	4.8
Employment								
1949-IV to 1953-III	3.6	4.1	4.9	[5.9]ᵃ	3.6	0.5	0.7	[0.9]ᵃ
1954-III to 1957-III	4.7	6.9	7.3		4.7	2.1	0.4	
1958-II to 1960-II	3.2	5.1			3.2	1.8		
1961-I to —	1.2	2.3	4.5	6.8	1.2	1.0	2.2	2.3
Nonagricultural employment								
1949-IV to 1953-III	4.3	5.6	7.4	[8.7]ᵃ	4.3	1.2	1.7	[1.2]ᵃ
1954-III to 1957-III	4.6	7.6	8.8		4.6	2.8	1.1	
1958-II to 1960-II	3.1	5.9			3.1	2.7		
1961-I to —	1.8	3.7	6.5	9.4	1.8	2.0	2.7	2.8

Sources: *Survey of Current Business* and *Employment and Earnings*.
ᵃ The data relate to the increase attained by the third quarter of 1953, in which the peak of the upswing occurred.

In each of these four upswings, the percentage increase in GNP was markedly greater during the first year of the upswing than in subsequent years, reflecting the ease with which rapid expansion can be achieved when the economy moves upward from a position of substantially underutilized capacity (Table 1). Although the percentage increase in GNP during the first year of the present upswing—from the first quarter of 1961 to the first quarter of 1962—was smaller than in the previous three upswings, the difference was pronounced only in comparison with the 1949–1953 upswing. In the second and third years, the rate of increase in the present upswing was considerably more impressive. The advance in the fourth year cannot be compared with that in any previous upswing, in view of the greater length of the continuing period of expansion. As R. A. Gordon's paper shows, however, the average annual rate of advance in 1960–1964 was substantially higher than in 1953–1957 or 1957–1960 and not far below that of 1948–1953.

When we turn to employment comparisons, we see a strikingly different picture. The percentage increase in employment in the first year of the present upswing was startlingly small compared with that in earlier upswings, and, in the second year, the advance was again less pronounced than in the two preceding upswings, though larger than that in the 1949–1953 expansion period. In the third year, on the other hand, the increase in employment accelerated and was more pronounced than in the only two previous upswings with which comparison can be made. The increase in the fourth year was slightly more rapid than that of the third year.

The differences are somewhat less sharp when comparisons are based on the behavior of nonagricultural employment, reflecting the influence of a pronounced drop in agricultural employment in the first few years of the present upswing which has no parallel in earlier upswings except for that of 1949–1953. The ratios in Table 2 indicate that the increase in employ-

TABLE 2. RATIO OF PERCENTAGE INCREASE IN GNP (IN 1954 DOLLARS) TO PERCENTAGE INCREASE IN EMPLOYMENT DURING POSTWAR UPSWINGS

(Quarterly, seasonally adjusted data)

Ratio and Dates of Upswing	Cumulative Increase				Noncumulative Increase			
	1st Year	2nd Year	3rd Year	4th Year	1st Year	2nd Year	3rd Year	4th Year
Percentage increase in GNP ÷ percentage increase in employment								
1949-IV to 1953-III	3.7	4.5	4.8	[4.5]	3.7	9.2	6.3	[2.4]
1954-III to 1957-III	2.1	1.5	1.8		2.1	0.3	6.8	
1958-II to 1960-II	3.1	2.3			3.1	1.1		
1961-I to —	6.7	5.1	3.8	3.3	6.7	3.5	2.1	2.1
Percentage increase in GNP ÷ percentage increase in nonagricultural employment								
1949-IV to 1953-III	3.1	3.3	3.2	[3.0]	3.1	3.8	2.6	[1.8]
1954-III to 1957-III	2.1	1.4	1.5		2.1	0.3	2.5	
1958-II to 1960-II	3.2	2.0			3.2	0.7		
1961-I to —	4.4	3.2	2.6	2.4	4.4	1.8	1.7	1.7

Source: Computed from data in Table 1.

ment—and to a less pronounced degree in nonagricultural employment—was not only sluggish in the first year of the present upswing but was smaller in relation to GNP then in earlier upswings.[2] In the second year of the present upswing, this was also true for total employment (except in comparison with the first upswing) and nonagricultural employment. In the third and fourth years, the response of employment to a given percentage increase in GNP tended to be considerably greater. Although the cumulative experience in this long upswing cannot be compared with that of any previous expansion period, by the last quarter of the third year the ratio of the percentage increase in GNP to that in employment was still high in comparison with the 1954–1957 upswing, although lower than in the 1949–1953 upswing. However, the experience in the 1949–1953 upswing was abnormal, for the increase in the size of the armed forces contributed to a tight labor-market situation which impeded the expansion of civilian employment.

We could express these relationships in terms of the absolute increase in employment associated with an increase of one billion dollars in GNP, but the results would not be substantially different.[3] In the first year of the present upswing, a billion-dollar increase in GNP (in 1964 dollars) was associated with a rise of only about 19,000 in employment as compared with an increase of approximately 66,000 in the first year of the 1954–1957 upswing.

The results of some regression analyses carried out by my research assistant, Lewis Perl, provide further evidence of these different relationships between increases in GNP and in employment and unemployment in postwar cycles. The variations in the regression coefficients expressing the increase in employment associated with a billion-dollar increase in GNP in the four postwar upswings might have been expected on the basis of the data considered thus far. What is striking is the extremely small and statistically insignificant coefficient of the present upswing. This apparently reflects, at least in part, the fact that the relationship between GNP and employment differed substantially between the earlier and later stages of the upswing. In other words, a nonlinear function might more satisfactorily express the relationship.

GNP and Employment—Changes Measured from the Previous Peak

The small increase in real GNP and the unusually small increase in employment in the early stages of the present upswing might partly have been explained by the fact that the economy was recovering from a mild and short downswing. The speed of recovery might have been expected to be less rapid than when the economy was recovering from a deeper recession, with the level of production further below capacity. The levels of production and employment attained by the end of the first year of the upswing might well have compared *relatively* more favorably with those of the previous peak than with the situation at the trough.

Pursuing this line of reasoning, we have computed percentages comparable with those shown in the first four columns of Table 1, except that the changes are measured from the peak quarter of the previous upswing (Table 3). The top figure in the first column of Table 3, for example, represents the percentage increase in real GNP from the fourth quarter of 1948 (the peak quarter of the 1945–1948 upswing) to the fourth quarter of 1950. Similarly, the top figure in the second column is the percentage increase from 1948-IV to 1951-IV, etc.

On this basis the performance of the economy in the first year of the present upswing compared unfavorably with its performance in the first year of previous upswings, except for the 1958–1960 expansion period. The percentage increase in GNP was slightly higher than in the first year of the 1958–1960 upswing, while the percentage increase in employment was equally low. On the basis of measurements from the trough, the percentage increase in employment in the first year of the 1958–1960 upswing was considerably greater than in the present upswing (Table 1), but the economy was recovering from a much sharper downswing in 1958–1960 and had more lost ground to recover by the end of the first year. Similarly, in the case of nonagricultural employment, the relative increase attained by the end of the first year of the 1958–1960 upswing turned out to be considerably smaller when measurements were made from the peak.

Again, on the basis of the measurements in Table 3, the percentage increase in GNP in the present upswing compared favor-

TABLE 3. PERCENTAGE INCREASE IN REAL GNP AND
EMPLOYMENT AT END (LAST QUARTER) OF EACH
YEAR OF POSTWAR UPSWINGS, MEASURED FROM
PEAK QUARTER OF PREVIOUS UPSWING
(Quarterly, seasonally adjusted data)

Variable and Dates of Upswing	1st Year	2nd Year	3rd Year	4th Year
GNP (in 1954 dollars)				
1949-IV to 1953-III	11.5	16.7	21.9	[24.5][a]
1954-III to 1957-III	7.4	8.1	11.0	
1958-II to 1960-II	5.6	7.6		
1961-I to —	6.1	9.8	14.9	20.4
Employment				
1949-IV to 1953-III	2.1	2.6	3.4	[4.4][a]
1954-III to 1957-III	2.6	4.8	5.2	
1958-II to 1960-II	0.9	2.7		
1961-I to —	0.9	2.0	4.2	6.6
Nonagricultural employment				
1949-IV to 1953-III	3.7	5.0	6.8	[8.1][a]
1954-III to 1957-III	2.3	5.3	6.4	
1958-II to 1960-II	1.3	4.1		
1961-I to —	1.4	3.3	6.0	9.0

Sources: *Survey of Current Business* and *Employment and Earnings.*
[a] The data relate to the increase attained by the third quarter of 1953, in which the peak of the upswing occurred.

ably with that of earlier upswings after the first year, while the percentage increase in employment did not begin to, on a cumulative basis, until after the second year.

The ratio of the percentage increase in GNP to employment, computed on this basis, was also high in the first year of the present upswing, but did not exceed those for the first year of the 1949–1953 and 1958–1960 upswings by nearly as much as when measurements were made from the trough (Table 4). In the second year, however, its relative position was more comparable with that of the corresponding ratio in Table 2.

The ratios expressing the relationship between the percentage

TABLE 4. RATIO OF PERCENTAGE INCREASE IN GNP (IN 1954
DOLLARS) TO PERCENTAGE INCREASE IN EMPLOYMENT AT
END (LAST QUARTER) OF EACH YEAR OF POSTWAR
UPSWINGS, MEASURED FROM PEAK QUARTER OF
PREVIOUS UPSWING

(Quarterly, seasonally adjusted data)

Ratio and Dates of Upswing	1st Year	2nd Year	3rd Year	4th Year
Percentage increase in GNP ÷ percentage increase in employment				
1949-IV to 1953-III	5.5	6.4	6.4	[5.6]
1954-III to 1957-III	2.8	1.7	2.1	
1958-II to 1960-II	6.2	2.8		
1961-I to —	6.8	4.9	3.5	3.1
Percentage increase in GNP ÷ percentage increase in nonagricultural employment				
1949-IV to 1953-III	3.1	3.3	3.2	[3.0]
1954-III to 1957-III	3.2	1.5	1.7	
1958-II to 1960-II	4.3	1.9		
1961-I to —	4.4	3.0	2.5	2.3

Source: Computed from data in Table 3.

increase in GNP and nonagricultural employment are less
changed when measurements are made from the previous peak.
They are not greatly different from the corresponding ratios in
Table 2, although again the position of the ratio for the first
year of 1958–1960 upswing is substantially altered.

Let us consider the relationship between changes in GNP and
employment in the upswing *as a whole* (as it developed through
the first quarter of 1965) in comparison with earlier upswings.
For this purpose measurements from the previous peak seem appropriate, and comparison can be made if we bring together the
relevant ratios from Table 4. The first line of figures relates the
percentage change in GNP to total employment; in the second
line the denominator represents the percentage change in nonagricultural employment.

	1948-IV– 1953-III	1953-III– 1957-III	1958-II– 1960-II	1960-II– 1965-I
$\dfrac{\Delta GNP \div GNP}{\Delta E \div E}$	5.6	2.1	2.8	3.1
$\dfrac{\Delta GNP \div GNP}{\Delta NAE \div NAE}$	3.0	1.7	1.9	2.3

The variations in these ratios from upswing to upswing, and within upswings, indicate that it is hazardous to predict the percentage increase in employment that will be associated with a percentage increase in GNP. Over longer periods, the relationship may be more stable. The unusually high ratio for the 1948–1953 period reflects not only the special characteristics of the increase in output associated with the Korean conflict but also the effects of the sizable withdrawal of manpower from the civilian economy to the armed forces. To some extent, these men were replaced by new entrants to the labor force, particularly women, but under the tight labor-market conditions prevailing in the early 1950's there were many unfilled job vacancies which were filled in the course of the 1953–1957 period with the flow of men back into civilian employment. Thus, it seems appropriate to compute the ratio of the percentage increase in GNP to the percentage increase in employment for the entire 1948–1957 period. It turns out to be 3.9, using the change in total employment as a base, and 2.5, using the percentage increase in nonagricultural employment as a base. These computations suggest somewhat greater stability in these ratios, at least under peacetime conditions, but variations over the cycle, and from cycle to cycle, may still be substantial.[4]

Employment, Unemployment, and the Civilian Labor Force

The sluggish response of employment in the first two years of the present upswing helps to explain the disappointingly slow decline in the unemployment rate during this period. The halting decline in unemployment cannot be explained by an unusually heavy increase in the labor force. Unlike the first years of previous upswings, the civilian labor force did not increase during the first year of the present upswing, but actually showed a slight decline. Evidently the increase in employment was too slight to offset the discouraging effects on labor-force participation of the high unemployment rate that had been prevailing for approximately four years.[5] In the second year of the upswing, the absolute increase in employment was nearly twice as large as in the first year and substantially exceeded the modest increase of 815 thousand in the civilian labor force. In the third and fourth years of the present upswing, although the increase in the civilian labor force has been greater and more in line with what underlying population trends and the upward trend in female labor-force participation would have led us to expect, the increase in employment has exceeded the increase in the labor force. Moreover, on a cumulative basis through the first quarter of 1965, the increase in employment in the present upswing has exceeded the increase in the civilian labor force. The increase in the total labor force in the last five years has been smaller than predicted, even on the basis of the revised interim projections in 1962, which reflected a downward revision of earlier projections.[6] But this is largely explained by the experience of 1961–1962.

As Gertrude Bancroft's paper shows, however, there have been important differences between men and women in this respect. For men aged 20 or more, the increase in employment has exceeded the increase in the civilian labor force, and unemployment has declined. In the case of women, although it has shown improvement in the more recent stages of the expansion, the situation has been less favorable. In the first quarter of 1965, employment of women in this age group was 2.3 million higher than in the first quarter of 1961 (on a seasonally adjusted basis), while the number of women aged 20 or more in the civilian labor force increased by 1.7 million.

The Sluggish Increase in Employment, 1961–1962

In searching for explanations of the sluggish increase in employment in the first two years of the present upswing, we shall consider (a) the behavior of agricultural and nonagricultural employment, (b) the composition of the increase in GNP, (c) the behavior of productivity, and (d) the behavior of hours of work.

Agricultural and nonagricultural employment. The heavy decline in agricultural employment in the first two years of the present upswing was an important factor in explaining the sluggish increase in total employment (Table 5). The contrast between the decline of 287,000 in farm employment in the first year and the increases that occurred in the corresponding stages of the two preceding upswings is noteworthy. Moreover, the decline in agricultural employment in the second year was unusually great, although pronounced declines also occurred in the corresponding stages of all three earlier upswings. The additional declines in farm employment in the third and fourth years, though smaller in magnitude, have acted as a continuing drag on the increase in total employment.

However, the heavy drop in agricultural employment was not the sole explanation of the sluggish behavior of total employment in the early stages of this upswing. The increase in nonagricultural employment was unusually slight in the first year, as we have seen, while in the second year the rise in nonagricultural employment was numerically smaller than in the two preceding

TABLE 5. CHANGES IN AGRICULTURAL AND NONAGRICULTURAL
EMPLOYMENT DURING POSTWAR UPSWINGS
(Quarterly, seasonally adjusted data, in thousands)

Type of Employment and Upswing	Cumulative				Noncumulative			
	1st Year	2nd Year	3rd Year	4th Year	1st Year	2nd Year	3rd Year	4th Year
Agricultural employment (household data)								
1949-IV to 1953-III	−103	−457	−908	[−1,014][a]	−103	−354	−451	[−106][a]
1954-III to 1957-III	326	47	−292		326	−279	−339	
1958-II to 1960-II	242	−190			242	−432		
1961-I to —	−287	−748	−968	−1,186	−287	−461	−220	−218
Nonagricultural employment (household data)								
1949-IV to 1953-III	2,196	2,858	3,763	[4,436][a]	2,196	662	905	[673][a]
1954-III to 1957-III	2,512	4,123	4,747		2,512	1,611	624	
1958-II to 1960-II	1,817	3,422			1,817	1,605		
1961-I to —	1,084	2,252	3,939	5,759	1,084	1,168	1,687	1,820

Sources: *Employment and Earnings* and *Monthly Labor Review.*
[a] Data do not represent a full year but are included to show the pattern of change in the last three quarters of the 1949–1953 upswing.

upswings, although, on a percentage basis in relation to increase in GNP, it was larger than in two out of three of the previous upswings (Table 2).

A factor holding back the increase in nonagricultural employment in the first two years of the present upswing was a decline in the number of nonagricultural self-employed and unpaid family workers. Since data on self-employment and unpaid family employment are not available on a seasonally adjusted basis and allowance must be made for sampling and other errors, the changes shown by quarterly data cannot be viewed as completely reliable. However, annual data indicate that there was a substantial decline in these two types of employment —which are closely related as unpaid family workers generally work for the self-employed—from 1961 to 1963, and a decline in the number of unpaid family workers in 1964. This development is closely associated with the behavior of business failures, which have displayed an upward trend throughout the postwar period, after reaching an abnormally low level during World War II. The number and rate of business failures reached a postwar peak in 1961, 17,075 and 64.4 per 10,000 listed enterprises, respectively.[7] Since then they have declined but have maintained a level above that of the first half of the 1950's.

As Mincer's paper reminds us, the amendments to the federal minimum-wage law adopted in the spring of 1961 provided for extensions of coverage to large numbers of workers in retail trade. This development may have played a role in forcing a number of small retail establishments out of business and thus have helped to explain the decline in self-employment. The sluggish behavior of total wage and salary employment in retail trade in 1961–1962 may be explained at least partially by this development.[8] Rees' paper goes into the question at greater length.

The composition of the increase in GNP. The sluggish rise in employment in the first two years of the present upswing might be explained in part by the composition of the increase in GNP, with increases occurring to a greater extent in industries characterized by rapid productivity increases. Unfortunately, data on changes in GNP by industry group are available only on an annual basis and are therefore unsatisfactory for an analysis of the characteristics of the early stages of the present upswing, since the recovery began early in 1961. With total real GNP in 1961 exceeding that in 1960, the year 1961 hardly serves satisfactorily as a trough year.

However, data on the behavior of consumption, private investment, and government expenditures—which *are* available on a quarterly, seasonally adjusted basis—show pronounced differences between the early stages of the present upswing and the two preceding ones, (Table 6). During the first year of the current upswing, the increase in personal consumption expenditures accounted for a smaller percentage of the increase in GNP than in any of the postwar upswings except that of 1949–1953. In the first year of the 1954–1957 upswing, on the other hand, the increase in personal consumption expenditures, especially for durable goods, accounted for a large percentage of the increase in GNP. This chiefly reflected a marked increase in expenditures for automobiles between 1954 and 1955. It was the 1954–1957 upswing in which the ratio of the increase in GNP to employment was low in the first year—that is, employment increased more rapidly in *relation* to the increase in GNP than in the other upswings.

A second characteristic of the first year of the present upswing was the large contribution made by the increase in federal government purchases of goods and services. Again, the contrast with the first year of the 1954–1957 upswing, when the contribution of federal purchases was negative, is of interest.

During the second year of the present upswing, gross private domestic investment contributed negatively to the increase in GNP. However, the sharply negative contribution of changes in business inventories, reflecting a smaller increase than in the preceding year, largely accounted for the poor showing of private investment.

The most significant difference in the behavior of components of GNP between the first two years of the present upswing and those of the two preceding upswings was the positive contribution of increased federal government purchases of goods and services. Moreover, most of the increase in the first year went for national defense, whereas in the second year the increases were almost equally divided between national defense and other types of expenditures.

TABLE 6. RELATIVE CONTRIBUTION OF COMPONENTS OF GNP TO INCREASE IN TOTAL GNP, IN 1954 DOLLARS, IN EACH YEAR OF POSTWAR UPSWINGS
(Quarterly, seasonally adjusted data)

Component	1949-IV-1950-IV	1950-IV-1951-IV	1951-IV-1952-IV	1952-IV-1953-III a	1954-III-1955-III	1955-III-1956-III	1956-III-1957-III	1958-II-1959-II	1959-II-1960-II	1961-I-1962-I	1962-I-1963-I	1963-I-1964-I	1964-I-1965-I
Increase in GNP (billions of 1954 dollars)	38.6	15.3	15.4	7.9	35.4	2.7	10.8	38.8	10.4	35.1	16.3	22.6	24.2
Per cent b	100.0	100.0	100.0	100.0	100.0	100.0	100.0	100.0	100.0	100.0	100.0	100.0	100.0
Personal consumption expenditures	20.7	18.3	67.5	73.4	59.0	129.6	92.6	46.9	122.1	44.7	78.5	61.5	81.4
Durable goods	9.6	-29.4	25.3	26.6	25.7	-166.7	17.6	17.8	-7.7	15.7	22.7	20.4	24.0
Nondurable goods	2.1	30.1	26.0	17.7	19.5	111.1	38.0	17.5	34.6	13.4	25.2	19.9	36.0
Services	9.1	17.6	16.2	27.8	13.8	185.2	37.0	11.3	94.2	15.4	31.3	21.2	21.9
Gross private domestic investment	77.5	-94.1	8.4	-27.8	42.4	-92.6	-23.1	55.2	-99.0	43.0	-0.6	23.9	24.8
New construction	10.6	-17.6	7.8	13.9	11.3	-70.4	-5.6	13.1	-9.6	6.8	8.0	12.4	-2.1
Residential nonfarm	6.7	-21.6	8.4	1.3	6.8	-81.5	-7.4	13.6	-25.0	8.3	6.7	7.5	-5.0
Other	3.9	3.9	-0.6	12.7	4.5	11.1	1.9	-0.5	14.4	-1.1	0.7	4.9	2.5
Producers' durable equipment	11.1	-3.9	-2.6	10.1	8.5	55.6	-2.8	6.7	-10.6	8.5	8.6	15.5	12.0
Change in business inventories	55.7	-71.9	2.6	-53.2	22.6	-77.8	-14.8	35.1	-78.8	27.6	-16.6	-4.4	14.9
Net exports	-2.3	23.5	-30.5	-1.3	1.7	70.4	6.5	-7.5	50.0	-6.6	—	18.1	-11.2
Government purchases	3.9	152.3	54.5	55.7	-2.8	-7.4	25.0	5.9	26.0	18.5	22.1	-3.5	5.0
Federal	2.3	148.4	51.3	44.3	-7.3	-51.9	12.0	—	2.9	15.1	14.1	-12.8	-2.9
State and local	1.6	3.3	3.9	11.4	4.5	40.7	13.0	5.7	24.0	3.7	8.6	8.8	8.3

Source: Computed from data in *Survey of Current Business*.
a Data do not represent a full year but are included to show the pattern of change in the last three quarters of the 1949-1953 upswing.
b Items do not always add to totals because of rounding.

There has been much discussion of the fact that with the shift from aircraft to missiles and the development of the space program, a dollar of defense procurement expenditures tends to generate less employment than it did a decade ago. Statistics compiled by the Department of Defense shed some light on this question, although the data are not fully satisfactory since the expenditure categories are not completely comparable with the employment categories.[9] The contrast between the 1960–1963 experience and that of 1955–1957 is striking. The increase of approximately 25 per cent in monthly expenditures for the selected categories (aircraft and missiles, ships and ordnance, vehicles, and related equipment) in 1960–1963 was accompanied by an increase of only 6 per cent in corresponding types of employment, whereas in the 1955–1957 period an increase of about 6 per cent in expenditures was associated with a rise of about 16 per cent in employment.

Turning to Table 7, which shows the contribution of each major industry group to the increase in GNP on an annual basis, we find that in 1961–1962 the contribution of the goods industries was distinctly smaller than in 1949–1950, 1954–1955, or 1958–1959. In making this comparison, we must keep in mind that 1961 serves less satisfactorily as a trough year than 1949, 1954, or 1958, because the trough month occurred very early in the year. I have shifted the transportation and utilities group to the goods sector, departing from Department of Commerce procedure, but following the practice of other analysts.[10]

Interestingly, it was not manufacturing which accounted to a great extent for the small contribution of the goods sector, as compared with earlier upswings, but construction and the transportation and utilities groups. Agriculture made no contribution, in contrast with the 1949–1950 and 1954–1955 situations, while mining made an insignificant contribution.

In view of the fact that productivity increases tend to be greater in the goods sector of the economy than the service sector, we should expect the increase in employment to be smaller in relation to the increase in GNP when the rise in GNP occurs predominantly in the goods sector of the economy. However, the reverse prevailed between the early stages of the present upswing and earlier upswings, particularly those of 1954–1957

TABLE 7. RELATIVE CONTRIBUTION OF EACH INDUSTRY GROUP
TO INCREASE IN GNP (IN 1954 DOLLARS) ANNUALLY,
1949–1953, 1954–1957, 1958–1960, AND 1961–1963

Industry Group	1949–1950	1950–1951	1951–1952	1952–1953	1954–1955	1955–1956	1956–1957	1958–1959	1959–1960	1961–1962	1962–1963
Total increase in GNP (billions of 1954 dollars)	25.4	23.7	11.7	15.5	29.6	8.2	7.7	27.3	11.3	28.5	16.2
Per cent[a]	100.0	100.0	100.0	100.0	100.0	100.0	100.0	100.0	100.0	100.0	100.0
Goods industries	68.1	61.2	30.8	56.1	68.9	37.8	20.8	63.0	26.5	53.7	54.9
Agriculture, etc.	3.9	−5.5	6.8	4.5	3.4	−4.9	−5.2	−0.4	9.7	—	4.9
Mining	3.5	3.8	−0.9	1.9	3.4	7.3	—	1.5	1.8	0.7	1.9
Construction	4.7	8.9	0.9	0.6	4.4	11.0	−3.9	4.0	−4.4	0.4	1.9
Manufacturing	42.1	39.7	25.6	44.5	43.6	−3.7	18.2	44.3	1.8	42.5	27.2
Durable	34.6	32.1	13.7	36.1	28.0	−17.1	2.6	30.4	2.7	29.1	n.a.
Nondurable	7.1	7.6	12.0	9.0	15.2	13.4	16.9	13.9	−0.9	13.7	n.a.
Transportation, communications, and utilities	13.8	14.3	−1.7	4.5	14.2	28.0	11.7	13.6	17.7	10.2	19.1

Service industries	44.1	35.9	47.9	27.1	34.8	79.3	61.0	39.6	54.9	40.0	57.4
Trade	26.0	0.4	15.4	16.1	19.6	20.7	—	21.2	4.4	16.1	21.0
Finance, insurance, and real estate	8.7	8.9	6.0	3.9	8.8	22.0	35.1	8.1	22.1	9.5	19.1
Services	5.9	1.3	6.0	8.4	6.4	29.3	16.9	8.1	18.6	7.4	11.1
Government	3.5	25.3	20.5	−1.3	—	7.3	9.1	2.2	9.7	7.0	6.2
Rest of world	0.4	−0.4	—	0.6	0.7	2.4	2.6	0.4	—	1.1	—
Residual	−11.8	3.4	21.4	16.8	−4.4	−15.9	16.9	−2.9	18.6	4.9	−12.3

Source: Computed from data in *Manpower Report of the President*, March 1965, p. 258.

[a] Items do not always add to totals because of rounding.

153

and 1958–1960. We must point to the inadequacy of annual data for this type of comparison. It should also be noted that within the service sector the contribution of trade to the 1961–1962 increase was smaller than in 1949–1950, 1954–1955, or 1958–1960, whereas the contribution of government was larger. We have commented on the character of federal government expenditures and their limited employment-generating effect. And there was a sizable positive residual item in 1961–1962, in contrast with negative residual items in the earlier years.

Another interesting phenomenon shown in Table 7 is the shift to the service group of industries as the major contributor to increases in GNP after the first year of the 1954–1957 and 1958–1960 upswings. (The 1949–1953 upswing was a mixed bag in this respect.) A sizable increase in the relative contribution of the service industries, with more employment-generating effects, also occurred in 1962–1963, but there was no corresponding drop in the contribution of the goods industries. (The behavior of the residual item plays a role.) The relative contribution of manufacturing fell off, but far less than in the two previous upswings, while those of the other goods sectors increased.

The behavior of productivity. The tendency of productivity to decline in a recession and increase sharply in the early stages of an upswing, at least in the manufacturing sector, has been clearly established.[11] The cyclical behavior of productivity changes in the nonmanufacturing sector appears to be similar, although it has not been studied as closely. Productivity changes in agriculture, on the other hand, seem to have followed a distinctive pattern of variation.

For our purposes the question is whether the increase in productivity in the early stages of the present upswing was unusually pronounced as compared to the earlier postwar upswings. The available annual data are not adequate for the purpose, but the answer to the question seems to be a qualified no. The overall increase in output per man-hour in 1961–1962 was equal to that in 1954–1955 and higher than that in 1958–1959, but lower than that in 1949–1950 (Chart 1). While the increase in productivity in manufacturing in 1961–1962 was as high as 5.5 per cent, this was exceeded by the increase in 1954–1955. Nor was the

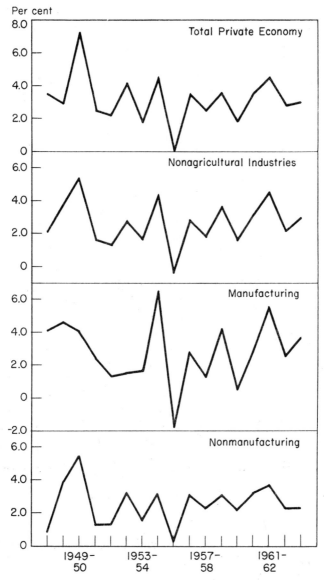

CHART 1. *Annual percentage changes in output per manhour, 1947–1948 to 1963–1964.* (*Source: U. S. Bureau of Labor Statistics.*)

increase in productivity in nonmanufacturing industries extraordinarily high in 1961–1962, although it was higher than in 1954–1955 or 1958–1959.

Let me repeat that annual data have their limitations. The increase in productivity in 1960–1961 was high. If we compute the percentage increase in output per man-hour from 1960 to 1962, it turns out to be higher (8.2 per cent) than the increase from 1953 to 1955 (6.4 per cent) or from 1957 to 1959 (6.2 per cent), although lower than for 1948–1950 (10.2 per cent).[12] This is not surprising in view of the fact that the downswing was short, from June, 1960 to February, 1961, and mild. The decline in productivity that occurred during the downswing was probably small, and, although the increase in the recovery period under such circumstances might be expected to be less pronounced than usual, the result was a high percentage increase for the two years combined. Productivity increases continued at high levels in the two following years.[13]

The behavior of hours of work. A small percentage increase in employment compared with GNP might reflect a pronounced increase in hours of work. Employers might achieve higher output by increasing hours of work to a greater extent than in previous upswings. Such a response would not be surprising, especially in view of the increase in the costs of fringe benefits as a percentage of total labor costs.

The increase in hours of work in the early stages of the present upswing was slight compared with previous upswings—and this is true whether we look at the annual or monthly data.[14] An unusual increase in hours of work apparently did *not* play a role in accounting for the sluggish increase in employment.

Accelerated Employment Increases, 1963–1965

Between the first quarter of 1963 and that of 1965, employment increases were more rapid and compared more favorably with the increase in GNP than in the first two years of the present upswing.

One reason for this was that although agricultural employment continued to decline, the drop was less pronounced than in the first two years of the upswing. Self-employment increased in the

third year of the upswing, although it declined between the first
quarter of 1964 and that of 1965.

Turning to the behavior of components of GNP (Table 6),
let us first consider the performance of private investment. In
the third and fourth years of the expansion, private investment
made a substantial contribution to the increase in GNP—smaller
than in 1961–1962, but displaying a more satisfactory performance than in the second and third years of the 1954–1957
upswing and the second year of the 1958–1960 expansion. Business inventories were stable, while investment in producers' durable equipment made a greater relative contribution than in the
first two years of the expansion. Construction behaved well in
1963–1964 but made a negative over-all contribution in
1964–1965. The sizable increase in private investment had a stimulating direct effect on employment, particularly in durable
goods manufacturing, as well as secondary effects in various sectors of the economy.

As far as personal consumption expenditures are concerned,
the most significant change was the increase in its relative contribution in 1964–1965, taking the form of a substantial increase
in the relative contribution of expenditures on durable goods and
on nondurables. The tax cut probably played a role here.

As a result of the combined effects of these favorable developments, employment in durable goods manufacturing increased
almost as much from 1963-I to 1965-I as in the preceding two
years, whereas in previous upswings the increase had slowed
down after the early stages of the expansion. In nondurable
goods manufacturing, the increase in employment occurred more
rapidly from 1963-I to 1965-I than in the first two years of the
expansion. Construction employment also increased rapidly
throughout this more recent period despite the falling off in construction investment from 1964-I to 1965-I.

On the other hand, the relative contribution of government
purchases of goods and services was negative in 1963–1964 and
only slightly positive in 1964–1965. The contribution of federal
government purchases in these years was negative, while that
of state and local expenditures was less important relatively than
in 1962–1963.

Unfortunately, annual data on GNP by industry group are not

available for 1964. There was an increase in the contribution of the service industries in 1962–1963, which may help to explain the accelerated increase in employment in the course of 1963. Within the goods sector the contribution of manufacturing fell off, but this change was probably reversed between 1963 and 1964, in view of the increases in the contributions of expenditures on durable and nondurable goods.

If we consider the expansion as a whole through 1963 in comparison with earlier upswings, measuring changes on a peak-to-peak basis and excluding agriculture, the differences between the present upswing and the preceding ones show up strikingly (Table 8). The contribution of the goods-producing industries, particularly manufacturing, was relatively greater than in any period since 1948–1953, while the contribution of the service industries was comparatively less important. Given the relatively greater productivity increases in the goods-producing industries, this would tend to make for relatively smaller increases in employment in relation to GNP.

As Table 9 shows, the overall-increase in output per man-hour was considerably higher than in the two preceding periods. This reflects larger increases in productivity in agriculture and in the manufacturing and nonmanufacturing sectors of the nonagricultural economy. Variations in average annual output per man-hour from period to period are consistent with variations in the ratios of the percentage increase in GNP to employment presented earlier.[15] Both sets of measures reflect changes in the composition of output as well as changes in "pure" productivity. We shall have more to say about the relative roles of changes in the composition of output and productivity in the next section.

Although the increased relative importance of expansion in the goods sector in 1960–1964 helps to explain the smaller increase in employment *relative* to GNP, as compared with the two preceding upswings, the average annual increase in employment *per se* in 1960–1964 was as high as in 1953–1957 and much higher than in 1957–1960 (Table 9). From the point of view of full employment policy, there would be no advantage in a set of fiscal policies which deliberately stimulated expansion of the service industries at the expense of the good industries. Such policies would be likely to retard *both* the rate of growth of output

TABLE 8. Relative Contribution of Each Industry Group
to Change in GNP (Excluding Agriculture),
1948–1953, 1953–1957, 1957–1960, and
1960–1963
(annual data)

Industry Group	1948–1953	1953–1957	1957–1960	1960–1963
Change in total GNP, excluding agriculture (billions of 1954 dollars)	75.6	38.5	30.0	51.9
Per cent[a]	100.0	100.0	100.0	100.0
Goods-producing industries	48.8	43.4	28.7	46.8
Mining	1.3	3.4	−1.3	1.3
Contract construction	5.0	5.2	−0.7	—
Manufacturing	34.3	15.3	14.0	31.8
Durable	26.2	1.6	0.7	n.a.
Nondurable	8.2	13.5	13.3	n.a.
Transportation, communications, and public utilities	8.2	19.5	16.7	13.7
Service-producing industries	44.0	57.7	61.3	49.9
Wholesale and retail trade	14.8	17.7	17.0	16.2
Finance, insurance, and real estate	10.3	21.6	21.0	15.2
Services	5.2	16.1	17.3	10.8
Government and government enterprises	13.8	2.3	6.0	7.7
Rest of the world	0.3	2.1	0.3	1.9
Residual	7.3	−3.4	9.3	1.2

Source: Computed from data in *Manpower Report of the President*,
March 1965, p. 258.
[a] Items do not always add to totals because of rounding.

and the rate of employment expansion, at least in the short run.
On the other hand, too much emphasis on expansion of the goods
industries could have disadvantages, also, in maintaining
balanced and sustained expansion and combatting structural unemployment. We shall return to this point in the concluding
section.

TABLE 9. Average Annual Change in Output per Manhour,
Output, Employment, and Manhours, 1948–1953,
1953–1957, 1957–1960, and 1960–1964[a]

	Average Annual Percentage Change			
	Output per Manhour	Output	Employment	Manhours
	1948–1953			
Total private economy	3.7	4.5	1.2	0.7
Agriculture	5.5	0.2	−4.6	−5.0
Nonagriculture	2.9	4.8	2.0	1.8
Manufacturing	2.7	5.4	2.4	2.6
Nonmanufacturing	3.0	4.4	1.8	1.4
	1953–1957			
Total private economy	2.5	2.8	0.9	0.3
Agriculture	4.9	1.4	−1.5	−3.4
Nonagriculture	2.1	2.9	1.3	0.8
Manufacturing	2.2	1.3	−0.5	−0.9
Nonmanufacturing	2.0	3.7	2.1	1.7
	1957–1960			
Total private economy	2.7	2.6	0.2	−0.7
Agriculture	5.1	1.9	−2.9	−3.0
Nonagriculture	2.3	2.6	0.5	0.3
Manufacturing	2.0	1.2	−0.8	−0.8
Nonmanufacturing	2.5	3.3	1.1	0.8
	1960–1964			
Total private economy	3.5	4.1	0.9	0.7
Agriculture	5.3	0.8	−4.1	−4.3
Nonagriculture	3.1	4.3	1.3	1.2
Manufacturing	3.6	4.8	0.7	1.1
Nonmanufacturing	2.9	4.1	1.6	1.2

[a] Calculated on the basis of indices (of establishment data) in *Manpower Report of the President*, March 1965, p. 256.

Employment by Major Industry Group

It is time to turn to a more intensive analysis of the behavior of employment in the present upswing. With respect to employment by industry we must rely on the nonagricultural employee (establishment) data which omit self-employed, unpaid family, and domestic workers.

Let us consider the relative contribution of each industry group to the total increase in the number of nonagricultural employees, on a peak-to-peak basis, in the four postwar upswings, with the annual data for the present upswing extending through 1964 (Table 10). Like the statistics relating to GNP in Table 8, these data reveal startling contrasts between the four postwar upswings in the relative contributions of goods and service industries—only more so! The large negative contribution of the goods-producing industries in the 1958–1960 upswing is striking. Although manufacturing and the transportation and utilities groups were making positive contributions to the increase in GNP, they were making negative contributions to the increase in employment in the 1953–1957 and 1957–1960 periods. In the transportation group, this chiefly reflects the heavy cutbacks in railroad employment in those years, although there was also a decline in employment in the telephone communication industry in 1957–1960.

Comparison of Tables 8 and 10 suggests that it may be worthwhile to analyze the changes that have occurred in the relationships between increases in GNP and employment in individual industry groups. In Table 11 percentage increases in employment have been subtracted from GNP for each of the postwar upswings, and the difference divided by the number of years involved. This method was chosen rather than the ratio method used with Tables 2 and 4 because in this case many negative ratios, of dubious meaning, would have resulted.[16] The data in Table 11 should not be looked upon as measures of productivity changes, although they tend to be related to such changes.

A study of this table, along with Tables 8 and 10, provides some clues to the roles of changes in the composition of GNP and of changes in productivity in individual industry groups in contributing to the variations in the relationship between increases in GNP and employment from period to period. For

TABLE 10. Relative Contribution of Each Industry Group
to Change in Number of Nonagricultural Employees,
1948–1953, 1953–1957,1957–1960, and 1960–1964

Industry Group	1948–1953	1953–1957	1957–1960	1960–1964
Increase in number of nonagricultural employees (in thousands)	5,341	2,662	1,309	3,983
Per cent[a]	100.0	100.0	100.0	100.0
Goods industries	44.8	−6.1	−58.7	15.6
Mining	−2.4	−1.4	−8.9	−1.9
Contract construction	8.5	11.3	−2.9	5.5
Manufacturing	36.8	−14.1	−28.9	12.7
Durable goods	33.4	−9.5	−30.3	9.7
Nondurable goods	3.4	−4.5	1.3	3.0
Transportation, communications, and public utilities	1.9	−1.8	−18.1	−0.7
Service industries	55.2	106.0	158.7	84.4
Wholesale and retail trade	18.3	24.0	38.6	20.0
Finance, insurance, and real estate	5.9	12.4	14.7	6.9
Services and miscellaneous	12.4	33.1	49.1	28.6
Government	18.6	36.5	56.3	28.9
Federal	8.3	−3.3	4.0	2.0
State and local	10.4	39.8	52.3	26.9

Source: Computed from data in *Manpower Report of the President*,
March 1965, p. 233.
[a] Items do not always add to totals because of rounding.

example, the low ratio of the increase in GNP to nonagricultural
employees in the 1953–1957 period reflected the decline in the
relative importance of the goods industries in contributing to
the upswing, as compared with the 1948–1953 period, but *also*
reflected marked changes in the relationship between increases
in GNP and employment in individual industry groups. One of
the most striking differences between the two periods was the
sharp drop in the contribution of durable-goods manufacturing

TABLE 11. PERCENTAGE CHANGES IN NONAGRICULTURE GNP AND NUMBER OF EMPLOYEES, BY INDUSTRY GROUP, AND ARITHMETIC ANNUAL AVERAGE OF DIFFERENCE, 1948–53, 1953–1957, 1957–1960, AND 1960–1963

Industry Group	Percentage Change in GNP				Percentage Change in Employment				Annual Average of Difference			
	1948–1953	1953–1957	1957–1960	1960–1963	1948–1953	1953–1957	1957–1960	1960–1963	1948–1953	1953–1957	1957–1960	1960–1963
Total	25.9	10.7	7.7	12.0	11.9	5.3	2.5	4.5	2.8	1.4	1.7	2.5
Mining	11.2	13.1	-3.6	6.5	-12.9	-4.4	-14.0	-10.8	4.8	4.4	3.5	5.8
Construction	28.4	11.6	-1.0	—	20.9	11.4	-1.3	3.4	1.5	0.1	0.1	-1.1
Manufacturing	30.1	5.3	3.6	13.5	12.6	-2.1	-2.2	1.2	3.5	1.9	1.9	4.1
Durable goods	42.8	1.0	0.3	n.a.	21.4	-2.5	-4.0	1.8	4.3	0.9	1.4	n.a.
Nondurable goods	15.6	11.3	7.8	n.a.	2.5	-1.6	0.2	0.6	2.6	3.2	2.5	n.a.
Transportation, communication, and utilities	23.4	22.9	12.4	15.7	2.4	-1.1	-5.6	-2.2	4.2	6.0	6.0	6.0
Trade	20.6	10.4	7.0	10.8	10.5	6.2	4.6	3.6	2.0	1.1	0.8	2.4
Finance, insurance, and real estate	24.1	20.7	13.0	14.4	17.3	15.4	7.8	7.6	1.4	1.3	1.7	2.3
Service	13.3	18.6	13.2	12.5	12.7	15.0	9.5	11.3	0.1	0.9	1.2	0.4
Government	39.1	2.4	4.7	10.1	17.6	14.6	9.7	10.1	4.3	-3.1	-1.7	—

Source: Computed from data in *Manpower Report of the President*, March 1965, pp. 233 and 258.

to the increase in GNP. However, the annual average difference between the percentage change in GNP and employment in this industry group was much smaller in 1953–1957 than in 1948–1953. This suggests that, in a period in which production is increasing very little or not at all, productivity gains may lag, for much the same reasons giving rise to decreases in productivity in recessions. Moreover, as Kuh has shown, changes in the composition of output toward low-productivity industries also played an important role in explaining the over-all behavior of productivity in durable goods manufacturing in this period.[17]

In 1957–1960, the difference between the percentage increase in GNP and the number of nonagricultural employees was higher than in 1953–1957, despite the greater relative importance of the service industries in contributing to the expansion. This is partly explained by the fact that the difference between the percentage increase in GNP and employment rose between the two periods in two industry groups in which GNP was rising more rapidly than over-all nonagricultural GNP—finance, insurance, and real estate, and services.

In 1960–1963, the goods industries played a relatively more important role in contributing to the increase in GNP than in either of the two previous periods, especially 1957–1960, so the larger difference between the percentage increase in GNP and employment is scarcely surprising.

Before leaving Table 11, the large increase in the annual average difference between the percentage rise in GNP and employment in manufacturing in the 1960–1963 period should be noted. This reflects the combined effects of a greater rise in sectoral GNP and shifts in composition back toward higher productivity industries, as well as changes in "pure" productivity. Conceivably of greater long-run significance was the sizable increase in the difference in trade. Does this mean rapid productivity increases are taking place in wholesale and retail trade? The continued expansion of supermarkets, the continued spread of branches of large department stores to suburban areas, and the decline of self-employment in retail trade all suggest this. The possible impact of the extension of coverage of the minimum wage law in 1961 has been mentioned earlier. There was also an increase in 1960–1963 in the difference between the percentage increase in

GNP and the number of employees in finance, insurance, and real estate, but something of a decline in the service sector.

The revival of employment in the goods industries in the current upswing has arrested, but not reversed, the relative gain in the service industries. If we consider the peak years—1948, 1953, 1957, and 1960—and 1964, the latest year for which annual data are available, we find that the percentages of nonagricultural employees in the goods industries were 51, 50, 48, 43, and 43. The drop between 1957 and 1960 was abnormally rapid and was largely explained by the lagging behavior of private investment and federal government spending during that period rather than by any unusual increases in productivity. Employment was sluggish in construction and durable goods manufacturing, and within durable goods manufacturing in the metal and machinery industries (affected by the decline in private investment) and the aircraft and parts industry (affected by the decline in federal government spending and the shift to missiles). These developments are brought out clearly in Charts 2 and 3.

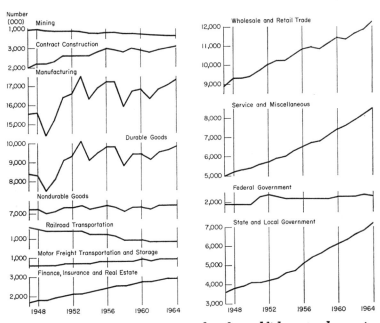

CHART 2. *Employees in nonagricultural establishments, by major industry group, 1947–1964. (Source: U. S. Bureau of Labor Statistics.)*

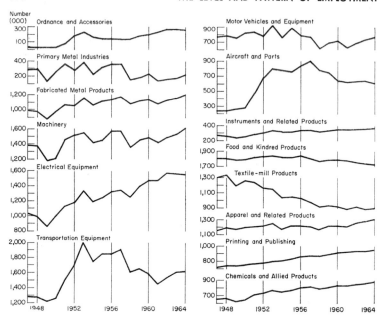

CHART 3. *Employees in selected manufacturing industries, 1947–1964.* (*Source: U. S. Bureau of Labor Statistics.*)

It seems unlikely that the long-run downward trend in the proportion of nonagricultural employees in the goods industries will be reversed.[18] There is no sign of abatement in the steady expansion of employment in the two large sectors of service industries and state and local government. Moreover, increased federal expenditures on health, education, training, and anti-poverty programs should have a stimulating effect on employment in those sectors. In the retail-trade sector, employment increases continue to be large in numerical terms even though there are indications of declining increases in percentage terms and in relation to increases in sectoral GNP.

In the next five years or so and perhaps over a longer period, employment in the goods sector may increase relative to employment in the service sector *if* there is continued relative expansion in the consumption of durable and nondurable goods and investment in producers' durable equipment,[19] *and* if the long-anticipated boom in residential construction in the latter part of the sixties materializes. The largest increases in the birth rate occurred in 1942 and the immediate postwar years. The cohort born in 1942 is now aged 22-23. Marriage and birth statistics tell us that a substantial proportion of this cohort is married and beginning to raise children. Its impact on the housing market is likely, given reasonably favorable labor market conditions, to be a buoyant factor in the late sixties, and this, of course, is only the first of a wave of increasing cohorts of young people approaching 25 to 30 years of age. True, those who lack an adequate level of education and skill will have difficulty maintaining steady employment, but if we can avoid a reversal in the downward trend of the unemployment rate, the over-all employment situation for young persons in their late twenties is likely to be favorable.

Before turning to changes in employment by occupation, we need to take account of the well-known increase in the proportion of nonproduction workers in manufacturing and certain other industries. In the industries for which data on the number of nonproduction employees are available, there was a substantial increase in the proportion of such workers from 1948 to 1964; from 9 to 22 per cent of all employees in mining; from 11 to 15 per cent in construction; from 17 to 26 per cent in manufacturing; and from 20 to 24 per cent in wholesale and retail trade.[20] However, in mining and manufacturing the shift has been less rapid since 1960 than in the middle and late fifties, while in construction there has been no change in the proportion of nonproduction workers since 1960. In manufacturing the proportion of nonproduction workers rose from 25 to 26 per cent between 1960 and 1961 but has tended to level off since. Thus, blue-collar workers have benefited more from the expansion of manufacturing employment than they would have if the proportion of nonproduction workers had continued to rise.

Employment by Occupation

The shift from blue-collar to white-collar employment has become a familiar story. Volumes have been written on its relevance to the structural-unemployment hypothesis and its implications for education, training, and retraining. In the light of all the data considered in this chapter, it is scarcely surprising

TABLE 12. PERCENTAGE DISTRIBUTION OF EMPLOYED PERSONS, BY MAJOR OCCUPATION GROUP AND SEX, 1948, 1953, 1957, 1960, AND 1964

Occupation Group	Both Sexes					Men					Women				
	1948	1953	1957	1960	1964	1948	1953	1957	1960	1964	1948	1953	1957	1960	1964
All employed workers	59,307	61,778	65,016	66,681	70,357	42,457	42,684	44,013	44,485	46,139	16,851	19,094	21,003	22,196	24,218
Per cent	100.0	100.0	100.0	100.0	100.0	100.0	100.0	100.0	100.0	100.0	100.0	100.0	100.0	100.0	100.0
Total white-collar workers	36.1	38.2	40.6	43.1	44.2	30.8	32.5	34.7	37.3	38.4	49.3	51.0	53.3	54.6	55.4
Professional, technical, and kindred workers	6.7	8.8	9.9	11.2	12.2	5.8	8.0	9.3	10.7	11.8	9.0	10.7	11.4	12.2	12.8
Managers, officials, and proprietors, exc. farm	10.7	10.4	10.3	10.6	10.6	12.9	12.7	12.9	13.4	13.7	5.2	5.1	4.9	5.0	4.6
Clerical and kindred workers	12.5	12.9	14.1	14.7	15.2	6.9	6.4	6.8	7.1	7.0	26.9	27.5	29.4	29.9	30.8
Sales workers	6.1	6.1	6.3	6.6	6.3	5.3	5.4	5.8	6.1	5.9	8.2	7.7	7.6	7.6	7.2
Total blue-collar workers	40.4	40.4	38.3	36.3	36.3	47.7	48.8	47.9	46.2	46.7	22.2	21.9	18.2	16.4	16.5
Craftsmen, foremen, and kindred workers	13.7	13.9	13.3	12.8	12.8	18.7	19.5	19.2	18.7	18.9	1.2	1.4	1.1	1.0	1.0
Operatives and kindred workers	20.9	20.6	19.3	18.0	18.4	21.1	20.9	20.5	19.4	20.1	20.5	19.9	16.6	15.0	15.1
Laborers, exc. farm and mine	5.9	5.9	5.7	5.5	5.2	8.0	8.3	8.2	8.1	7.7	0.5	0.6	0.4	0.4	0.4
Total service workers	10.2	11.3	11.7	12.5	13.2	6.1	6.5	6.4	6.6	7.1	20.5	21.9	22.9	24.5	24.7
Private household workers	3.0	3.0	3.2	3.3	3.3	0.3	0.1	0.1	0.1	0.1	9.5	9.5	9.8	9.8	9.3
Service workers exc. private household	7.2	8.3	8.5	9.2	9.9	5.7	6.4	6.3	6.5	6.9	11.0	12.5	13.2	14.7	15.4
Total farm workers	13.3	10.1	9.3	8.1	6.3	15.4	12.3	11.1	9.9	7.8	8.0	5.2	5.6	4.5	3.4
Farmers and farm managers	7.9	6.2	5.1	4.2	3.3	10.4	8.6	7.2	6.0	4.7	1.6	0.9	0.7	0.5	0.5
Farm laborers and foremen	5.4	3.9	4.2	3.9	3.0	5.0	3.7	3.9	3.9	3.1	6.5	4.3	4.9	4.0	2.8

Source: *Manpower Report of the President*, March 1965, pp. 202–203.

to find that the shift has slowed down, but not been arrested, since 1960 (Table 12).

The gains in the relative importance of professional, technical, and clerical workers have continued since 1960, but nonfarm managers have just held their own, and sales workers have declined as a percentage of all employed workers. (This latter development, contrasting as it does with a relative gain in the number of sales workers in 1957–1960, is consistent with our finding that the percentage increase in employment in retail trade has been declining.)

The decline in the proportion of blue-collar workers has been arrested, but not reversed. Craftsmen and foremen have held their own, the proportion of operatives has increased, and the percentage of nonfarm laborers has declined. In the light of the data we have been examining, it is no surprise to observe that the proportion of blue-collar workers fell between 1960 and 1961, recovered only slightly in 1962, and made its chief gain, back to its former level, in 1963 (annual data not shown in Table 12).

The proportion of service workers continued its long-run increase, while the proportion of farm workers continued to decline, at an accelerated rate compared with 1957–1960.

Changes in the occupational distribution of the two sexes were similar, but female nonfarm managers lost ground as a percentage of employed women, whereas men in this category gained ground. On the other hand, in the clerical field the women made the relative gains, while male employment in this category declined as a proportion of all employed men.

Since 1957 more detailed information has been available on occupational changes from the Monthly Labor Force Survey. There have been a number of interesting differences in the rates of change in the 1957–1960 and 1960–1964 periods for some of these more detailed categories, as well as some reversals in the direction of change.

In two important professional categories—medical and other health workers and teachers, except college—the percentage increase in employment in the four-year period from 1960 to 1964 was considerably smaller than in the three years from 1957 to 1960. Moreover, there was a sharp drop in the rate of increase for men, but only a modest decline in the rate of increase for women. It may be that there was an abnormally large flow of men into these occupations in 1957–1960 at least in part because of less favorable employment opportunities in a number of other occupations. And it was approximately during this period that the children born in the high-birth-rate war years, 1942 to 1944, reached the high-school level. (The birth rate reached an even higher point in 1947, but the increase from 1941 to 1942 was sharp.)

Within the managerial group, employment of salaried workers increased at a more rapid rate in 1960–1964 than in the three previous years. On the other hand, there was a sharper decline in the number of self-employed workers in retail trade in the more recent period, and a more pronounced decline for other self-employed nonfarm workers.[21]

Other changes worthy of special comment are (a) the continued, but much less sharp, decline in the employment of carpenters in the more recent period, (b) the reversal from a slight decline to a fairly sharp increase in the case of mechanics and repairmen, (c) the reversal from decline to increase for foremen, (d) the reversal from decline to increase for nearly all operatives' categories, but particularly for those in durable goods manufacturing, (e) the slowing down of the rate of increase for private household workers (a phenomenon which has occurred before in periods of improved over-all employment opportunities), (f) the sharp jump in the rate of increase for protective service workers, which has been associated with the increase in the crime rate in recent years, (g) a pronounced rise in the rate of increase for waiters, cooks, and bartenders, (h) a decline in the rate of increase for other service workers, and (i) the sharply accelerated decline in the employment of farm laborers, which reflects the influence of improved opportunities for nonagricultural employment as well as deteriorating job opportunities in agriculture.

A final word is in order about the implications of 1960–1964 occupational changes with respect to the problem of structural unemployment. On the whole, changes in the structure of employment were less pronounced than in the 1957–1960 period. If returning to Table 12 we add the percentage point changes (disregarding sign) in occupational distribution for the 11 major groups between 1957 and 1960, we get a total of 9.0 percentage points. The corresponding figure for the four-year period from 1960 to 1964 was 6.1 percentage points. Moreover, the revival in blue-collar employment in the latter period was an advantageous development in relation to the problem of structural unemployment. But the problem of shrinking relative job opportunities for those with no specialized skill or training was, if anything, exacerbated. Although the proportion of service workers continued to increase, the decline in the percentage of nonfarm laborers was substantial, the drop in the proportion of farm laborers was sharp, and the decline in the proportion of sales workers (often an entry occupation for young persons and married women) was disadvantageous for the untrained.

Even though there is a possibility of a relative gain in employment in the goods industries in the next five years, as suggested in the previous section, there may be a need for greater emphasis on job-creation programs, at least for a time, to meet the employment needs of the unskilled. Retraining programs alone cannot make a large dent on the problem. By the end of 1964, after more than two years of operation, only 190,000 persons had been enrolled in training under the Manpower Development and Training Act and far fewer under the Area Redevelopment Act. The numbers involved in training programs can be increased, but, as I have stressed elsewhere, the scope of retraining programs cannot be expanded sharply without incurring a growing risk of insufficient job opportunities for those completing training.[22]

The scope of job-creation programs sponsored by the federal government is undergoing substantial expansion. The newly-enacted Public Works and Economic Development Act (replacing the previous Area Redevelopment Act) and a number of the programs being developed under the Economic Opportunity Act will provide financing for a great number of permanent or temporary jobs, as well as work-study or work-trainee positions.

Conclusions

1. The chief conclusion to be derived from this chapter is that the amount of employment generated by a given increase in

GNP—measured in absolute or percentage terms—can vary greatly from period to period, depending on the composition of the increase in aggregate demand and the behavior of productivity in various sectors of the economy. As the present upswing has proceeded, the percentage increase in employment relative to the percentage increase in GNP, which was small in the early stages, has tended to rise. If comparisons are made on a peak-to-peak basis, the performance of the economy in generating employment in the current upswing compares more favorably with that in the two previous upswings than when percentage increases are measured from the trough of the previous recession.

2. The fact that employment has not increased as rapidly in *relation* to GNP in the present period of expansion as in the two previous upswings reflects the combined influence of the greater importance of the goods industries, with their generally higher rates of increase in productivity, in contributing to the expansion, and of increased rates of gain in productivity in a number of nonagricultural sectors of the economy, especially manufacturing.

3. On the other hand, the actual percentage increase in employment on an average annual basis was substantially greater from 1960 to 1964 than in 1957–1960, and equal to that in 1953–1957. A general policy of deliberate stimulation of the service industries at the expense of the goods industries, purely because of their lower productivity increases, would be disadvantageous *both* in relation to the goal of rapid growth and to the goal of full employment.

4. Nevertheless, for purposes of maintaining balanced expansion in the short run, stimulating increased rates of growth in the long run, and meeting a variety of important social needs, there is a strong case for increased public spending on some of the service industries, particularly education.

5. The decline in the proportion of workers employed in the goods industries as compared with the service industries, which has characterized much of the postwar period, has been arrested in recent years, reflecting the greater importance of the goods industries in contributing to the increase in GNP. From a long-run point of view, however, it seems unlikely that the decline has been arrested. Similarly, it is not at all clear that the inter-

ruption in the decline of the percentage of workers in blue-collar employment, which has been associated with the revival of the goods industries (chiefly manufacturing), represents a reversal of the long-run trend, although it has served, at least for the present, to curb exaggerated fears of the impact of automation on employment. Through 1964, the revival of blue-collar employment chiefly affected the semiskilled category. There was a continued decline in the proportion of workers employed as laborers, both farm and nonfarm, while skilled craftsmen barely held their own as a percentage of all employed workers. If it is true, as many of the contributors to this volume seem to believe, that the difficulty we are experiencing in reducing the over-all unemployment rate to 4 per cent or below is increasingly stemming from changes occurring on the supply side of the labor market, we must nonetheless recognize that poor employment opportunities for certain types of unskilled workers are continuing to present something of a problem on the demand side.

6. Finally, although I am generally optimistic about the prospect for continued expansion in both GNP and employment, *provided*, as suggested earlier, we can maintain a satisfactory rate of expansion until the prospective boom in residential construction begins to develop, I am much less optimistic about the outlook for unemployment. I should like to call attention to the aspect of the postwar unemployment experience that impresses me most. It was *only* during the immediate postwar years, when there were tremendous backlogs of consumer demand, and during the Korean conflict, that we succeeded in maintaining an average annual unemployment rate below 4 per cent. R. A. Gordon's analysis of structural unemployment indicates that exacerbation of the problem occurred largely in the period immediately following the Korean conflict.[23]

In the light of these considerations, *and* the prospect of an accelerated increase in the labor force, I am not optimistic about the possibility of pushing the unemployment rate below 4 per cent if we continue to rely on tax cuts as the chief method of stimulating aggregate demand, with a modest retraining program as our main approach to the structural program. Along with the Clark Subcommittee on Employment and Manpower, Myrdal, Galbraith, and others, I believe we need greater emphasis on substantially increased government spending, directed in part toward job-creation programs for the unskilled, at least for the next few years. And, as I have pointed out in a number of previous articles, I would advocate expansion and liberalization of income-maintenance programs for the unemployed and those out of the labor force.[24]

It is necessary to add that the increase in defense expenditures which has occurred as a result of further involvement in Vietnam since these passages were written has altered the short-run outlook. Whether and to what extent the longer-run prospects will be affected cannot be predicted at this time.

NOTES

1. I should like to acknowledge the valuable assistance of Marian Lacklen, Lewis Perl, and David Solomon in the preparation of this paper.

2. The ratios can be regarded as measures of the reciprocal of the elasticity of the response of employment to a given percentage increase in GNP. Since this chapter was completed, the Department of Commerce has published revised estimates of GNP and its components. Although the percentages and ratios in my tables would be altered slightly by these revisions, I have concluded on the basis of a good deal of sample checking, that the relationships shown in the tables and the conclusions drawn from them would not be altered if the revised GNP data were used.

3. For an earlier use of this general approach, see Richard C. Wilcock and Walter H. Franke, "Will Economic Growth Solve the Problem of Long-Term Unemployment?", *Proceedings of the Fourteenth Annual Meeting of the Industrial Relations Research Association, 1961*, pp. 37–59.

4. Okun has estimated that an increase of 1 per cent in real GNP is required to bring about a decline of one-third of a percentage point in the unemployment rate. Our computations indicate that in the present upswing an increase of 1 per cent in GNP has been associated with an increase of one-third of a percentage point in employment. The two measures are related, but the behavior of the labor force will affect the relationship between them. See Arthur M. Okun, "Potential GNP: Its Measurement and Significance," *1962 Proceedings of the Business and Economic Statistics Section*, American Statistical Association, pp. 98–104.

5. For a review of recent literature on the relationship between labor force participation, employment, and unemployment, see the chapter by Jacob Mincer in the present volume.

6. See Sophia Cooper, *Interim Revised Projections of the U. S. Labor Force, 1965–1975*, Special Labor Force Report, No. 24 (Washington, D. C.:

U. S. Bureau of Labor Statistics, 1962). The most recent projections may be found in Sophia Cooper and Denis F. Johnston, *Labor Force Projections for 1970–1980*, Special Labor Force Report, No. 49 (Washington, D. C.: U. S. Bureau of Labor Statistics, 1965).

7. See *Economic Report of the President*, January 1965, p. 274.

8. See *Manpower Report of the President*, March 1965, p. 233.

9. See *Statistical Abstract of the United States*, 1960, p. 241; and 1964, p. 256. Revised employment data have been supplied to me by the U. S. Bureau of Labor Statistics. For purposes of the comparisons made in the text, I have omitted data relating to the electronics and communications industry, since the revised employment data relating to this industry for recent years are not comparable with the data for years before 1958.

10. See Victor R. Fuchs, *Productivity Trends in the Goods and Service Sectors, 1929–1961*, Occasional Paper 89 (New York: National Bureau of Economic Research, 1964).

11. For a recent detailed analysis of this phenomenon, see Edwin Kuh, "Cyclical and Secular Labor Productivity in Manufacturing," *Review of Economics and Statistics*, XLVII (February, 1965) 1–12.

12. These percentages are computed from indexes of output per man-hour, on a 1957–1959 base. See *Manpower Report of the President*, March 1965, p. 256.

13. For further discussion of the implications of recent changes in productivity, see Leon Greenberg, "Technological Change, Productivity, and Employment in the United States," and Ewan Clague, "Effects of Technological Change on Occupational Employment Patterns in the United States," papers presented at the Conference on Manpower Implications of Automation, Washington, D. C., December 8–December 10, 1964 (available from the U. S. Bureau of Labor Statistics).

14. For annual data, see *Manpower Report of the President*, March 1965, pp. 236–237. Monthly data are regularly reported in *Employment and Earnings, Monthly Labor Review,* and *Monthly Report on the Labor Force.*

15. See page 145. The ratios were based on data for peak quarters, whereas the changes in output per man-hour were computed from annual data.

16. Probably a preferable method would have been to compute the annual average rates of increase in GNP and employment, and then take the difference. However, since each period includes relatively few years, the results would not differ appreciably from those obtained by this simpler method.

17. Kuh, *op. cit.,* p. 4.

18. On the basis of a careful analysis of the factors underlying the growing importance of employment in the service industries since 1929, Fuchs comes to the cautious conclusion that the changes in this period do "not suggest an inevitable trend." See Victor R. Fuchs, *The Growing Importance of the Service Industries* (New York: National Bureau of Economic Research, unpublished manuscript, 1965), p. 28.

19. R. A. Gordon's paper suggests continued expansion at the high rates recently experienced is unlikely, while Eckstein expresses some disagreement with this view.

20. Computed from data in *Manpower Report of the President,* March 1965, pp. 233–235.

21. Annual data show that the decline for the two groups combined was pronounced between 1962 and 1963 and was slightly reversed in 1963–1964. However, these two detailed categories of self-employed workers account for only about half of all nonagricultural self-employed workers, as revealed in the data relating to classes of workers. For the more inclusive group the sharpest drop occurred between 1961 and 1962 and there was a modest increase in 1963–1964. (See *Manpower Report of the President,* March 1965, p. 200.)

22. See the concluding chapter of my report, *Retraining and Labor Market Adjustment in Western Europe* (Washington: U. S. Government Printing Office, 1965).

23. See his article, "Has Structural Unemployment Worsened?", *Industrial Relations,* III (May 1964), 53–78.

24. See "Poverty and Income Maintenance for the Unemployed," in Margaret S. Gordon, editor, *Poverty in America* (San Francisco: Chandler Publishing Co., 1965), and "U. S. Welfare Policies in Perspective," *Industrial Relations,* II (February 1963), 33–61.

Discussion

BY SOLOMON FABRICANT

"The chief conclusion to be derived from this chapter," writes Mrs. Gordon, "is that the amount of employment generated by a given increase in [real] GNP—measured in absolute or percentage terms—can vary greatly from period to period, depending on the composition of the increase in aggregate demand and the behavior of productivity in various sectors of the economy." I agree with this conclusion.

It is, indeed, pretty clear that the ratio of change in employment to change in real GNP is not fixed. It varies from business cycle to business cycle; and within a business cycle, from one stage to another. The reasons are well known: (1) output per worker in most, if not all, sectors or industries rises at a rate that fluctuates cyclically; (2) industries differ in rate of growth of output per worker and level of output per worker, and change in relative importance from cycle to cycle and over the several stages of each cycle. These sources of change in the ratio of real GNP to employment are sources of change in the ratio of the increments (measured in absolute or percentage terms) of employment to real GNP. The ratio varies over time not only systematically but irregularly. A dynamic economy is not characterized by uniform or even smooth trends, if for no other reason than the strong erratic element in technological change. While business cycles are more alike than economists used to believe, and some economists still believe, it is also true that every business cycle is to a large degree a unique member of its species. For these reasons, irregularities must pervade patterns of change in productivity and industrial composition, and changes must occur in the kind and degree of correlation between change or level of productivity and change in industrial composition. Therefore, we should expect to find, as Mrs. Gordon finds, that the ratio of the increments of employment to GNP can, and does, vary greatly from period to period.

I do not mean to suggest that her conclusion is altogether obvious. It was worthwhile to illustrate the variability of the ratio over the last few cycles, for economists too often assume that the ratio of change in employment to GNP is stable. Also it is not the general fact that the ratio varies over time which Mrs. Gordon is interested in as much as the peculiarities of its variation over the current expansion and the particular sources of these peculiarities. She wishes to shed light on the special characteristics of the behavior of employment (and thereby of unemployment) since 1961; and this certainly could not be done without an examination of the recent period. I think her chapter succeeds in illuminating the period, even with an analytical apparatus that is rather simple by modern standards. The results suggest that a "fancier" statistical analysis might be worth the trouble.

The fact that "the amount of employment generated by a given increase in GNP can vary greatly" is important. It means that no one can be sure just what the employment and unemployment consequences of any particular policy to change aggregate demand will be. There is the additional fact, already mentioned at this conference, that the value of the multiplier is uncertain; and also what I suppose many here would agree with, at least after listening to Mincer's paper, is that structural unemployment is neither insignificant nor constant. If we ponder these statements, will we not come to recognize that policy to reduce unemployment by raising aggregate demand must be uncertain as to the magnitude and timing of its effects; that policy to reduce unemployment should not rely too heavily on raising aggregate demand; that caution, alertness, and flexibility in the application of policy is essential; and that continuous attention to the unfolding of events is required in order to detect peculiarities as early as possible? Less can legitimately be claimed for the quantity and quality of economic knowledge than some of us imply in our anxiety to deal with economic problems; and I would ask whether a larger portion of the time and energy and patience of economists should not be reserved for the improvement of economic knowledge, and a smaller portion spent on following current events and arguing over current policy.

Two additional points: First, I felt uncomfortable when Mrs.

Gordon spoke of employment being "generated" by increase in GNP. Employment can be generated by increase in aggregate demand, but aggregate demand is not quite the same as GNP, as I am sure she fully understands. Second, it should be admitted that knowledge even of the simple facts of recent change is imperfect. In the case of the industrial composition of real GNP, this is indicated by the "residual" to which Mrs. Gordon refers—the residual that is the difference between GNP measured as the sum of final products and GNP measured as the sum of industry products. This residual is annoyingly large when one is interested in short-term changes.

Discussion

BY HAROLD GOLDSTEIN

The unique and valuable contribution of this chapter is its emphasis on analysis of the *composition* of the increase in aggregate demand and behavior of productivity and hours in the various sectors of the economy to gain understanding of the effect of the increase in aggregate demand upon employment. The complex relationships shown and the varied effects of differential demand growth upon employment caution us against making facile judgments using aggregate data alone.

I think the author is right in concluding that an analysis should not be hung on the changes from trough to peak, especially in dealing with the recovery since 1961. As she points out, the 1960–1961 recession was very mild; employment, seasonally adjusted, declined very little in that period, 200,000 to 300,000 from the peak in the second quarter of 1960 to the trough in the second quarter of 1961, and about all of this drop was in agriculture. This was not a trough; it was a dimple. The subsequent recovery, therefore, does not exhibit the rebound characteristic of the first year of recovery in other recessions.

In seeking light on changes in the relationship between production and employment, we typically look first to productivity and the factors which affect it, and this is a significant part of the total subject with which Dr. Gordon deals. Her chapter brings out some interesting questions.

She remarks that productivity usually declined in recession periods, and this is a common observation one finds in dealing with individual industries. It does not show up, however, in the annual data. There are smaller than average increases in productivity in recession periods, such as 1953–1954 and 1957–1958. There was a greater than average increase in 1960–1961, consistent with the thesis that this was not much of a recession.

Another subject dealt with in the chapter is the productivity gain in agriculture. In most industries productivity gains are directly associated with technological changes. In agriculture, they are made possible by technological improvements, but the cause and effect relationship takes place over a much longer period of time. The farms that do not or cannot introduce technological improvements—the small farms, the less fertile farms—become marginal long before the workers leave them. Unlike nonfarm employees, farm owners have the option of remaining or leaving, and are encouraged to remain by a favorable farm policy and a host of sociological and emotional factors. Only when they do leave, sometimes after a generation has elapsed, do the productivity gains show up in the statistics. What the productivity figures measure, then, is the migration out of agriculture, rather than its technological improvement. This defeats attempts to analyze agricultural productivity developments in relation to current production levels, technological change, or other factors normally considered.

Second to the significance of differential productivity growth rates in explaining the relationship between increases in GNP and employment is the analysis of the employment effects of different patterns of demand or expenditure. In making this analysis we cannot be sure that the nature of the industry or the expenditure—capital goods, consumer goods, services—is *per se* the differentiating factor in the direct or the indirect effect on employment of each billion dollars spent. One can argue that the real differentiating factors are the wage levels in the industry, the returns to capital, and the tax rates applicable to both. If wages in services are lower than those in goods-producing industries we are likely to get more employment per dollar spent. The same is true of the effect of federal expenditures on purchases of goods compared to federal expenditures on research and development because of the high average pay of technical personnel. Aside from factor returns, the nature of the industry—whether it has a high value-added ratio or the materials and services it purchases amount to a large proportion of the value of its sales—determines not the total employment effect but whether it is localized in the industry or pervasive in the economy.

Dr. Gordon's basic focus is on determining which components of employment are growing faster in the recovery period and why. Her finding that goods-producing industries grow faster than services early in the recovery, and the reverse occurs in the later stages of expansion, is explainable on the basis of the more severe decline in goods-producing employment in the recession phase of the cycle: it drops more, so it bounces back faster. On the other hand, services' long-term growth trend, which is more steady and consistent, gives them a higher rate of growth after the initial recovery phase.

I am glad to see her conclusion that despite the big increase in production worker employment in manufacturing in the recovery period (though only 75 per cent of the employees in manufacturing, production workers have provided 85–90 per cent of the employment gains in the last year or so) the long-term decline in the ratio of blue-collar to white-collar workers has been only arrested, not reversed. My own judgment is that the strong showing of production worker employment is a cyclical phenomenon. After one removes the cyclical effect, the trend of the ratio of production workers to total employment shows not a reversal in the decline, but a leveling off, which on the basis of long-term projections of the changing occupational composition of each industry, I believe will be temporary. Further growth of service industries, which employ a higher proportion of white-collar workers, will also increase their relative importance.

Dr. Gordon's major policy conclusion is on the limited possibilities of employment growth to be achieved through further increases in retraining activity as compared with job creation activity. Her conclusion is supported by an additional piece of evidence: the preliminary information on job vacancies which has been collected through the pilot studies made by the Labor Department and the National Industrial Conference Board. Job vacancies have run about 1 to 2 per cent of the level of employment in each of the 17 areas surveyed. If this is true of the United States as a whole, it means that there would have been from three-quarters of a million to a million and a half vacant jobs at a time when there were three and a half to four million people unemployed. It is apparent that with a maximum training and retraining program, we could not employ all of the unemployed at current levels of demand. Without denigrating the importance of training and retraining, this evidence argues for the need for job creation programs, either direct, as in the Neighborhood Youth Corps and the special campaign for job promotion in the services, or indirect, through general stimulation of demand.

Discussion

BY STANLEY LEBERGOTT

Having agreed to give the first Herbert Spencer lecture some years ago, Santayana observed that to read Spencer's works by way of preparation "would have been too severe a penance." I suspect that most of us, charged with Dr. Gordon's responsibility for reviewing postwar employment and GNP changes, would have reacted similarly. Fortunately for us, she has not shirked, giving us instead this absorbing and perceptive chapter. I should like to make a number of comments extending some of her findings, then note two differences of opinion.

The chapter focuses on "an explanation of the sluggish increase in employment for the first two years of the present upswing." After a review of individual postwar periods, Dr. Gordon notes that employment increases during 1963–1965 were substantially more rapid and compared more favorably with the increase in GNP than in the first two years of the present upswing. Let me note how recently we were all fretting about the reverse problem, low productivity gains, because rising output levels did not justify large real-wage increases. However, perhaps it is inevitable that we alternate between pessimistically discovering that the bottle is half empty, and optimistically finding it to be half full.

Dr. Gordon's explanation of this change in pace and what she says is the main conclusion to be derived from this chapter is ". . . the amount of employment generated by a given increase in GNP . . . can vary greatly . . . depending on the composition of the increase . . . and the behavior of productivity in the various sectors." This conclusion is worth the full emphasis and elaboration given it in her chapter. While agreeing with its central importance (overlooked in many discussions of the subject), let me add a qualification with respect to one period.

The relatively restricted amount of employment generated per dollar of GNP from 1961-I to 1962-I, as contrasted with 1949-IV to 1950-IV, is perhaps the most obvious feature of Table 2. But a central factor in this difference is the massive $22 billion inventory buildup in the earlier period as compared to a mere $5 billion in the later. Now it is a reasonable possibility that we are not seeing any difference in the structure of production nor efficiency of the economy here. Of the $22 billion rise, we may estimate $7.5 billion in the form of materials accumulation by manufacturers, with complementary speculative increases all along the line. Such accumulation was predominantly in anticipation of price rises, shortages, and outright rationing, and we should not expect a minimizing of immediate costs, but rather find employment per unit of such output rising proportionately much more than during periods of more prudent inventory accumulation, such as 1961–1962. We must partial out the war-related responses of 1949–1950 before we can use that period for contrasts with later ones.

Seeking to explain productivity changes from reference-cycle trough to peak, the chapter makes it possible to deal directly with many current explanations put in that framework—but at an excessive cost in constraining the analysis. How tolerable any of us finds "the morning after" depends in part on how abandoned the night before was. The NBER cycle dating is not intended to reflect the severity nor the nature of conditions at the trough. Therefore, we are going to miss some critical dimensions when we seek to explain changes from trough to peak or peak to peak. (Presumably it is a comment on this difficulty when Dr. Gordon reminds us that employment gains following a short and mild recession might be relatively slight in percentage terms.)

One way out would be to eschew explanations of changes over "the" cycle and instead develop a model to explain potential GNP by a production function, with variables to explain a short fall from potential.[1] These variables might or might not involve reference to the stage of the cycle.

In the course of her analysis, Dr. Gordon suggests that "in a period in which production is increasing very little or not at all, productivity gains may lag." Insofar as slow gains in production are more than a proxy for hesitations in final demand and for slackened capital investment (ready vehicle for embodying new techniques), the point suggests that some technical aspects of the structure of production have hitherto been overlooked. As such it deserves fuller analysis. Table 11 permits us to surmise an hypothesis for manufacturing but the link is less clear or does not appear at all in other sectors. The contrast suggests the complexity of the forces involved; forces to be unraveled by a more extensive study.

"It seems unlikely that the downward trend in the proportion of nonagricultural employees in the goods industries will be reversed," Dr. Gordon writes. Although I would place a bet on the same number, we require more extensive study of man-hour-demand linkages by sector and of trends in final demand before accepting this statement as more than shrewd surmise. Further studies would constitute an updating of the NBER retardation studies that were cut short by the war. These could now be continued, taking advantage of the advances in econometric techniques.

If one compares, say, the change of employment from 1947 to 1962 with the change from 1900 to 1929, one may discern retardation in that notable goods industry, manufacturing, but also see retardation in finance and, surprisingly, trade.[2]

One might even expect some future retardation in service-industry employment as well. A continuing rise of wages in service industries plus a decline in capital costs as computing and vending machinery experience the price declines characteristic of new products might occur. A more complex analysis is required before we can tell whether retardation will come at a greater rate in goods industries than service industries, particularly since the long-run declines in farming and mining may have brought these industries close to some sort of asymptote.

If we have a basis for projecting a rising share of government and service components in GNP, however, the foregoing considerations may prove to be unimportant. Experience suggests that nonprofit activities are insulated from cost pressures more than enterprise activities and hence do not tend to force increases in labor productivity. Moreover, the difficulties that consumers have in assessing the quality of such services makes possible quality deterioration rather than disemployment as a way of meeting cost pressures. (May not the quality of teachers, judges, hospital attendants, or generals, deteriorate without consumers of their services knowing or acting?)

Peripheral to the chapter's main analysis is a comment with which I disagree, namely that "the problem of shrinking relative job opportunities for those with no specialized skill or training was, if anything, exacerbated" from 1960 to 1964. Table 12 conveniently shows us the full record from 1948 to 1964—over which period no significant gain appears for managers and officials, craftsmen, sales workers, or male clerical workers. Skill does not appear to have been at a premium. On the other hand, the major gains that did appear were in professional and technical—surely skilled; in female clerical, no more skilled than operatives, who declined; and in service workers, not excessively skilled, some hotel or restaurant or barber-shop patrons would contend. This mixed pattern suggests that skill *per se* hardly explains shrinking or growing opportunities during this 16-year period, and to sort out the skill variable during a much shorter period, when overlaid with output mix changes, requires a much fuller showing.

A second point of disagreement relates to Dr. Gordon's lack of optimism about an "unemployment rate below 4 per cent if we continue to rely primarily on tax cuts" plus "a modest retraining program." I would agree wholeheartedly with this conclusion if retraining were to remain what it now is. However, her solution via an "expansion and liberalization of income-maintenance programs for the unemployed" is not the way to get below 4 per cent. It is a way to keep unemployment up—conceding that many of us might favor it to achieve other goals. If the primary goal here is to bring unemployment down to or below 4 per cent, then any such expansion must be linked to requirements that would (a) give the worker greater incentives toward reemployment, and (b) enrich his capacities so that he would become more readily re-employed. Such conditions strike me as consistent with the spirit, even if not the letter, of Dr. Gordon's proposal.

NOTES

1. Among a number of recent models, one might note Charles Schultze, "Short-Run Movements of Income Shares," in Conference on Research in Income and Wealth, *The Behavior of Income Shares,* Studies in Income and Wealth, Vol. 27 (Princeton: Princeton University Press, 1964), and Edward Kuh, "Cyclical and Secular Labor Productivity in U. S. Manufacturing," *Review of Economics and Statistics,* XLVII (February 1965).

2. Using data from the writer's *Manpower in Economic Growth* (New York: McGraw-Hill, 1964), Tables A-3, A-5.

P A R T **IV**

THE PATTERN OF UNEMPLOYMENT

CHAPTER 5

Lessons from the Pattern of

Unemployment in the Last Five Years

BY GERTRUDE BANCROFT

Summary

Writing just after the close of the great first quarter of 1965, the cheerful unemployment watcher could suggest that the experience of the last five years has taught the following lessons:

1. Automation and technological changes in the last few years have *not* permanently and drastically reduced the number of blue-collar jobs and left stranded, as chronically unemployed or out of the labor force, increasingly large numbers of American workers without college or high school education. Output per man-hour in manufacturing recorded the largest increase between 1963 and 1964 of any year since 1949 except for the recovery years of 1961–1962, 1958–1959, and 1954–1955. Neverthe-

less, from 1963 to 1964 manufacturing employment rose by 300,000.

2. A strong increase in demand has not yet brought back into the labor force an army of discouraged workers who have been lurking in the wings disguised as nonworkers but really unemployed.

3. Expansion of total employment has not been seriously limited by shortages of professional and skilled workers or workers with extensive education. The rapid growth in the labor force, and also, perhaps, a good deal of job mobility, have supplied manpower far in excess of the number of unemployed in specific sectors.

4. None of the work-sharing programs that have been proposed from time to time has been necessary to reduce unemployment. We did not have to abolish moonlighting, send married women back to the kitchen, or develop plans for wholesale early retirement. Even with record-breaking overtime in manufacturing, factory worker unemployment reached a nine-year low in early 1965.

5. The heterogeneous character of unemployment has been repeatedly underscored, particularly in the last three years. The impression created by aggregative data on the proportions of joblosers, jobchangers, and jobseekers, the major constituents of unemployment, entering or re-entering the labor force, has been misleading. Joblosers have diminished in importance while jobchangers and new jobseekers have increased. The early reduction in the unemployment rates for married men is testimony of the fact that where the supply of workers is practically fixed and the propensity to work almost invariable, recovery and rising economic activity can come close to wiping out all but frictional unemployment. On the other hand, the recent very large population increase among older teenagers and young people in their early twenties have injected into the labor force just those very types whose jobseeking rates are highest—both because they nearly all are seeking their first permanent jobs and because they often don't find what they want to begin with. Unemployed adult women include joblosers, but a substantial proportion are entering or re-entering the labor force. Industries and occupations to which adult women generally have easy access have been ex-

panding rapidly, but since 1962 the female labor force has also been growing at a brisk pace. Some of the stickiness in their unemployment rate is attributable to the high proportion of labor-force entrants.

6. Further evidence of the heterogeneous character of unemployment lies in the developments among full-time and part-time workers. Full-time employment has expanded, and the number of workers looking for full-time jobs has dropped since early 1963, when these data began to be collected. Voluntary part-time employment has also grown, though more modestly, and there has been little or no reduction in those seeking part-time jobs. Thus, the supply of workers who need and want to work full time has not exceeded the demand for such workers as much as in the case of regular part-time workers.

7. The evidence of the importance of structural unemployment in the first quarter of 1965 as compared with the first quarter of 1957 is mixed. On the basis of the simple test of dispersion of unemployment rates around the average there is clear evidence that manufacturing workers, blue-collar workers, and workers with the least education have a smaller disadvantage among the various groups than was true earlier. This reflects the strong expansion since 1962. On the other hand, certain population groups are worse off than in 1957—teenage girls in particular.

Not much progress has been made in reducing the greater risk of unemployment for nonwhites, but at least the unemployment rate for nonwhite adult men is only slightly higher than in 1957, and the gap between their rate and that of white men has narrowed a little. Nonwhite women have returned, if not to 1957, to their pre-1961 recession rates, but teenaged boys and girls are in very serious difficulties in the job market.

Long-term unemployment, considered one measure of structural unemployment, had fallen in the first quarter of 1965 to only 1.1 per cent of the labor force, seasonally adjusted, the lowest rate since the last quarter of 1957 (1.0 per cent). If the rate had been reduced to the *early* 1957 level of 0.8 per cent of the labor force, the number of long-term unemployed in the first quarter of 1965 would have been 600,000, adjusted for seasonality, instead of 840,000.

The concentration of long-term unemployment among young workers, those in clerical and service occupations, and those in trade and service industries, gives greater hope for its further reduction. These are the more mobile workers who may eventually be guided to or trained for available jobs.

Introduction

The path of recovery from the 1960–1961 recession is quite familiar by now. Every analyst has pointed out that the 1960–1961 recession was a shallow one, that recovery started later in unemployment than in many sectors of the economy, and that those labor-force groups that took the sharpest cuts bounced back most rapidly. We have been astonished by the experience of the married men, whose unemployment rates started to fall in the third quarter of 1961 and fairly early not only reached the prerecession level but returned almost to the 1957 lows. We have been puzzled by the adult women, on the other hand, whose rates remained sticky until after the tax cut. And we have worried and stimulated others to worry about teenagers. Their always high unemployment rates have risen higher as the postwar baby-boom age classes have passed through the early teens to arrive at age 18 this year. What was once only a demographer's dream is this year a threatening reality that dominates not only statistics but life in the world outside.

Increased demand in almost every sector of the economy and recordbreaking increases in employment have been accompanied by only mild reductions in the number of unemployed. From 1961-I to 1965-I, employment rose 4.7 million, while unemployment dropped only 1.4 million (seasonally adjusted), but the experience of the two sexes differed substantially. For men, employment rose by 2.5 million, while unemployment fell about 1.2 million. In the case of women, employment rose 2.2 million, but unemployment fell only 250,000.

One of the obvious reasons for this lies in the pattern of labor-force growth and the demographic changes underlying them— most of which have been in line with earlier projections. None of the labor-force changes that have occurred in the last five years has been unpredicted except for the slow-down in growth between 1961 and 1962. What has not been fully anticipated is the difficulty of reducing unemployment rates when the volume of additions to the labor force is expanding.

Path of Recovery and Expansion[1]

In the following pages, changes in unemployment rates for the various population groups in the last five years will be traced, and comparisons made with 1957, the last year in which the over-all rate approached 4 per cent. The teenage problem will be examined in some detail. Hopefully a better understanding of the remaining unemployment problem, as of the first quarter of 1965, will emerge.

Age, sex, and color. Starting from a cyclical low of 5.2 per cent in 1960-I, the over-all unemployment rate rose to a peak of 7.0 per cent in 1961-II and slipped back to 5.6 per cent in 1962-I. Through 1962 and 1963, the rate did not move from this plateau. In 1964-I it began to slide. By 1964-III it was back to the 1960 low point and by 1965-I had reached 4.8 per cent. The absolute number of unemployed workers, seasonally adjusted, was the same in 1965-I as in 1960-I. During this five-year period, the number of new workers (those who had never had a job lasting two weeks or more) rose by 50 per cent. Hence the reduction in the rate for experienced workers from 4.6 per cent in 1960 to 4.0 per cent in 1965 was larger than for the total.

The pattern of the over-all rate seems to have been chiefly determined by what was happening to adult unemployed women and to some extent, teenagers. The rate for women aged 25 and over fell from the recession high of 6.1 per cent in 1961-II to 4.9 per cent in early 1962, and remained at that level (4.8 to 4.9 per cent) for nine quarters—1962-I through 1964-I (Chart 1). Only then did it fall, and by 1965-I was back to 4.2 per cent—below the 1960 low but still above the rate in 1957-I (3.7 per cent).

The teenage unemployment rate has behaved somewhat erratically, and although it did fall below the 1961 high occasionally, it showed no firm signs of real reduction even by 1965-I. Teenage white boys fared better than other teenagers (Chart 2); their rate in 1965-I (11.5 per cent) was back to the level of 1960 and not far above the comparable quarter in 1957 (10.4 per cent). The rate for nonwhite boys showed recovery from

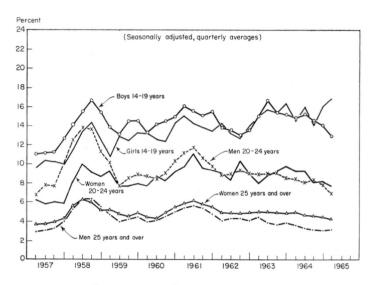

CHART 1. *Unemployment rates, by age and sex. (Source: U. S. Bureau of Labor Statistics.)*

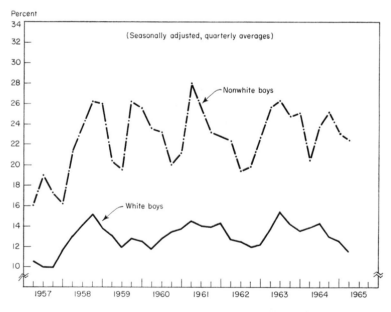

CHART 2. *Unemployment rates, white and nonwhite teenage boys. (Source: U. S. Bureau of Labor Statistics.)*

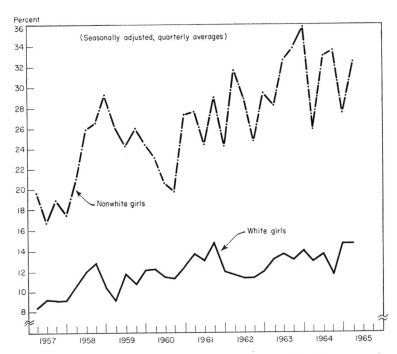

CHART 3. *Unemployment rates, white and nonwhite teenage girls. (Source: U. S. Bureau of Labor Statistics.)*

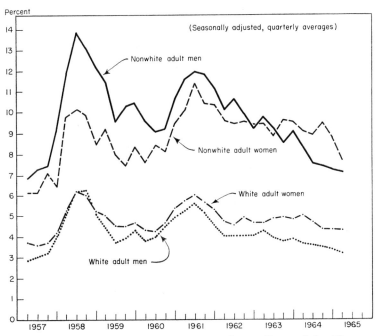

CHART 4. *Unemployment rates, white and nonwhite, adults 20 years and over. (Source: U. S. Bureau of Labor Statistics.)*

the highest points in 1961 but, at 22.4 per cent in 1965-I, it was far above the rate of 15.9 per cent recorded in early 1957. Both white and nonwhite teenage girls, particularly the latter, had high unemployment rates in early 1965, still above the prerecession low, and almost twice as high as in early 1957 (Chart 3).

The age groups 20 to 24 had patterns that were midway between those of the teenagers and of adults aged 25 and over (Chart 1). After an initial drop from the high second quarter of 1961, there was no further improvement for young men or young women until the second or third quarter of 1964. By early 1965 the rate for 20- to 24-year-old men was 6.8 per cent, below 1960 and not significantly different from the 1957-I rate of 6.6 per cent. For young women, the rate in 1965 was back to the level of 1960-I (7.7 per cent), but above the 6.2 per cent rate of 1957-I.

In sharp contrast to the slow recovery for these groups was the experience of adult men, aged 25 and over (Chart 1), particularly married men. The rate for men 25 and over declined almost steadily from its 1961 high of 5.5 per cent, and by 1963-I was back to its 1960 low (3.9 per cent). In 1965-I it was 3.1 per cent—practically the same as the 1957-I rate of 2.9 per cent. The rate for married men (not shown in Chart 1) followed the same path at a somewhat lower level. In 1964-IV it reached 2.6 per cent. Only in late 1955 and 1956 was it really below this, during the period in which these data have been collected on a monthly basis. In April 1952 and April 1953, during the Korean War, the rate was lower than in April 1965 by about one percentage point.

These differential patterns suggest that the normal course of recovery from the 1960–1961 recession must have led to the rehiring of both men and women with seniority rights. We see this in the rise of 620,000, seasonally adjusted, in employment in manufacturing, from the 1961 low quarter to the first quarter of 1962. Thereafter, jobs in durable goods manufacturing continued to expand, and construction began to pick up, too. The momentum increased. Between 1964-I and 1965-I, employment in construction and durable goods manufacturing together rose by 650,000.

The recovery of employment in nondurable goods manufacturing and trade, where women and younger workers tend to concentrate and where the recession had been rather shallow, was also mild, and it was not until 1963 that trade employment started to soar. Nondurable goods employment was fairly flat until 1964. Employment in state and local government and services did not show any setback at all in the recession years, but each continued to grow about 300,000 to 400,000 a year.

Labor force changes. Why these rapidly expanding sectors did not absorb more of the unemployed can be partially answered in terms of labor-force growth, which began to assume large proportions toward the end of 1962 (Table 1).

TABLE 1. CHANGES IN THE CIVILIAN LABOR FORCE, BY AGE AND SEX
(Annual averages, in thousands)

Age and sex	1962–1963	1963–1964
Total	+1,122	+1,257
Male	+ 487	+ 543
14 and 15	− 42	− 7
16 and 17	+ 144	+ 177
18 and 19	− 6	− 10
20 to 24	+ 235	+ 240
25 to 34	− 46	—
35 to 44	+ 72	− 32
45 to 54	+ 121	+ 120
55 to 64	+ 114	+ 66
65 and over	− 106	− 12
Female	+ 635	+ 714
14 and 15	− 55	+ 6
16 and 17	+ 108	+ 100
18 and 19	− 24	− 17
20 to 24	+ 157	+ 251
25 to 34	+ 71	+ 6
35 to 44	+ 126	+ 14
45 to 54	+ 122	+ 177
55 to 64	+ 134	+ 115
65 and over	− 6	+ 61

Source: U. S. Bureau of Labor Statistics.

The over-all increases in the civilian labor force—1.1 million in 1962–1963 and 1.3 million in 1963–1964—were in line with Bureau of Labor Statistics projections based on extrapolation of long-term demographic and social trends. (These data have not been adjusted for introduction of 1960 Census data into the estimation procedure.) There was no "catch-up" of earlier deficits, and certainly no sign of the greater-than-usual labor-force growth that was widely expected to occur when the economy started to move again. The only group whose declining labor-force rates showed any sign of turning upward was that of men 65 to 69 years old. Their labor-force rate rose from 40.9 per cent in 1963 to 42.6 per cent in 1964, and the number of workers in this group increased by 40,000. Independent evidence from the Social Security system also suggests a very small reduction in retirement rates.

The preceding table shows the effect of the two baby booms associated with World War II. The first jump in the birth rate occurred in 1942, and babies born at that time were swelling the 20-to-24-year-old labor force by 1962. The effects of the second boom, immediately following the War, will be visible in the number of 18-year-olds entering the labor force this year, and account for the 16-to-17-year old bulge in the last two years. A third twist in the structure of the labor force is the lack of growth among 25-to-34-year-olds, the depression babies.

Men aged 25 and over were the prime source of full-time workers as over-all demand increased and the expansion in construction and durable goods manufacturing continued its upward thrust, long after the recovery from the recession. Altogether, the number of men 25 years and older in the civilian labor force grew only 155,000 in 1962–1963, and only 145,000 in 1963–1964 —0.4 per cent each year. Not too many additional jobs were required, therefore, to absorb the slowly growing number of workers and to reduce their unemployment substantially. These labor-force increases did not represent new workers, for the most part, but simply the aging of workers already in the labor force (from the under 25 to the 25 and older group).

The number of adult women aged 25 and over in the labor force increased much more than the number of adult men, because their labor-force participation rates were rising. About

825,000 women aged 25 and over were added to the civilian labor force between 1962 and 1964, an increase of 4 per cent. Their employment increased by 825,000, and unemployment remained unchanged:

	Men	Women
Civilian labor force	+300,000	+825,000
Employed	+600,000	+825,000
Unemployed	−300,000	0

This bit of arithmetic does not, of course, mean there were no unemployed women finding jobs, but it does point up the sharp differences in labor-force growth and a reason for the different patterns of unemployment rates. Among the added women workers were many who went through a stage of unemployment before finding jobs after they had entered the labor force. Some, or perhaps all, of those unemployed at the start got jobs, but in the turnover process the unemployment rate stayed up.

Some evidence recently accumulated by the BLS, to be published shortly, reinforces this speculation. In December 1964, one third of women aged 25 and over reported as unemployed that month indicated they were entering or re-entering the labor force, and therefore looking for jobs. The comparable group of unemployed men of this age constituted only one fifth; the other four fifths were "disemployed"—they were looking for work because they had left their last jobs voluntarily or involuntarily. The classification of reasons for looking for work underlying these statistics is rough but the results appear reasonable and are consistent with those from a similar experimental survey made in June 1964.

The high unemployment rates for both men and women aged 20 to 24 are due at least partially to the expansion of these age groups, since so many are entering the labor force for the first time on a permanent basis. Over the two-year period 1962 to 1964, the male civilian labor force aged 20 to 24 grew by 475,000 (11 per cent); the female labor force by 400,000 (15 per cent). These are very large changes for a five-year age group in such a short time, and are not accounted for by changes in labor-force participation rates.

Again, a substantial part of the unemployment in this age group is associated with labor-force entrance and with job changing and inexperience. (A BLS survey of job mobility in 1961 showed that the highest rate of job changing among the unemployed was in this age group.[2]) Furthermore, young workers are likely to have little seniority when employed and a much higher than average proportion of the men in this age group are operatives and nonfarm laborers, more subject than other workers to layoffs and intermittent employment. Employed young women in this age group, on the other hand, are highly concentrated in clerical jobs (almost one half)—in which the demand is strong but turnover for reasons of marriage and family formation is high, and therefore few are laid off.

With all these reasons for unemployment, marriage has a powerful effect on the unemployment rate for men in the age group 20 to 24, and about half of the men in the labor force in this age group are married. Their unemployment rate in 1964 was 4.3 per cent, as compared with 8.1 per cent for all men of this age and 11.9 per cent for single men. For women, the differential between the rates for the married and single is not so great. Single women have the lower rates:

UNEMPLOYMENT RATES BY MARITAL STATUS AND SEX FOR PERSONS
20 TO 24 YEARS OLD, 1962, 1963, 1964
(Annual averages)

	Married, Spouse Present			Single		
	1962	1963	1964	1962	1963	1964
Men 20 to 24 years	5.5	5.1	4.3	12.2	12.2	11.9
Women 20 to 24 years	9.9	9.4	9.1	7.6	7.6	7.1

Unless one assumes that only the most presentable, best educated, and most employable men in their early twenties are married—not a safe assumption at any age but most indefensible for this group—one must conclude that family responsibilities force men to take and stay with available jobs and eliminate some of the voluntary jobseeking that is reflected in the over-all unemployment rate. In September 1963 the induction of married men into the Armed Forces was halted and, until the summer of 1965, when the exemption of recently married men was discontinued, they may have had an advantage in jobseeking over those not married. However, draft calls in 1963 and 1964 were so small they could hardly account for much of the difference between married and single men, a difference that existed in earlier years too.

Unemployment of young workers. The teenage unemployment problem has not yielded to the various forces that have had an impact on other groups. The persistently high unemployment rates of teenagers have been interpreted and explained in many ways. To some the problems of young workers can be accounted for by such evils as the disappearance of entry jobs with the growth of automation, inadequate education and preparation for working life, inability to acquire the experience that leads to job security and seniority, and a disorganized labor market with insufficient job guidance by public authorities in the schools and the public employment services. Others are inclined to blame high minimum wages and unrealistic expectations on the part of young people today which lead them to refuse the jobs available or to move from one to another in a state of dissatisfaction, with repeated spells of unemployment. (Except for 20-to-24-year-olds, teenagers *are* most likely to be unemployed at some time during a calendar year, but a smaller proportion than those of older ages have repeated spells of jobseeking.) Since many live with their families, they can afford to be choosy because they have bed and board at least.

Both the group that blames the system and the group that blames the teenagers agree that the growing number of teenagers in the population makes it harder to find jobs, whether the youngster in question is a "bird dog" or a "kennel dog" in his search for work.

Information from the Current Population Survey for March 1965 showing the family income of the unemployed gives some background and perspective to the teenage problem. The average (median) family income in 1964 of teenagers unemployed in March 1965 was $6,019. Those looking for part-time work, most of them still in school, were in families with a median income of $7,201. Those looking for full-time work (about 55 per cent) had family incomes that averaged $5,295, but 100,000, or one fifth, were in families with incomes under $3,000. The nonwhite unemployed teenager was much worse off. The median family income of this group was $3,667 and about 40 per cent of the nonwhite unemployed teenagers were in families with less than $3,000. In the white population, then, the average unemployed teenager living at home is probably not suffering economic distress, and may be justified in taking his time to find a job. This is not so in the nonwhite population.

Although we are all guilty of thinking of teenagers as a group, it is impossible to assess the gravity of their problems without separating those in school from those who have left school. In 1964, during the school year, unemployment of teenagers had the following dimensions:

UNEMPLOYED TEENAGERS AND UNEMPLOYMENT RATE,
SCHOOL YEAR 1964

School Status[a]	Total 14–19 Years	14 & 15 Years	16 & 17 Years	18 & 19 Years
In school	418,000	61,000	252,000	105,000
Unemployment rate	13.2	6.7	15.6	16.0
Not in school	419,000	6,000	113,000	300,000
Unemployment rate	15.5	9.0	21.4	14.2

[a] These data on school status are based on major activity during the survey weeks (excluding June, July, and August). They tend to understate the number enrolled in school.

Teenagers who had left school had much higher unemployment rates in the ages 16 and 17 but were about on a par with those still in school in ages 18 and 19. However, most of those out of school (93 per cent) were looking for full-time jobs while only one in five (22 per cent) of those in school were seeking full-time jobs. So far, we have seen little improvement in the rates for out-of-school youngsters.

In the past, unemployment rates have fallen rapidly with age up through the mid-twenties, and this can be expected to continue. Whether the declines will be as rapid with the large incoming age-cohorts is not so certain. Based on annual averages for the years 1962, 1963, and 1964, rough estimates of the pattern can be made:

UNEMPLOYMENT RATES OF OUT-OF-SCHOOL YOUTH, BY AGE
AND SEX, ANNUAL AVERAGE, 1962–1964

Age	Male	Female
16	18.9	20.3
17	19.1	22.3
18	17.5	22.3
19	12.2	16.9
20	11.6	10.2
21	9.5	9.5
22	8.4	7.7
23	6.4	8.0
24	6.1	7.5

At ages 16 and 17 the unemployed are largely high school dropouts and a few who have graduated but are prevented by their youth from taking certain jobs. At age 18 the composition of the group changes, but a large proportion start looking seriously for their first regular jobs. If so many American high-school students did not customarily work part-time while in school, we would expect much higher unemployment rates at the time of graduation. Also, many are able to line up jobs while still in school.

A detailed study of out-of-school youths 16 to 21 years of age conducted by the Census Bureau for the Bureau of Labor Statistics in February 1963, showed that almost 30 per cent had jobs waiting for them when they left school, and over 50 per cent looked for work; a majority of both graduates and dropouts found jobs within five weeks of starting to look (Table 2). Success rates in the search for jobs differed by amount of education,

TABLE 2. Job Experience on Leaving School, for Persons
16 to 21 Years Old Not in School in February 1963

Educational Attainment	Had Job Waiting	Per Cent of 16 to 21 Year Olds Who Looked for Work		
		Total	Found Job in:	
			Less than 5 Weeks	15 Weeks or More
All persons[a]	27.8	54.1	29.4	7.0
Less than 4 years high school	21.7	53.5	28.1	8.1
4 years of high school	32.7	55.2	29.7	6.7
Nonwhite[a]	18.1	60.9	27.9	10.4
Less than 4 years high school	24.2	54.4	26.2	10.4
4 years of high school	10.8	69.0	26.9	12.3

Source: Vera C. Perrella and Forrest A. Bogan, *Out of School Youth,
February 1963*, Special Labor Force Report, No. 46 (Washington, D. C.:
U. S. Bureau of Labor Statistics, 1964), Table B-1.
[a] Includes persons with 1 to 3 years of college.

of course, and, as would be expected, were not very high for
the nonwhite group.

The disorganization of the labor market, particularly for young
persons, can be seen in the small proportions who got their first
full-time job through school or a public or private employment
agency: 14 per cent over-all, but only 9 per cent of the nonwhites. The dropouts received much less help from these institutions than the high-school graduates or those who had had some
college training. In fact, the state employment offices sent approximately twice as many young people with some college education to their jobs as they did high-school graduates and four
times as many as they did dropouts. The largest proportion of
all these out-of-school youths found their first jobs through direct
application to an employer—41 per cent. But nonwhites most
frequently credited friends and relatives with obtaining them
their first full-time jobs, the most casual and undirected method.

Although they may not always recognize job guidance when
they receive it, only 22 per cent of the dropouts said they had

had guidance from the school and/or the employment service. The proportion of graduates aware of guidance, although more than twice as large, was only 56 per cent.

The survey gave only indirect evidence on the question of whether their unemployment is prolonged because their wage demands are too high or because they are not worth the legal minimum wage in the eyes of prospective employers. The median earnings of dropouts on their first full-time jobs were just $50 a week for boys and under $40 for girls. For high-school graduates (some with one to three years of college) median earnings for boys were about $65 a week and for girls about $52. These amounts are not far from minimum wage levels; for girls who dropped out of school, they are below the current federal minimum and reflect their heavy concentration in service jobs—almost half, including private household work.

The special survey furnishes one piece of evidence after another of the extreme employment problems of nonwhite girls, even those who graduated from high school. About one in five had been unemployed most of the time since leaving school—higher than the proportion found for boys, white or nonwhite, and more than three times the proportion for white girls. Fewer had jobs waiting for them when they left school and it took them longer to find their first jobs or their first full-time jobs. In February 1963, the time of interview, their unemployment rate was 30 per cent, with no difference between graduates and dropouts. As a group, nonwhite girls had less formal education and less post-school vocational or commercial training than white girls. When they found jobs, they were more often in private household and other service work, where part-time and intermittent employment is common and working conditions often disagreeable. It has also been suggested that they must compete with adult nonwhite women for such jobs and because of their immaturity may be at a disadvantage in the competition. Again and again the statistics give evidence that the jobs generally open to nonwhite girls who have completed a high-school education are not particularly desirable and are poorly paying. If the girls increasingly refuse such jobs, preferring to remain unemployed, their unemployment rate cannot be expected to move down from its extremely high peak until white-collar jobs are opened to them, not only in government offices and a modest number of private establishments but all over the country.

For nonwhite boys the unemployment situation is bad enough —one in four or five of the teenagers and only a moderately lower fraction of the 20-to-24-year-olds have been unemployed, on the average, since 1958. Unlike the young nonwhite girls, however, the boys are not markedly worse off than at the start of the 1960 recession.

Nonwhite boys, whether graduates or dropouts, seem to find employment chiefly as operatives and laborers, both farm and nonfarm. The growth of these jobs in the nonfarm sector in the past several years may have given them a slight advantage over the nonwhite girls in this age group. Disappearance of farms and farm jobs, on the other hand, has cut down a common type of work for these boys.

A recent study of the economic status of Negroes[3] has pointed out the lack of employment growth in manufacturing in the 11 Northern and Western cities with the largest Negro populations in 1960, and suggests that this is a major explanation for the persistence of high unemployment rates for Negro male workers in spite of a generally rising level of economic activity for the country as a whole. Total nonfarm employment in those areas has also moved rather sluggishly, affecting the job prospects of all Negroes living in the areas. The 1960–1964 increase was only 4 per cent compared with 7.4 per cent for the country as a whole.

Effect of Changing Age-Sex Structure of Labor Force on Unemployment Rate

With the marked shift in the age composition of the labor force since 1957 it is reasonable to suspect that some of the difference between the 4.3 per cent unemployment rate in 1957 and the 5.2 per cent rate in 1964 is due to the increased number of young workers (with their typically high unemployment rates). Higher participation rates for women—37.4 per cent in 1964 *versus* 35.9 per cent in 1957—should give a similar upward push to the rate since the female unemployment rate tends to be slightly higher than the male rate. Assuming the 1964 age-specific unemployment rates and standardizing the 1964 labor force on the 1957 composition by age and sex would reduce the over-all rate in 1964 by 0.2 percentage points and account for 22 per cent of the difference in the over-all rate—almost all among women. Thus, we would have had an average of 150,000 fewer unemployed in 1964 if the age and sex composition of the labor force had not changed.

The combined effect of changing age-structure and differential unemployment rates between 1957 and 1964 amounted to roughly 675,000. (The remainder of the difference in the abso-

EFFECT OF CHANGING AGE-SEX COMPOSITION AND UNEMPLOYMENT RATES ON 1964 LEVEL OF UNEMPLOYMENT

Age	Difference between Actual and Estimated 1964 Unemployment Standardized for 1957 Labor-Force Composition and Unemployment Rates	Due to Age-Sex Structure of Labor Force	Due to Changing Unemployment Rates
Total	+675,000	+150,000	+525,000
14 to 19 years	+335,000	+120,000	+215,000
20 to 24 years	+190,000	+110,000	+ 80,000
25 years and over	+150,000	− 80,000	+230,000

lute level (940,000) is due to labor force growth alone.) We are therefore trying to explain a rise in unemployment due to rising unemployment rates amounting to 525,000, more than half of it among young workers under 25. Among adult workers 25 years and over some of the estimated additional unemployment due to rising rates was offset by the effect of changing age-sex structure of the labor force. Thus, on balance, it can be estimated that if a half million more persons out of a total of 74.2 million in the labor force had found jobs—0.7 per cent of the total—all of the excess over 1957 that remained in 1964 would have been eliminated except for the effect of the growing population and larger numbers in the labor force. If the improvement recorded in the first quarter of 1965 continues throughout the year, it is not impossible that this bright prospect might be realized, but it would require further substantial job expansions for those age groups whose unemployment rates were most resistant until the tax cut.

Changes in Unemployment by Occupation

The recovery and expansion of the past five years have been paced by the blue-collar worker group, judging by the pattern of unemployment rates (Charts 5 and 6) and the occupation employment statistics. Not only are the unemployment rates among blue-collar workers below the 1960 peak, they are at 1957 levels or lower. Employment in blue-collar occupations has risen by 1.7 million since 1960-I and by 1.25 million since 1957-I. Nevertheless, blue-collar workers are not so large a part of the labor force as they were in 1957—37 per cent *versus* 39 per cent—having lost out slightly to white-collar and service workers.

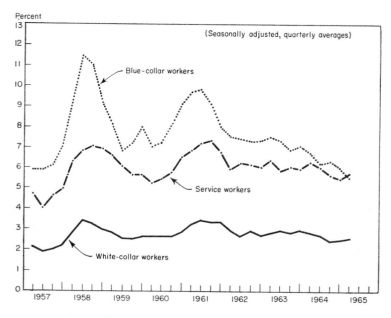

CHART 5. *Unemployment rates of white and blue-collar workers and service workers. (Source: U. S. Bureau of Labor Statistics.)*

Only about one half of blue-collar workers are in manufacturing, and the gains in recent years are not all to be credited to the revival of factory employment. According to the 1960 Census of Population, sizable nonmanufacturing occupations included in the craftsmen, foremen, and kindred worker group are: construction craftsmen, linemen, and servicemen in the communications and power industries, mechanics and repairmen, stationary engineers, and inspectors. Operatives in other than manufacturing include attendants in auto service and parking, bus, truck, and taxi drivers; deliverymen and routemen; dressmakers and seamstresses; laundry and dry cleaning operators; mine operatives and laborers; and miscellaneous operatives in nonmanufacturing, chiefly trade and construction. Only one third of nonfarm laborers are in manufacturing.

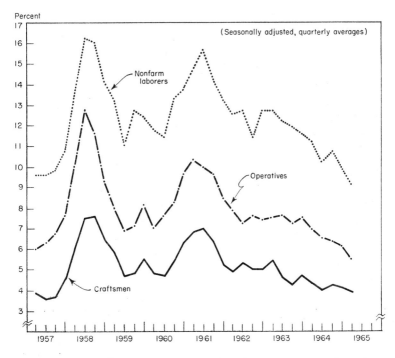

CHART 6. *Unemployment rates of craftsmen, operatives, and nonfarm laborers.* (*Source: U. S. Bureau of Labor Statistics.*)

A substantial proportion of blue-collar employment is therefore correlated with population growth. Even with some gains in productivity through automation and other means, high rates of economic activity in both goods-producing and service-producing sectors should continue to be reflected in strong demands for blue-collar workers.

Between 1960-I and 1965-I employment rose 5.2 million and unemployment of experienced workers fell only 176,000 net. (Employment in nonfarm occupations rose 6.1 million.) In blue-collar occupations, however, unemployment showed a net reduction of 323,000 against an increase in employment of 1,738,000 (Table 3). Operatives, largely the semiskilled, accounted for most of these changes.[4]

These net changes suggest that the blue-collar expansion was achieved through employment of some of the new workers added to the labor force, a substantial transfer from the farm

TABLE 3. CHANGES IN EMPLOYMENT AND UNEMPLOYMENT BY
MAJOR OCCUPATION GROUP, 1960–I TO 1965–I
(Quarterly, seasonally adjusted data, in thousands)

Major Occupation Group	Change in Employment	Change in Unemployment
Total	+5,217	−176
White-collar workers	+3,502	+ 68
Professional and technical	+1,531	+ 33
Managers, officials and proprietors	+ 334	− 1
Clerical	+1,334	+ 30
Sales	+ 303	+ 6
Blue-collar workers	+1,738	−323
Craftsmen	+ 476	− 72
Operatives	+1,023	−149
Nonfarm laborers	+ 239	−102
Service workers	+ 890	+107
Farm workers	− 913	− 28
Farmers and farm managers	− 568	+ 4
Farm laborers	− 345	− 32

Source: U. S. Bureau of Labor Statistics.

sector, and the reduction in unemployment. Since it is unlikely that many blue-collar and service workers moved to white-collar jobs, most of the additional white-collar workers probably came from outside the labor force—recent graduates and women returning to the labor force.

In service occupations, where employment and unemployment increased, the effect of the increment of new young workers, many of whom start off in service jobs, can be seen.

By 1965-I, unemployment rates in all major occupation groups except the service sector had returned to the level of 1960-I, with, as indicated, the best performance shown by blue-collar workers. This sector also showed the best record over the longer term; the unemployment rates were at the 1957-I level or below. No other occupation group, except farm laborers, had unemployment rates as low as those of 1957-I.

Unemployment by Industry

Recovery from the 1960–1961 rise in unemployment was pretty well complete by 1964-I in all major nonfarm industry groups except trade and the service industries, where many of the labor-force entrants and re-entrants were seeking jobs. (The unemployment rate in agriculture was above that of 1962-I and was probably affected by extreme weather conditions at one period or the other.) Most of the decline from the 1961-II peak rates had already taken place by 1962-I (Chart 7).

The additional reductions between 1964-I and 1965-I were universal (except for mining), and in some major groups larger than had occurred in the two-year period from 1962 to 1964. The rate for experienced wage and salary workers in manufacturing fell in this period by 1.2 percentage points, to 4.1 per cent—one half of its recession peak. For some of the smaller groups within manufacturing—primary metals, machinery (except electrical), and automobiles—the rates were below 3 per cent, not seasonally adjusted, in 1965-I.

Even with the 1964-I to 1965-I reductions, the unemployment rates for trade and service industries were no lower than they had been in 1960, before the recession started. There has been no lack of growth in these sectors; more than half of the 5.3

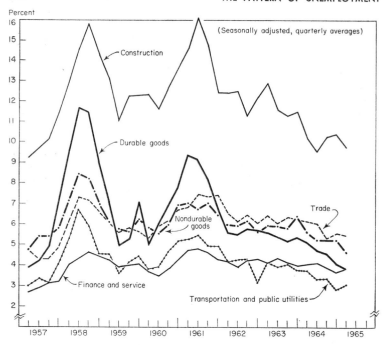

CHART 7. *Unemployment rates, by industry. (Source: U. S. Bureau of Labor Statistics.)*

million increase in nonfarm jobs between 1960-I and 1965-I was in trade and service industries. This suggests again that the large number of unemployed who are teenagers and married women and whose previous employment was in trade and service are responsible for holding up the rates in these sectors as they come into the labor force and look for work.[5]

The unemployment rate for experienced wage and salary workers in 1965-I was within 0.3 percentage points of the 1957-I rate of 4.2 per cent. The record was best for workers whose last job was in manufacturing; in both durable and nondurable goods the 1965-I rates were as low as those in 1957-I. The rates for those in transportation and other public utilities and for public administration were close to the 1957-I rates, and the differences for other groups (except mining) were no greater than one percentage point.

Changes in Unemployment by Education

The changing relationship of unemployment to amount of education is difficult to detect with the infrequent observations available to us. The sampling variability of the numbers for one month in the year is high, and increases or decreases for specific groups can be misleading and overinterpreted.[6]

Preliminary data for 1965 seem to be consistent with more reliable statistics on the changing patterns by occupation and age group (Table 4). High unemployment rates for teenagers,

TABLE 4. UNEMPLOYMENT RATES BY YEARS OF SCHOOL
COMPLETED AND SEX

Years of School Completed and Sex	March 1957	March 1959	March 1962	March 1964	March 1965[a]
Male					
Total, 18 years and over	4.1	6.3	6.0	5.2	4.4
Less than 8 years	6.9	9.8	9.2	8.4	6.6
8 years	4.4	7.3	7.5	6.9	5.2
High school					
1 to 3 years	4.7	8.1	7.8	6.6	6.8
4 years	3.0	4.9	4.8	4.1	3.4
College					
1 to 3 years	2.7	3.3	4.0	3.8	3.1
4 years or more	0.6	1.4	1.4	1.5	1.4
Female					
Total, 18 years and over	4.1	6.0	6.0	6.1	5.3
Less than 8 years	5.7	9.9	7.6	9.1	7.3
8 years	5.6	6.5	6.4	6.2	4.7
High school					
1 to 3 years	5.9	9.3	9.2	8.5	8.6
4 years	2.9	4.7	5.7	5.6	5.0
College					
1 to 3 years	3.2	3.8	3.2	5.2	3.6
4 years or more	1.0	1.3	1.5	1.6	1.3

Source: U. S. Bureau of Labor Statistics.
[a] Preliminary.

the increasing number of inexperienced workers among the unemployed, and the brisk expansion in blue-collar employment
are manifested again in the education data. Workers with the
least education have scored the most spectacular reductions in
unemployment. For the first time in the period 1957 to 1965 for
which data are available the highest unemployment rates are
for persons who have gone to high school but have not graduated. Some of these were still in school in March 1965 but most
are probably dropouts. Between 1964 and 1965 there were reductions in the unemployment rates of every group except this one,
although the changes may not all be statistically significant.

In the recovery and expansion after early 1962, the growth
of blue-collar jobs appears to have benefited nonwhite men
about equally with white men at the lower end of the educational ladder. At the higher levels, the gap in their unemployment rates has been somewhat narrowed, although nonwhite
rates are still high. (It is necessary to combine the data into
broad categories in order to provide sufficiently reliable
comparisons.)

UNEMPLOYMENT RATES BY EDUCATIONAL ATTAINMENT
AND COLOR FOR MEN 25 TO 54 YEARS OLD

| Educational | March 1962 | | March 1964 | | March 1965 | |
Attainment	White	Nonwhite	White	Nonwhite	White	Nonwhite
Total	4.4	11.5	3.7	8.2	3.1	7.1
8 years or less	7.9	11.0	6.7	8.6	5.4	8.1
High school						
1 to 3 years	5.5	16.1	5.0	8.6	4.8	7.9
High school						
4 or more						
years	2.6	8.8	2.2	7.2	1.8	5.6

If the preliminary figures for March 1965 really stand up, they
show that the current reduction in unemployment has brought
the jobless rates of some of the least advantaged workers back
to 1957 levels. The unemployment rates for men with less than
an elementary-school education and for women with only an

eighth-grade education are below those for 1957. Men with high-school education or better are slightly more likely to be unemployed than they were in 1957, as are women with some college education. The largest relative increase over 1957 is seen in the unemployment rate for women who have finished high school, from 2.9 to 5.0 per cent. Whether these unexpected patterns reflect only vagaries in the figures or flaws in the doctrine of the inevitability of increasing risk of unemployment for the less skilled and poorly educated workers, only time can tell.

Some of both the employed and unemployed older workers with little education have left the labor force because of retirement, death, or discouragement and have been replaced by younger ones who have gone further in school.[7] There is no denying the fact that the unemployed in early 1965 are a much better-educated group than the unemployed in 1957; one third of the men and one half of the women were high school graduates or better in 1965 whereas in 1957 the comparable proportions were one-fourth and one-third. But the entire labor force is better-educated, and despite the curious reversals of the recent past, education is still some insurance against unemployment, especially if the course, short or long, is completed. High-school dropouts in the adult population are currently more likely to be unemployed than workers who have never entered high school.

Evidence on Changing Structure of Unemployment

The recovery and expansion since 1960 have left us, at least temporarily, with less variation in unemployment rates among different occupation groups and more variation among age groups. By 1965-I, there was a marked reduction in the comparative disadvantage of blue-collar workers, those in manufacturing, nonwhite men, and the poorly educated, and an increase in the disadvantage of youth, particularly nonwhite, workers in service occupations and industries, and those in trade (Tables 5, 6, 7, and 8). Men who had not yet finished high school or had dropped out along the way had much higher unemployment rates relative to the total in 1965 than in previous years studied.

We have been using the situation in 1957 as a model of what

TABLE 5. Ratios of Unemployment Rates by Age, Sex, and
Color to Total Unemployment Rate
(Quarterly averages, seasonally adjusted)

Age, Sex, and Color	1957-I	1960-I	1961-II	1962-I	1964-I	1965-I
Total unemployment						
rate (per cent)	4.0	5.2	7.0	5.6	5.4	4.8
Ratio	1.00	1.00	1.00	1.00	1.00	1.00
Male	0.93	0.96	0.97	0.95	0.91	0.88
14 to 19 years	2.73	2.54	2.22	2.45	2.70	2.69
20 to 24 years	1.65	1.65	1.66	1.57	1.56	1.42
25 years and over	0.73	0.75	0.78	0.73	0.67	0.65
Female	1.15	1.08	1.07	1.13	1.20	1.25
14 to 19 years	2.40	2.54	2.02	2.54	2.69	3.48
20 to 24 years	1.55	1.48	1.57	1.59	1.70	1.60
25 years and over	0.93	0.85	0.88	0.88	0.91	0.88
Male						
White	0.83	0.83	0.87	0.82	0.81	0.77
Nonwhite	1.90	2.10	1.89	2.00	1.74	1.77
14 to 19 years						
White	2.60	2.27	2.01	2.27	2.56	2.40
Nonwhite	3.98	4.52	3.64	4.00	3.78	4.67
20 years and over						
White	0.70	0.73	0.78	0.71	0.67	0.65
Nonwhite	1.70	1.85	1.71	1.80	1.54	1.48
Female						
White	1.05	0.98	0.96	0.98	1.07	1.13
Nonwhite	1.83	1.69	1.77	2.07	1.94	1.90
14 to 19 years						
White	2.10	2.35	1.86	2.09	2.43	3.08
Nonwhite	4.93	4.44	3.42	5.68	4.78	6.79
20 years and over						
White	0.93	0.83	0.85	0.84	0.93	0.90
Nonwhite	1.53	1.46	1.63	1.71	1.69	1.58

Source: U. S. Bureau of Labor Statistics.

TABLE 6. Ratios of Unemployment Rates by Major
Occupation Group to Rate for
Experienced Workers
(Quarterly averages, seasonally adjusted)

Major Occupation Group	1957-I	1960-I	1961-II	1962-I	1964-I	1965-I
Unemployment rate for all experienced workers (per cent)	3.6	4.6	6.3	4.8	4.7	4.0
Ratio	1.00	1.00	1.00	1.00	1.00	1.00
White-collar workers	0.58	0.57	0.54	0.60	0.60	0.63
Professional and technical	0.39	0.35	0.33	0.40	0.38	0.43
Managers, officials, and proprietors	0.28	0.28	0.30	0.33	0.34	0.33
Clerical workers	0.83	0.83	0.79	0.83	0.87	0.90
Sales workers	0.75	0.78	0.70	0.88	0.70	0.88
Blue-collar workers	1.64	1.52	1.56	1.56	1.43	1.38
Craftsmen and foremen	1.08	1.04	1.11	1.02	0.91	0.98
Operatives	1.67	1.52	1.59	1.63	1.47	1.38
Nonfarm laborers	2.67	2.57	2.49	2.60	2.38	2.28
Service workers	1.31	1.13	1.14	1.23	1.32	1.43
Private household workers	1.00	0.96	1.00	0.98	1.09	1.13
Other service workers	1.42	1.17	1.19	1.31	1.38	1.53
Farm workers	0.61	0.54	0.49	0.42	0.64	0.60
Farmers and farm managers	0.11	0.07	0.05	0.04	0.06	0.13
Farm laborers and foremen	1.22	1.09	0.94	0.83	1.21	1.10

Source: U. S. Bureau of Labor Statistics.

TABLE 7. RATIOS OF UNEMPLOYMENT RATES BY MAJOR INDUSTRY
GROUP TO RATE FOR EXPERIENCED WAGE AND SALARY WORKERS
(Quarterly averages, seasonally adjusted)

Major Industry Group	1957-I	1960-I	1961-II	1962-I	1964-I	1965-I
Unemployment rate for all experienced wage and salary workers (per cent)	4.2	5.2	7.1	5.6	5.2	4.5
Ratio	1.00	1.00	1.00	1.00	1.00	1.00
Agriculture	1.62	1.75	1.45	1.39	1.90	1.71
Mining	1.29	1.81	1.58	1.18	1.23	1.49
Construction	2.19	2.35	2.27	2.21	1.96	2.18
Manufacturing	1.00	1.04	1.13	1.04	1.02	0.91
Durable goods	0.93	0.96	1.30	1.00	0.98	0.84
Nondurable goods	1.12	1.12	0.94	1.07	1.08	1.02
Transportation and public utilities	0.64	0.73	0.76	0.73	0.71	0.67
Wholesale and retail trade	1.12	1.02	1.04	1.16	1.17	1.20
Service industries[a]	0.71	0.71	0.68	0.73	0.77	0.84
Public administration	0.40	0.50	0.39	0.34	0.52	0.42

Source: U. S. Bureau of Labor Statistics.
[a] Includes forestry and fishing.

the rates of unemployment would be given a close-to-4 per cent
unemployment rate. However, the distribution of unemployment
in early 1965 is in some respects improved over 1957. Some types
of workers who traditionally have had the most unstable employment experiences have gained an advantage or moved closer to
their appropriate share of the unemployment burden, in view
of their share in the labor force. Using R. A. Gordon's[8] measure
of the comparison of the contribution of each segment to unemployment and the labor force we find that the most significant
changes are the increment of new workers and the improvement
for workers in the more cyclical industries and occupations
(Table 9). A negative sign indicates that relatively fewer work-

ers in the specified group are unemployed than are in the labor force.

The underlying changes appear more clearly by occupation, with the marked drop in the over-representation of blue-collar workers and the increased over-representation of service workers among the unemployed (Table 10).

Two other developments should be noted. One is the rapid decline since early 1963, when the figures began to be collected on a monthly basis, in the unemployment rates for full-time workers and the much less rapid reduction in the rate for part-

TABLE 8. RATIOS OF UNEMPLOYMENT RATES BY YEARS OF
SCHOOL COMPLETED AND SEX TO TOTAL UNEMPLOYMENT RATE

Years of School Completed and Sex	March 1957	March 1959	March 1962	March 1964	March 1965[a]
Males					
18 years and over	1.00	1.00	1.00	1.00	1.00
Less than 8 years	1.68	1.56	1.53	1.62	1.50
8 years	1.07	1.16	1.25	1.33	1.18
High school					
1 to 3 years	1.15	1.29	1.30	1.27	1.55
4 years	0.73	0.78	0.80	0.79	0.77
College					
1 to 3 years	0.66	0.52	0.67	0.73	0.70
4 years or more	0.15	0.22	0.23	0.29	0.32
Females					
18 years and over	1.00	1.00	1.00	1.00	1.00
Less than 8 years	1.39	1.65	1.27	1.49	1.38
8 years	1.37	1.08	1.07	1.02	0.89
High school					
1 to 3 years	1.44	1.55	1.53	1.39	1.62
4 years	0.71	0.78	0.95	0.92	0.94
College					
1 to 3 years	0.78	0.63	0.53	0.85	0.68
4 years or more	0.24	0.22	0.25	0.26	0.25

Source: U. S. Bureau of Labor Statistics.
[a] Preliminary.

TABLE 9. Difference Between Percentage of Unemployed
and Percentage of Labor Force in Each Industry Group—
1957-I and 1965-I
(Not seasonally adjusted)

Industry Group	1957	1965
Experienced wage and salary workers	+ 6.5	− 0.9
Agriculture	+ 2.7	+ 2.0
Mining	+ 0.4	+ 0.3
Construction	+11.0	+ 9.9
Manufacturing	+ 0.4	− 3.5
Durable goods	− 1.2	− 3.1
Nondurable goods	+ 1.6	− 0.4
Transportation, communication, public utilities	− 1.8	− 2.1
Trade	+ 3.3	+ 2.3
Services	− 7.0	− 6.8
Public administration	− 2.4	− 3.1
Self-employed and unpaid workers	+12.7	−10.0
New workers	+ 6.1	+10.9

time workers.[9] For teenagers neither the full-time nor part-time
unemployment rate has shown any real improvement.

Unemployment Rates of Full-time and Part-time Labor
Force, April 1962, 1963, and 1964

	Full-Time Labor Force			Part-Time Labor Force		
Age	April 1963	April 1964	April 1965	April 1963	April 1964	April 1965
Total	5.6	5.2	4.5	5.9	6.4	6.2
Men 20 and over	4.6	3.9	3.5	6.2	5.5	5.4
Women 20 and over	5.5	5.6	4.7	3.4	3.5	3.1
Teenagers	21.4	22.9	20.8	9.7	10.8	10.7

The figures suggest that some of the changing structure of
unemployment may be the result of shifts in proportions of "vol-

TABLE 10. Difference Between Percentage of Unemployed
and Percentage of Labor Force in Each Occupation Group—
1957-I and 1965-I
(Not seasonally adjusted)

Occupation Group	1957	1965
White-collar workers	−22.7	−22.9
Professional and technical	− 7.6	− 8.9
Managers, officials, and proprietors	− 7.8	− 7.5
Clerical	− 5.2	− 4.9
Sales	− 2.1	− 1.6
Blue-collar workers	+19.1	+11.7
Craftsmen and foremen	+ 1.3	+ 0.2
Operatives	+ 8.4	+ 4.2
Nonfarm laborers	+ 9.4	+ 7.3
Service workers	—	+ 1.8
Private household	− 0.9	− 0.4
Other workers	+ 0.9	+ 2.2
Farm workers	− 2.4	+ 1.5
Farmers and farm managers	− 4.2	− 2.6
Farm laborers and foremen	+ 1.8	+ 1.1
New workers	+ 6.1	+10.9

untary unemployment"—the unemployment of secondary workers free to choose whether or not to look for work. Although
the expansion of full-time employment since 1960 has been
greater in absolute terms (3.3 million nonagricultural workers
on full-time schedules as compared with 1.4 million voluntary
part-time workers), the proportion of the labor force who are
voluntary part-time workers has been increasing slowly but
steadily each year. The failure of the unemployment rates of
the part-time labor force to come down has had some effect in
holding up the total rate. In view of the anticipated expansion
of the labor force, it is doubtful that the unemployment rate
of part-time workers could be much affected by increases in aggregate demand or in the improvement of the mechanism of the
job market.

Long-term unemployment, sometimes taken as an indicator of
structural unemployment, was at the rate of 1.1 per cent of the

civilian labor force, seasonally adjusted, in the first quarter of 1965. In 1957, it was 0.8 per cent in the first three quarters of the year and 1.0 per cent in the last quarter. Thus, the total number of long-term unemployed, seasonally adjusted, is within about 240,000 of the number who would have been in that category with early 1957 rates.

The composition of long-term unemployment has altered. A greater proportion are young workers under age 25 (29.4 per cent in 1964 compared with 23.5 per cent in 1957). Clerical and service workers are more numerous (26.8 per cent vs. 21.6 per cent), as are workers in trade and service industries (33.9 per cent vs. 26.4 per cent). These types of workers are perhaps the most mobile in the labor force and could be more readily trained and directed into available jobs.

Conclusion

Even with the remarkable improvements outlined, unemployment of the dimensions of early 1965 is certainly still too large in terms of numbers of people. But when the numbers are disaggregated, converted to rates, compared with 1957 or periods of more nearly full employment, and scrutinized for guidance on causes and types of unemployment, the evidence seems to lead to one conclusion on the possibilities of further reduction. To be sure it is a risky business after 52 months of upswing to make a prophecy for publication some months in the future. It appears to me that increases in aggregate demand may produce some additional, moderate declines in unemployment among the hard core of full-time workers in the labor force, but the prospective labor-force expansion could hold up the unemployment rates of young workers and adult women for a long time to come. (The special problems of nonwhite workers do not need to be restated or labeled. They will yield only to a very varied set of measures.)

The frictions generated when large numbers of people come into the labor force, particularly when they are competing for the same kinds of jobs, will be reflected in continuing unemployment for these groups. To some extent the problem will be one of insufficient training and poor labor market mechanisms, and further steps can be taken to improve these. However, it seems unlikely that any institutions we can imagine in the short run can change very radically the voluntary, undirected, and sometimes aimless mobility into and out of the labor force so prevalent in this country.

NOTES

1. See "The Employment Situation in Early 1965, "*Monthly Report on the Labor Force,* April 1965, for a detailed description of developments through the first quarter of 1965.
2. *Job Mobility in 1961,* Special Labor Force Report, No. 35 (Washington, D. C.: U. S. Bureau of Labor Statistics, 1964), Table 4.
3. Dorothy K. Newman, "The Negro's Journey to the City, Part II," *Monthly Labor Review,* LXXXIII (June 1965).
4. Between 1964-I and 1965-I employment of operatives increased by 500,000, mostly in durable goods manufacturing—autos and other metals and metal-using industries. The additional male operatives were preponderantly young workers. See "The Employment Situation in Early 1965," *The Monthly Report on the Labor Force,* April 1965.
5. Rather dramatic evidence of the effect of labor-force growth can be seen in a comparison of the changes in employment of women with changes in their unemployment in specific industry groups. Data for 1962-I and 1965-I show that there was no relationship between the two in these cross-sectional figures.

EMPLOYMENT AND UNEMPLOYMENT OF WOMEN
(Changes—1962-I to 1965-I—in thousands)
(Not seasonally adjusted)

	Employed	Unemployed experienced workers
Total women	+1,889	−47
Manufacturing	+604	−22
Durable goods	+161	+15
Nondurable goods	+443	−37
Trade	+365	−26
Service	+885	+18
Personal	−224	−24
Professional	+916	+43

6. At least for the population 25 and over, the BLS is planning to compile quarterly or annual averages of data by educational attainment beginning in 1966.

7. Between March 1957 and March 1965 the number of persons in the labor force who had never gone to high school fell by 4.6 million, but the number in the population fell by close to five million. The composition of the changes by employment status and sex is shown below:

CHANGES IN NUMBER OF PERSONS WITH EIGHT YEARS OF
EDUCATION OR LESS, MARCH 1957 TO MARCH 1965
(in thousands)

	Total	Male	Female
Population	−4,959	−2,687	−2,272
Labor force	−4,597	−3,772	− 825
Employed	−4,366	−3,579	− 787
Unemployed	− 231	− 193	− 38
Not in labor force	− 362	+1,085	−1,447

8. R. A. Gordon, "Has Structural Unemployment Worsened?," *Industrial Relations,* III (May 1964), 53–77.

9. The full-time component is comprised of (a) persons actually at work 35 hours or more, (b) regular full-time workers temporarily on part time for noneconomic reasons (holidays, illness, bad weather, etc.), (c) workers on part time for economic reasons including the usually full-time and usually part-time groups (both categories of workers on part time for economic reasons are included in the full-time group, since all of them presumably wanted full-time work and their short workweeks were involuntary. This is consistent with the inclusion of all the unemployed who sought full-time jobs; some of the latter would probably accept part-time work if a long search for a full-time job proved fruitless), (d) the unemployed seeking full-time work, and (e) an estimated proportion of the persons who had jobs from which they were absent the entire survey week. The part-time component of the labor force is comprised of (a) voluntary part-time workers (those who usually work less than 35 hours a week for noneconomic reasons), (b) the unemployed seeking part-time work, and (c) a proportionate number of persons with jobs but not at work.

CHAPTER 6

The Composition of Unemployment
and Public Policy[1]

BY EDWARD D. KALACHEK

Between 1948 and 1961, given the over-all rate, the composition of unemployment was quite stable. Several investigators found consistent relationships between the over-all unemployment rate and the rate for specific demographic, occupational, and industrial groups.[2] Changes in the over-all rate led to predictable changes in unemployment within various labor-market subgroups. This general stability of relationships provided a framework for the interpretation of instability. If unemployment in specific activities turned out to be unusually high or low, given the over-all rate, the deviation was interpreted as indicating an alteration in relative supply or demand conditions. This was interpreted as indicating a shift in the relationship between unemployment and the annual rate of price change.

In general the relationships between specific unemployment

227

rates and the over-all rate demonstrated for earlier cycles have persisted during the current expansion. When unemployment declined after the 1960–1961 recession and in 1964, the sharpest reductions were among groups traditionally most sensitive to fluctuations in aggregate supply-demand conditions. As always, however, there were departures from average experiences. In particular, unemployment remained unusually high among teenagers and women while reaching quite low levels among adult men. These departures from normal have been explained on the basis of demand shifts—the increasing sophistication of production processes—or supply shifts—the population explosion in the younger age groups.

Such interpretations tend to be overly simple. The composition of unemployment depends not only on its level but on a weighting of current and preceding inflows and outflows.[3] The regularity of the cycle during the 1948–1961 period was such that preceding flows could be ignored at the cost of only minor distortion. However, the pattern of preceding inflows which characterizes this expansion differs sharply from the pattern associated with other periods when the unemployment rate was in a similar range. The central theme of this chapter is that the currently high unemployment rates among women and teenagers can be satisfactorily explained only by taking account of these differences.

The Demographic Composition of Inflows

Let us begin with the fact that people become unemployed mainly as the result of layoffs, voluntary quits, and labor force entrance. They can find their paths of exit from unemployment by recall, new hire, and labor-force departure. Workers of every age and sex will enter unemployment through the channels mentioned above, but each channel will nonetheless have a characteristic demographic composition.[4] Labor-force entrants and re-entrants will primarily consist of teenagers and women. (The relative proportion of these two groups will vary over time. If the proportion of teenagers in the population rises, their share of entrants will increase, whereas, if care of the home becomes more efficient and more women are free to enter the labor market, the female share will rise.) There will also be a disproportionate number of women and teenagers among voluntary quits, but this channel will have a larger representation of men in their twenties and some of more advanced ages. Layoffs will consist of a still more widely diversified demographic sampling; in particular, there should be a higher proportion of men aged 25 to 54 than in the other two groups. This brings us to an obvious but important point. Whenever the relative importance of the quit rate, layoff rate, and labor-force entrance rate varies, so will the age-sex composition of unemployment unless there are exactly offsetting changes in the probability of exit.

In order to concentrate attention on the factors which concern us, let us hold a wide number of other forces constant. Let us assume constancy in the size of the population, its demographic composition, social customs, the rate of increase of output per man-hour, the factor bias of technical change, employer hiring preferences, and the skills of the labor force. Having done this, it becomes clear that the layoff rate depends on different factors than the quit and labor-force entrance rates. It is reasonable to assume that changes in the layoff rate are determined by aggregate changes in planned output and the dispersion of individual establishment experience around this national average. This presumably results in layoffs leading cyclical turns, reaching a low some time in the recovery phase and remaining at about that level while expansion continues. The layoff rate is thus not closely tied to the unemployment rate. Layoffs can vary greatly at any unemployment rate, depending on whether that rate is reached as the result of contraction, recovery, or steady expansion. In contrast, the inflow of quits and labor-force entrants to unemployment will be determined by the ratio of job vacancies to unemployment.

At any given time the composition of the unemployment stock will depend on preceding as well as current inflows and outflows. In other words, the relative contribution of quits, entrances, and layoffs to unemployment will depend on earlier as well as present unemployment rates and rates of change in output. There is no normal composition for unemployment at any unemployment rate, even after taking account of our sweeping constancy assumption, unless time paths are stipulated. The composition of unemployment associated with any given unemployment rate,

encountered at two different moments in time, will be the same
only if moving down the same path. For instance, any unemployment rate encountered at a specific point along a cyclical path
will be associated with a distinct composition of unemployment
only if the economy has exactly regular unemployment and output contours. This requires the unemployment rate always to
reach the same high during recessions and the same low during
expansions, and to spend the same amount of time at its peak
and trough levels and in the intervening periods of expansion
and contraction. Further, any specific point on the cyclical path
must be associated with the same rate of change in output. Only
then will any given unemployment rate always be associated
with the same weighting of inflows, both current and past, and
consequently with the same composition.

Many unemployment rates will of course be encountered twice
during a cycle—during the recession and recovery phases. Current inflows and the inherited stock of unemployment will differ
between the two points. For instance the inflow to unemployment from layoffs will be lower during the recovery but the proportion of laid off workers may be higher, since changes in the
composition of the stock will lag behind changes in the magnitude of inflows. As a matter of fact, though not of necessity,
this phase difference appears to be sufficiently moderate so that
when cyclical regularity is even roughly approximated, most of
the variance in the composition of unemployment can be explained by changes in the over-all unemployment rate.

A Change in Paths

Imagine that an economy, previously cyclically regular in the
fashion described above, begins to follow a different time path.
In emerging from a recession, it arrives at an unemployment
rate U, typically a recession-recovery rate. Cyclical recovery then
ceases. Output continues to increase, but at a pace which merely
keeps up with the growth in aggregate supply at the unemployment rate. Since the net size of the labor force has been assumed
constant, the economy is not generating additional jobs. The
unemployment rate will then stabilize at U.

As the economy moves through time, the members of the unemployment stock who entered through layoff will eventually

consist solely of persons laid off after the unemployment rate reached U. The weighted average of layoff rates for recent periods will necessarily be lower than it was when U was reached in recession, with an inheritance of periods of output decline. Generally it should also be lower than when U was reached in recovery and the pertinent heritage consisted of periods of recession and recovery.[5] If the probability of laid-off workers finding reemployment relative to the probability of quits and entrants is no worse along this growth path than during the course of the usual cyclical pattern, layoffs will account for a smaller proportion of the unemployment stock. New entrants and quits will then account for a higher proportion; the stabilization of the unemployment rate at U will have increased their susceptibility to unemployment.

Building on this highly reasonable conclusion, some interesting results follow. Women and teenagers account for a larger proportion of labor-force entrances and quits than layoffs. They will consequently account for a higher proportion of the unemployed. An unusually heavy concentration of unemployment among women and teenagers can thus occur without any shift in employer hiring patterns or in the industrial composition of jobs or in population composition.

The industrial and occupational composition of unemployment will now diverge from what was normal at U when that unemployment rate was encountered during recession or recovery periods. There will be less unemployment among workers attached to cyclically sensitive activities because the layoff rate or the accumulation of past layoffs in these activities will be lower than during recession or recovery periods. We do not know whether the offsetting concentration of unemployment will occur among entrants, quits, or both. If it occurs among entrants, there will be more unemployment in activities which are large providers of beginning jobs for new workers, part-time jobs, and part-year jobs. This will be attributable to the work habits of many entrants and to the official system for classifying unemployed workers.

Many teenagers and women do not remain continuous members of the labor force. Dependent on family and personal financial needs, the pressures of school schedules, and the availability of jobs, they periodically enter and leave the labor market. If they have had two full weeks of work experience, they are classified as experienced workers when reentering. If they become unemployed on reentering, their unemployment is attributed to the activity in which they were employed during their last labor-market stay. If labor-force entrants have a higher probability of unemployment (when the rate is at U along a growth path rather than in the course of the cycle), unemployment will tend to rise in those occupations and industries they frequent. If quits are more susceptible to unemployment, this too will be attributed to industries which employ large numbers of women and young people.

The Experience of the Current Cycle

The preceding discussion indicates that comparing the composition of unemployment at different moments in time may lead to spurious conclusions unless allowance is made for differences in time paths. It also provides a plausible framework for explaining changes in the composition of unemployment during the current expansion. It predicts the direction of change with considerable accuracy.

First, the current situation is aptly described by the case of an unemployment rate originally encountered only in the course of cyclical fluctuation but later met in a period when output was growing as rapidly as potential supply. From the beginning of the postwar period through 1961 unemployment rates in the range of 5 to 6 per cent were encountered only during recession and recovery periods. Using annual data, the unemployment rate was in this range in what were clearly recession and recovery periods in 1949–1950 and in 1954. The years 1959 and 1960, while tinged with more ambiguities, also belonged in the same category.[6]

The current expansion cannot be so classified. Unemployment reached 5.5 per cent in March 1962 and fluctuated with no apparent trend through early 1964. It then fell mildly, reaching 5 per cent in December 1964, and averaging 5.2 per cent for the year as compared with 5.6 per cent for 1962 and 5.7 per cent for 1963. During the 1962–1964 period, then, the unemployment rate was in the 5 to 6 per cent range while the economy was experiencing steady growth.

Second, if we consider the behavior of labor-turnover rates for manufacturing, we find the unemployment rate remained 5 per cent *despite* a considerably smaller inflow of layoffs than is normally characteristic of periods when unemployment is in this range. The average annual layoff rate, 2.3 per cent in 1954, 2 per cent in 1959, and 2.4 per cent in 1960, was 2 per cent in 1962 and declined to 1.8 per cent in 1963 and 1.7 per cent in 1964. In contrast, the quit rate fluctuated within a relatively narrow range and reached its high point for this period in 1964.[7] As a result of declines in layoffs and relative stability in quits, the absolute inflows from employment to unemployment were, according to BLS gross-flows data, actually lower in 1964 than in these other years despite significant growth over the period in the number of persons employed. In relative terms, previously employed persons accounted for 66 per cent of the gross flow into unemployment in 1954 and 60 per cent in 1959. They accounted for a still lower and continuously falling porportion during the current expansion—57 per cent in 1962, 55 per cent in 1963, and 48 per cent in 1964. As the current expansion progressed, flows into unemployment were thus increasingly dominated by labor-force entrants.[8]

Third, these lower layoff rates resulted in lower unemployment among adult males most sensitive to cyclical layoffs. Table 1 shows the marked improvement in the unemployment experience of adult males from 1959–1960 to 1962 and from 1962 to 1964. This improvement significantly exceeded expectations based on correlations of unemployment rates in specific age-sex groups with the over-all unemployment rate. Steady expansion in output at an unemployment rate normally encountered only in the course of cyclical fluctuations results in low unemployment rates among those most susceptible to layoff. It also leads to high unemployment among labor-force entrants and/or quits. Women and teenagers constitute the bulk of these groups. The marked deterioration of their unemployment position is shown in Table 1.

Finally, low layoff rates result in low unemployment among workers attached to cyclically sensitive occupations such as craftsmen, operatives, and nonfarm laborers, and to cyclically

TABLE 1. Unemployment Rates for Selected Categories,
Selected Years
(Per Cent)

Category	1959-1960	1962	1963	1964	Change from 1959-1960 to 1964 Expected[a]	Actual
Total	5.5	5.6	5.7	5.2		
Age-sex						
Adult males						
25 to 34 years	4.8	4.5	4.5	3.5	−0.3	−1.3
35 to 44 years	3.8	3.6	3.5	2.9	−0.3	−0.9
45 to 54 years	4.1	3.9	3.6	3.2	−0.3	−0.9
55 to 64 years	4.6	4.6	4.3	3.9	−0.3	−0.7
High entry groups						
Male teenagers	13.9	13.3	15.5	14.5	−0.7	0.6
Males aged 20-24	8.8	8.9	8.8	8.1	−0.6	−0.7
Women	5.9	6.2	6.5	6.2	−0.3	0.3
Industry						
Experienced wage and salary workers	5.7	5.5	5.5	5.0		
Cyclically sensitive indus-tries[b]						
Durable-goods manu-facturing	6.2	5.7	5.4	4.7	−1.1	−1.5
Mining	9.6	8.6	7.5	7.6	−1.2	−2.0
Construction[c]	12.1	12.1	11.9	9.9	−0.9	−2.2
Entry industries[d]						
Wholesale and retail trade	5.9	6.3	6.2	5.7	−0.5	−0.2
Nondurable-goods manufacturing	6.0	5.9	6.0	5.3	−0.7	−0.7
Services	4.2	4.3	4.4	4.1	−0.4	−0.1
Finance, insurance, and real estate	2.5	3.1	2.7	2.5	−0.3	0.0
Occupation						
Experienced workers	4.9	4.8	4.9	4.4		
Cyclically sensitive occu-pations[b]						
Craftsmen	5.3	5.1	4.8	4.2	−0.6	−1.1
Operatives	7.8	7.5	7.4	6.5	−0.9	−1.3
Nonfarm laborers	12.5	12.4	12.1	10.6	−1.3	−1.9
Entry occupations[d]						
Service	6.2	6.4	6.2	6.1	−0.5	−0.1
Sales	3.7	4.1	4.2	3.4	−0.2	−0.3
Clerical	3.8	3.9	4.0	3.7	−0.4	−0.1
Professional	1.7	1.7	1.8	1.7	−0.1	0.0

Source: *Manpower Report of the President,* March 1965.
[a] On the basis of the simple correlation of unemployment in specific groups with the appropriate over-all rate for the 1947-1961 period.
[b] Those activities in which the unemployment rate fluctuates proportion-ately more than the over-all rate are classified as cyclically sensitive.
[c] Construction may represent a special case, since its cyclical sensitivity is due not so much to its own declines in employment as to the inflow of dis-employed labor from other sectors.
[d] Activities are classified as entry activities if women and teenagers com-prised over 35 per cent of the employed workforce at the time of the 1960 decennial census.

sensitive industries such as durable goods manfacturing and mining. The counterpart is high unemployment in activities which are major providers of employment for women and young men, a phenomenon illustrated by Table 1. Fluctuations in the quit rate have been moderate, while there has been a sharp rise in the inflow of labor-force entrants to unemployment. Since new entrants to the labor force cannot be classified in the unemployment data as being attached to any occupation or industry, the high unemployment rates in entry activities probably reflect to a considerable extent the unemployment of reentrants formerly attached to these activities.

There is one important divergence between our model and the experience of the current expansion. We have demonstrated that steady expansion occurring at an unemployment rate normally associated with recession or recovery periods can result in unusually large concentrations of unemployment among teenagers and women even under the assumption of constancy in the size of the population, its age-sex composition, and social customs. But population has been rising, the younger age cohorts have been increasing in importance, and the steady modification of social customs has led to rising labor-force participation among women. These supply changes may be an additional cause of higher unemployment among teenagers and women. Since our analysis has been impressionistic and functions have not been fitted, there is no way of determining whether compositional changes during the current expansion can be explained without taking account of these supply changes. However, changes in the composition of unemployment have been moderate, as can be seen in Table 1. A significant portion of these changes must be attributed to the peculiar characteristics of this expansion. Unemployment rates in the 5 to 6 per cent range have been experienced during a period of steady expansion rather than during a period with current high layoff rates or with a heritage of earlier high layoff rates. It follows that recent dramatic changes in the composition of labor supply can have had only a modest impact on unemployment rates.

The Displacement Version

The displacement version of the rise in structural unemployment hypothesis merits reappraisal in light of developments during the current expansion. It was originally inspired by the shifts in the composition of employment from goods production to services and from blue-collar to white-collar work. With slack economic conditions, these shifts resulted in absolute employment declines during part of the 1950's among manufacturing and other industrial workers and among operatives and nonfarm workers. Many of these displaced workers flowed into the unemployment stock. It was hypothesized that the changed composition of unemployment meant any increase in aggregate demand would result in larger price increases and smaller real output and employment increases than hitherto.[9] In an earlier paper I tested this hypothesis by estimating the normal relationship between unemployment rates for the affected activities and the experienced worker unemployment rate for the 1948–1957 period.[10] These relationships were used to predict the activity composition of unemployment in 1959–1960. Actual unemployment among industrial workers, operatives, and nonfarm laborers corresponded very closely with expected unemployment when given the experienced worker rate. An unusual concentration of unemployment among these workers was the *sine qua non* for an increase in hiring costs or efficiency wages. In its absence the hypothesis was refuted.

Can this type of test, which relates specific-activity unemployment rates solely to experienced-worker rate be reconciled with the broader approach to the composition of unemployment presented in this chapter? It can be for 1959–1960 since in that period an unemployment rate averaging 5.5 per cent for the two years was encountered in the process of cyclical expansion and contraction. The years subsequent to 1961 are a different matter. In those years high unemployment rates were not attributable to high layoff rates or to prior accumulation of a large stock of laid-off workers. Consequently specific-activity unemployment rates cannot be accurately predicted unless allowance is made for this difference. The data now contain a built-in bias against the displacement hypothesis. Those activities which were the focus of concern of the hypothesis are by coincidence the activities most highly sensitive to cyclical fluctuations. The decline in output and the increase in layoff rates, associated with recession, are concentrated in durable goods manufacturing, mining, and among operatives and nonfarm laborers. Unemployment rates of workers attached to these activities should be lower during the current expansion than would have been predicted on the basis of the experience of the 1950's.

During the late 1950's, when net displacement was occurring among industrial and low-to-medium-skill blue-collar workers, there was no unusual concentration of unemployment. There is no longer a relevant test for the impact of industrial displacement, but there is also no need for one. There is no net displacement among industrial workers or medium to low-skill workers in the nonfarm sector. Their employment has been rising since 1961 and is currently above the levels reached in 1959–1960.

Public Policy

The distinction between inflows to unemployment and the stock of unemployed workers they generate is an invaluable aid in explaining changes in the composition of unemployment. It is also essential in determining the correct policy mix for coping with unemployment.

Imagine that the rate of price change per period of time is inversely related to the unemployment rate. The schedule *PP* (price-unemployment schedule) in Chart 1 describes the attainable combinations of price change per period of time and unemployment rates.[11] Imagine further that policy makers regard price increases and unemployment as being discommodities and are willing to contemplate tradeoffs—to consider how much unemployment to endure for the sake of stable prices and how much price increase to tolerate for the sake of low unemployment. Policy makers' preferences are summarized by the set of concave indifference curves in Figure 1. More desirable positions are attained by moving in a southwesterly direction, where unemployment and rate of price change are lower. The tangency of an indifference curve with the price-unemployment schedule at point *u* determines the prescribed goal for fiscal-monetary policy. The resulting annual rate of price change will then be *OA* and the unemployment rate will be *OB*.

The position of the price-unemployment schedule is not necessarily fixed over time. It can, for instance, be shifted in a south-

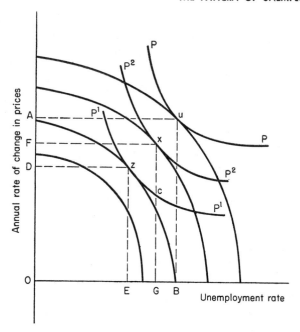

CHART 1

westerly direction by labor-market policy. If point u represents the lowest level of unemployment and rate of price change attainable, given other goals and constraints, rather than merely being the turn-off point for aggregate demand policies, it is necessary that expenditure on labor-market policy be at an optimum level.[12] Where this level is depends on the ability of labor-market policy to satisfy social wants. It is determined in the following fashion. First, the impact on unemployment of varying amounts of expenditure on labor-market measures must be analyzed to determine the net reduction in unemployment that will result from a given amount of expenditure. Second, the social value of this reduction may be determined by computing the sum of the additional stream of output resulting over time from reemployment[13] and the social premium attached to reducing unemployment because it is bad in itself or has adverse social consequences. Next, we must add the social premium attached to a reduction in the annual rate of price change.[14] We can then solve for the highest discount rate which equates this future stream of real and imputed returns to the cost of labor-market policy. We now have a rate of return on labor-market policy as a function of expenditure for this purpose. Such policy is pursued until this rate of return is brought into equality with the rate of return on other investments.

Imagine that the full perception and exploitation of opportunities for labor-market policy which meet these criteria for the rate of return result in shifting the price-unemployment schedule from PP to P^1P^1. The new tangency with a more preferred indifference curve occurs at z, where the annual rate of price change is OD and the unemployment rate is OE. In contrast with u, the position z is an authentic optimum. Unemployment of OE is preferred to a rate of price increase greater than OD or to a larger allocation of resources to labor-market policy.

What if biased technical change or some other disturbance now shifts the price-unemployment schedule from P^1P^1 to P^2P^2? The cut-off point for fiscal-monetary policy now occurs at x with an unemployment rate of OG and an annual rate of price change of OF. The previous lower unemployment level of OE will be reattained only if expenditure on labor-market policy is increased. Should it be? Those who interpreted the net displacement of industrial workers during part of the 1950's or the recent high rates of unemployment among teenagers as indicating an upward shift in price-unemployment schedules took this shift to be *prima facie* an indication of the need for more labor-market expenditure. However, their conclusion is valid only under certain restrictive circumstances. The more general rule is that if expenditure on labor-market policy was optimum before the upward shift in the price-unemployment schedule, it should now be increased only if (a) the social premium attached to reducing unemployment by one person rises with the number of unemployed, or (b) if the productivity of labor-market policy is favorably affected.[15] Unfortunately, there is no way of telling in advance how a shift in the price-unemployment schedule will affect the productivity of labor-market policy. The productivity of such policy can be raised, lowered, or left unchanged. An upward shift in the price-unemployment schedule can thus

result in a higher, lower, or unchanged level of labor-market expenditure, on the basis of our criteria.

This is an ambiguous conclusion, scarcely satisfying to those concerned about the current level of unemployment. Happily, however, it can be demonstrated that many of the possible disturbances in the price-unemployment schedule are largely resolvable by fiscal-monetary measures. Consider the two events already mentioned: the net displacement of industrial and low-to-medium-skill blue-collar workers during part of the 1950's, and recent high unemployment rates among teenagers. It has been demonstrated that net displacement did not lead to higher structural unemployment in 1959–1960, and this chapter indicates that a plausible explanation of higher teenage unemployment rates can be constructed without invoking structural change. Nonetheless, for illustrative purposes, imagine these events associated with upward shifts in the price-unemployment schedule. We have already seen that net displacement was a temporary phenomenon; it seems quite reasonable to assume that higher teenage unemployment rates would also be temporary. They would be due to relative wages and hiring specifications responding slowly to changing population composition rather than to their inability to respond at all. If so, neither of these disturbances has altered the permanent composition of inflows to unemployment. They can be characterized as one-time stock disturbances, as contrasted with permanent flow disturbances. To differentiate more fully between these two types of disturbances it is necessary to specify the length of the time horizon of policy makers. The contemplated tradeoff confronting them is between unemployment and annual rate of price change. How many years are taken into account when calculating annual rate of price change? In most instances the time horizon relevant for decision-making should be considerably longer than a year but still of moderate duration. We will call this time span the planning period, and assign it an arbitrary length.

Now assume that biased technical change reduces the marginal product of semi-skilled labor while increasing the marginal product of some more skilled labor group. Real wages of employed semi-skilled workers are rigid downward. The result is that employment declines among these workers. From the point of view of employers on the edge of hiring, this net displacement together with the change in relative marginal products reduces the desirability of the unemployment stock. Random hiring from the stock will result in higher efficiency wages after the displacement than before since either training expenditure must be increased or quality standards allowed to decline. The price-unemployment schedule shifts upward.[16] If biased technical change leads to displacement during each year of the planning period, and the resulting increase in efficiency wages plus price-markup were equal each time to cx, the price-unemployment schedule would then shift from P^1P^1 to P^2P^2. In the absence of additional labor-market expenditure the unemployment rate would rise by EG to the new level of OG.

Contrast this with a one-shot bias in technical change which leads only once to the displacement of semi-skilled workers. Such a disturbance does not shift the price-unemployment schedule from P^1P^1 to P^2P^2. In the absence of additional labor-market policy, the preferred position will not be moved as far northeast as x. Rather, barring additional disturbances, the lower rate of unemployment and price change z on P^1P^1 can be experienced until the end of time. To obtain this desired end, it is only necessary to endure for one year the annual rate of price change of cx. Alternatively, the position z can be secured simply by waiting long enough for the one-shot disturbance to decay. This decay will occur if the reservation wages of unemployed workers deteriorate more rapidly than their skills (where reservation wages are realistically defined to include attachment to specific occupations, industries, and areas, as well as wage rates). The disturbance will also be self-liquidating, even if reservation wages decline only as rapidly as skills, provided the displaced workers represent only a small proportion of their skill group. Deaths, retirements, and promotions among the employed will create vacancies which they then can fill. If either instance holds, it will be found that biased technical change did not alter the permanent composition of inflows to unemployment or the permanent probability of exit. Over the longer run, the composition of the unemployment stock and the position of the price-unemployment schedule will have been unaffected by the temporary stock disturbance.[17]

The identification of some types of structural change as temporary stock disturbances suggests the need for a reappraisal of the role of fiscal-monetary policy. Such a policy can be used more freely in attaining low unemployment rates than was thought when one-shot disturbances were indiscriminately lumped together with permanent flow alterations.[18] This can be redemonstrated by incorporating the amount of inflation associated with the temporary disorder into the price-unemployment schedule. For any unemployment rate, sum the annual price increases which would have occurred over the length of the planning period in the absence of the disturbance. Add the price rise resulting from the disturbance. Discounting this sum to the present yields one point on a new price-unemployment schedule. Following the same procedure for all unemployment rates generates a new price-unemployment schedule. If a permanent flow disturbance would have shifted the schedule from P^1P^1 to P^2P^2, a temporary stock disturbance necessarily shifts it into the range between P^1P^1 and P^2P^2. Its position in this range depends on the length of the planning period. The longer the planning period, the closer will be the new schedule to P^1P^1. If the planning period has any significant duration, the new schedule will be relatively close to P^1P^1 and quite far from P^2P^2. The new preferred position will not be very far from z, and the preferred unemployment rate not very far from OE.

Fiscal-monetary policy will always be used to cope with a higher unemployment rate when it results from temporary stock rather than permanent flow disturbances. This is so because reductions in unemployment can be bought at a smaller cost in terms of the planning-period rate of price change. Only one burst of inflation is required. It would be a different matter if a large number of such temporary disturbances were expected. This is not the case under consideration, nor is there reason to consider it a realistic case.

Since labor-market policy is generally far too slow and expensive in dealing with transitory problems of the type under discussion, this is fortunate. The start-up costs for a governmental unit, particularly the costs of recruiting and training appropriate personnel, are high. The optimum design of policy is never known in advance, but is discovered, if at all, by costly experimentation with less effective policies. Starting-up and learning costs cannot be amortized over any lengthy period of time since the agency is seeking to cope with a transitory problem. Converting the agency to other functions after its task is finished is also costly, even if they are similar functions. Perpetuating its routine is totally wasteful, but if the agency is to be discontinued and this is known in advance, recruiting and staffing problems would be greatly complicated. The social productivity of labor-market policy in coping with stock disturbances is probably quite low. Expenditure on labor-market policy should be directed toward more persistent frictions so that early costs can be amortized over time and benefits allowed to accrue with experience.

NOTES

1. This chapter is a preliminary report of a larger study on the flexibility of specific labor markets conducted under National Aeronautics and Space Administration Grant NSG-342. The author would like to thank Hugh Folk, Fred Raines, and Irvin Sobel for critical comments on this chapter.

2. See the correlation of unemployment in various age-sex groups with the rate for prime working age males in Hugh Folk, *Private Pensions and Labor Market Policy*, Bulletin No. 1359 (Washington, D. C.: U. S. Bureau of Labor Statistics, 1963), and the correlation of unemployment in various occupational and industrial groups with the experienced-worker rate in *Higher Unemployment Rates, 1957–1960: Structural Transformation or Inadequate Demand*, U. S. Congress, Joint Economic Committee (Washington, D. C., 1961).

3. For an elaboration of the relationship between unemployment flow and stocks, see Charles Holt and Martin David, "The Concept of Job Vacancies in a Dynamic Theory of the Labor Market," a paper presented at a research conference on *The Measurement and Interpretation of Job Vacancies* held by the National Bureau of Economic Research, February 11–13, 1965. To be published.

4. For instance, in 1964 men accounted for 69 per cent of the previously employed workers who became unemployed but for only 40 per cent of the labor-force entrants who moved into this category.

5. It is logically necessary that the weighted average be lower than when U was reached in recession. There may be some question, however, about the recovery period comparison. If the layoff rate were a simple function of the rate of change in output it would reach a low during the recovery and rise thereafter. This tendency may be modulated by the lack of coincidence between the general cyclical trough and the low point for specific industries. In any event, the weighted average of layoff rates contributing to U in the recovery will reflect the influence of low layoff rates in some

recovery months and of high layoff rates in some recession months.

6. In January 1959, with recovery under way, the unemployment rate was 6 per cent. By June it had fallen to 5 per cent, but by November had risen to 5.8 per cent as the result of a prolonged steel strike whose impact on layoffs and unemployment in many ways duplicated that of a cyclical recession. Unemployment declined to a low of 4.9 per cent in February 1960 and rose thereafter as general economic conditions weakened.

7. In the years mentioned the quit rate averaged 1.4, 1.5, 1.3, 1.4, 1.4, and 1.5 per cent respectively.

8. Persons in or leaving school accounted for the major portion of the increasing flow of entrants into unemployment, but there was also an appreciable increase in the number of housewives who became unemployed on entering the labor market.

9. A rise in structural unemployment is defined as an alteration in the composition of the demand or supply of labor or in the mechanisms bringing workers and jobs together which increases (at some stipulated unemployment rate) the efficiency wages or hiring costs which must be borne by employers in the market for additional labor. Let the ratio of real aggregate demand to the aggregate supply forthcoming at some relevant unemployment rate be the same in time 1 and time 2. Let the two periods be the same in all significant respects except that structural unemployment is higher in the second period. Higher structural unemployment means that prices will rise by more and output by less in time 2 than in time 1.

The net displacement of industrial and low-to-medium-skill workers will not necessarily lead to such a result. It is necessary to hypothesize further that displaced workers have inappropriate backgrounds for some of the jobs in the expanding sectors and sticky reservation wages too high for others. We then have the same over-all demand for goods and services in both periods, but with a worsening in the second period of the match between the attributes of unemployed workers and the preferences of prospective employers. Employers in the market for additional labor must pay higher efficiency wages to produce the output being demanded. Efforts to obtain properly trained labor can assume many forms. Overtime can be increased for employed workers or wages raised to attract qualified workers from other firms, from among the unemployed, or from outside the labor force. Jobs can at some cost be redesigned and simplified to make use of the skills of displaced workers. Employers can hire these workers, paying their reservation wages, and then increase training expenses or allow quality standards to decline. If the additional money demand is not satisfied in any of these fashions the number of unfilled jobs will rise. There are thus a wide number of adjustments that can be made to reconcile excess supply (with relatively rigid downward real wages) in some labor markets with excess demand in others. The unusual concentration of unemployment among the groups newly subject to net displacement is what causes these adjustments in the first instance, and under any reasonable set of assumptions this concentration will persist—so long as the problem does.

10. *Higher Unemployment Rates, 1957–1960: Structural Transformation or Inadequate Demand* (cited in footnote 2).

11. The price-unemployment schedule is a modified Phillips curve. The assumption that the rate of change of wages is a function of the unemployment rate is supplemented by the assumption that the rate of change of prices is a function of the rate of change of wages. The many oversimplifications involved in constructing this schedule are well known, but the schedule itself in many instances including the present permits a realistic portrayal of policy alternatives. For an elaboration of the relationship between price-unemployment schedules and policy-makers' preference functions, see Richard G. Lipsey, "Structural and Deficiency-Demand Unemployment Reconsidered," in Arthur M. Ross, Editor, *Employment Policy and the Labor Market* (Berkeley: University of California Press, 1965).

12. The position and slope of the price-unemployment schedule are influenced by a wide variety of forces besides labor-market frictions. These forces may be the prime determinants of the schedule, but labor-market policy should still have some capacity for shifting it.

13. This is a tenable first approximation. One might also wish to consider such factors as the psychic advantages and disadvantages of employment for unemployed workers, and the enhancement or deterioration of human and nonhuman capital as the result of higher employment.

14. Mr. Lester Thurow has pointed out that reduction in unemployment due specifically to increased labor-market expenditure will exceed the net reduction in unemployment, given the policy makers' preference schedules shown in Chart 1. As labor-market expenditures are increased, policy makers will choose to take part of the benefits in the form of a lower annual rate of price change and will consequently conduct a less expansive fiscal-monetary policy.

15. In addition, the shift in the price-unemployment schedule may result in a more expansionary monetary-fiscal policy and a lower interest rate. The lower interest rate will represent a decision to engage in more of all types of investments, including investments in labor-market policy.

16. The new schedule will be parallel to the old in the case of a disturbance of this type only under unusual circumstances—if, for instance, employers hire on a random basis.

17. It was thus never very surprising that unemployment among industrial and low-to-medium-skill blue-collar workers was at normal levels in 1959–1960. First, employment declines were of relatively moderate magnitude. Second, irregular occurrences aside, employment in these activities declined on net balance only during the 1957–1958 recession and after the cyclical turning point in 1960. Treating only net magnitudes, the average worker permanently displaced from an industrial or blue-collar job during the 1957–1958 recession had 18 months by 1959 and 30 months by 1960 in which to adjust to the changed pattern of demand for labor.

18. This holds for the type of preference function we are assuming but may not hold if there is an absolute upper limit to policy makers' tolerance for inflation.

Discussion

BY CHARLES C. KILLINGSWORTH

This is the third occasion in recent months at which I have been asked to give a five-, ten-, or fifteen-minute commentary following an hour or several hours of exposition of what has come to be called (incorrectly) "the aggregate demand viewpoint." Following each of the preceding occasions, someone remarked to me that I didn't really answer all of the other side's points. I have taken this lesson to heart, and have also noted that on this occasion I am not only outnumbered—I am surrounded, with Kalachek preceding me and Thurow following. I therefore ask you to recognize that in the time assigned to me I cannot undertake a full refutation of everything with which I disagree in the main papers nor offer a fully substantiated analysis of all aspects of the current unemployment problem as I see it.

My purpose is more limited, though undoubtedly still too ambitious. I merely want to toss a few apples of discord into this little den of consensus. I recognize, of course, that there has been a measure of disagreement among the participants in this conference. Some speakers seem to have argued that tax-cutting is the only thing that matters in employment policy, and others have disagreed, saying tax-cutting is only the most important thing. Perhaps I will merely induce these disputing factions to close ranks by asserting that another point of view is possible—that we have now reached the point at which *exclusive* or even *primary* reliance on tax cuts for further stimulation of aggregate demand is likely to yield a rising level of unemployment, perhaps accompanied by rising prices if the tax cuts are big enough. I believe that with a reported unemployment rate of 4.6 per cent last month (May 1965) virtually all the excess unemployment which remains is *structural* in character. It seems possible that some transitory factors may have temporarily reduced even structural unemployment.

Now that I have used that non-U term "structural unemployment" I want to comment briefly on what has come to be widely accepted, even by otherwise careful scholars, as "the structural unemployment hypothesis." As you know, Kalachek is almost universally regarded as the ultimate authority on how the "hypothesis" should be formulated. Kalachek, in his paper for this conference (Chapter 6), notes that in a previous paper he demolished this "hypothesis." And he did. But what has been generally overlooked is that what Kalachek demolished is only one possible formulation of the "structural hypothesis," and that it would be difficult to fabricate a more implausible statement of the hypothesis than his.

In his monograph for the Joint Economic Committee Kalachek made the claim that his formulation of the "structural hypothesis" drew together the thoughts of "various commentators."[1] I have sought long and hard to find these "various commentators" and have failed. My conclusion is that Kalachek's "structural hypothesis" is at best a crude caricature of what was being argued concerning structural unemployment back in 1961 and 1962. Neither I nor anyone else that I know about has ever argued that there was a "great upsurge" of structural unemployment *after* 1957. Furthermore, there is no basis for assuming that an increase in structural unemployment, whenever it occurred, would be precisely and uniformly concentrated on certain categories of workers as defined by our nineteenth-century system of occupational classification, or on industry groupings. Since I have discoursed at some length on other occasions on how untenable these assumptions are, I will not pursue this matter further here. But there are people present today who, although they have reason to know better, have attributed to me the absurdities incorporated in Kalachek's hypothesis. Therefore, I want to reiterate the point that what Kalachek's creative imagination has really given us is simply a straw man—and one of the most battered straw men in the history of recent economic discussion. It is unfortunate that so many able people have been so busy aiming new blows at this straw man they have lacked the time to read what was actually being said about structural unemployment by analysts other than Kalachek and those who quote him.

I turn to Gertrude Bancroft's paper, to which I was specifically asked to address myself. Her main point seems to be that under present circumstances the 4 per cent unemployment "target" is unreasonable and we must accept a higher level as the irreducible minimum. I must question whether such a redefinition of the goal is an acceptable way to attain "full employment." As best I can recall, hardly anyone had seriously suggested that an unemployment rate as high as 4 per cent should be regarded as "full employment" until the Council of Economic Advisers first advanced this figure—somewhat apologetically—in 1962 as the "interim target." I agree that the policies which are now being given the greatest emphasis, especially tax cutting, in all likelihood cannot reduce unemployment even to the 4 per cent level; but this does not prove that greater emphasis on other policies such as direct job creation for disadvantaged groups in the labor force cannot yield a rate even lower than 4 per cent.

At the outset of her paper Miss Bancroft mentions a number of things that have *not* happened during the recent expansion, which implies that somebody had predicted that they *would* happen. Regrettably, she fails to mention the most important thing which has not happened although it was repeatedly predicted by eminent authority. We have not achieved the 4 per cent unemployment rate which Walter Heller said again and again during 1963 was the probable if not absolutely certain result of the tax cut then under discussion.[2] Most of the things that Miss Bancroft says have *not* happened are things that I, for one, was expecting to happen somewhere *below* 5 per cent unemployment and *above* the 4 per cent rate that Heller was predicting, for example, serious bottlenecks in the supply of certain kinds of highly-trained manpower. Since we were much closer to the 5 per cent rate than to 4 per cent in the first quarter of 1965, there is no basis for an implication that my predictions, among others, have been proved false.

Perhaps it is not inappropriate to add one more point. Neither I nor anyone else that I know about who debated this matter in 1963 argued that tax-cutting would achieve *no* reduction in unemployment; in fact, my guess, now a matter of public record, was that the proposed tax cut would probably get us a little below a 5 per cent unemployment rate. I mention this only because of the constant reiteration in recent months of the myth that a lot of people were saying in 1963 that the tax cut would not reduce unemployment at all. It is difficult to see how such misrepresentation helps us learn the lessons of recent experience.

In the first sentence of Miss Bancroft's chapter are statements which seem to be seriously misleading if not factually erroneous. She writes: "Automation and technological change in the past few years did *not* permanently and drastically reduce the number of blue-collar jobs and eliminate employment opportunities for large numbers of American workers without college or high school education."

But what are the facts? In the last ten years agricultural employment has decreased by about 2,000,000. At the beginning of 1965 *total* manufacturing employment was as high as it had been in 1953; but there were about a million fewer blue-collar workers and a million more white-collar workers in manufacturing in early 1965 than in 1953. In the last five years (1959 to 1964), the employment of workers with an eighth grade education or less has decreased by 2,470,000; this decline was nearly twice as great, in percentage terms, as the population decrease at this level of education.[3] Perhaps Miss Bancroft believes that factors other than technological change were wholly responsible for these great employment changes, but her chapter does not reveal what these other factors are.

It is true, as Miss Bancroft points out in a later passage, that unemployment rates for less-educated workers have declined during the recent years of expansion. I believe that employment and unemployment trends by level of education are much more meaningful than the comparable figures broken down by occupation and industry. But even the published unemployment figures by level of education cannot be properly interpreted without studying the labor-force participation rates associated with them. And it is important to understand that the *averaging* of participation rates for a number of different age and education classifications very often yields results that are worse than meaningless because they are highly misleading. There have been marked changes in the patterns of lifetime participation rates by level of education over the last fifteen years and we can learn a great deal from them if we give attention to the detailed patterns instead of obliterating them by excessive aggregation.

Among the adult male population 18 years of age and over, the following broad generalizations seem justified: (a) in any given year there is a fairly close relationship, by age group, between years of school completed and participation rate, with the lowest participation rates at the lowest levels of education and vice versa;[4] (b) participation rates in most age groups have been declining among the less educated men, including high school dropouts, and the less the education the sharper the decline; (c) participation rates by age group at the middle levels of education have been fairly steady (except at age 65 and over); (d) participation rates by age among college graduates have shown a generally upward trend, except in age groups which already had rates around 99 per cent and in the 65 and over group.[5]

In recent years it is possible to find a combination of declining employment, generally declining participation rates by age, and declining unemployment rates. This was the situation among men with eight or fewer years of education from 1962 to 1964. It is also possible to find a combination of rising employment, rising participation rates, and rising unemployment, the situation among the youngest and oldest male college graduates from 1962 to 1964. In the first case the unemployment rate was declining despite slack demand and in the second the unemployment rate was rising despite briskly rising demand.

These facts lead me to suggest that it may be naive to interpret declining unemployment rates for poorly educated workers as evidence that their labor market position has markedly improved. Especially among males in this group, one form of adjustment to declining job opportunities has been to drop out of the labor force (as the labor force is somewhat unrealistically defined).

We can get an impression of the magnitude of this type of adjustment by calculating what the 1964 male labor force at the lower educational levels would have been if there had been no declines in participation rates, by age and education, since 1957. This calculation yields a labor-force increase of 377,000 among men 18 to 64 years of age with less than nine years of school; for the 18 to 64 age group with nine to eleven years of school it yields an increase of 113,000 in labor force size, or a total of 490,000 for all men 18 to 64 with less than a high school diploma. So far as the 65 and over group is concerned, if the participation rates of the less educated men had declined from 1957 to 1964 only in proportion to the decline of rates for male college graduates of the same age classification, the labor force of men 65 and over with less than a high school diploma would have been 474,000 larger in 1964 than it was.[6]

I question whether complacency or mild jubilation over this kind of adjustment to shrinking job opportunities is justified. We have not tried to find out very much about these labor-force dropouts. We don't know who they are, where they are, how they live, what it would take to make them employable, and so on. Surely we ought to have some knowledge about them before we conclude that the recent substantial shrinkage in the less-educated male labor force by this means can be neglected in labor-market analysis.

Miss Bancroft's heavy reliance on the first quarter of 1965 as the terminal point for many of her comparisons raises a question which is relevant not only to her conclusions but to many others that have been presented in this conference. Otto Eckstein, in his discussion, places great reliance on comparisons between May 1964 and May 1965. To what extent was the state of the economy in early 1965 attributable to the effect of the tax cut of 1964 and to what extent to temporary distortions of the level and pattern of demand in certain sectors of the economy? We know there was an abnormally high rate of inventory buildup during this period in the automobile and steel-using industries, plus catch-up sales of automobiles, and these abnormalities may have caused others less obvious now. There seems to be an implicit assumption in much of the discussion here that all of the employment changes since the tax cut are solely due to the tax cut. Eckstein went even further in answer to a question that I put to him yesterday; he said additional tax cuts would create a pattern of increases in employment even more favorable to the low-skilled and otherwise disadvantaged groups in the labor force than the May 1964–May 1965 pattern of increases. Among other things, this prediction seems to assume an even more rapid rate of increase in agricultural employment than the abnormal increase between these two dates; as we all know, one of the best established long-run trends in the labor market is the decline in agricultural employment. The experience of the past few months, with their obvious abnormalities, provides an inadequate basis for concluding either that many long-run employment trends have been reversed or that another tax cut of great magnitude would have the same or even more beneficial effects. I believe it will be another six months or so before we can sort out the effects of the tax cut and of the temporary distortions unquestionably present now.

Even if we assume, however, that all of the recent gains in employment that Miss Bancroft and Mr. Eckstein emphasize are solely attributable to the 1964 tax cut, one of the most basic assumptions of the so-called aggregate-demand school would remain essentially unverified. This assumption is that when the supply of more desirable kinds of workers gets tight employers will greatly increase their hiring of teen-agers, older workers, nonwhites, and less educated workers and will concurrently engage in wholesale retraining and job redesign programs. Stated a little differently, with a high level of demand the substitutibility of various kinds and grades of labor is very high. With unemployment still only a little below 5 per cent, we are scarcely on the threshold of a testing of this crucial assumption. The only evidence offered on this point is a reference to wartime conditions. Such a reference ignores some highly pertinent considerations. The wartime patterns of demand for labor were very different from current patterns; the training that took place was almost wholly financed by government; where there was redesign of jobs, it was generally in response to extremely large increases in the volume of production, as in shipbuilding and aircraft, and again the cost was borne by the government. There has been virtually no empirical investigation of how employers will respond under present-day conditions to moderate increases in demand; and there haven't even been guesses as to how much private retraining programs and job redesign might add to unit labor costs and prices.

By mid-1965 the great tax cut of 1964 had helped to move the unemployment rate from a little above to a little below 5 per cent. One major reason why we are here is to consider how we can move closer to full employment—defined as 4 per cent or 3 per cent unemployment or something in between. I presume hardly any of you would argue that further reductions in the unemployment rate will be easier, or at least no harder, to achieve than the reduction in the last twelve months. The question which confronts us is whether it is time for a change in priorities in employment policy. There is wide-spread and profound misunderstanding among professional economists concerning the position of those who would give tax-cutting a much lower priority in the future. The view has been expressed recently in several quarters that talk about structural unemployment is the last refuge of reactionary scoundrels who are against significant action by government. It is exceedingly curious for the recent bedfellows of Henry Ford II, the Chamber of Commerce, the American Bankers Association, and others of like persuasion to be trying even by implication to pin the "reactionary" label on men like Galbraith, Myrdal, Hansen, etc. This attempt at labeling wholly obscures the real policy issue.

Let me pose the issue in terms of a choice which was not hypothetical six months ago. Suppose one group in the Administration is proposing an adult counterpart of the Neighborhood Youth Corps to subsidize useful community employment (and indirectly, rehabilitation) for about 700,000 hard-core unemployed at an annual cost of two billion dollars. Suppose further that the Administration has already proposed a cut in excise taxes realistically expected to amount to about four billion dollars. Suppose finally that the best political judgment is that if the adult jobs program were proposed and passed the excise tax cut would probably be held down to about two billion dollars. In other words, the choice is between two billion in tax cuts plus two billion for the jobs program *versus* four billion for tax cuts and no jobs program. Please note that the choice is NOT between a four billion dollar stimulus to aggregate demand and no stimulus at all; the choice is between exclusive reliance on tax-cutting to stimulate aggregate demand and equal emphasis on tax cutting and a new expenditure program to achieve approximately the same *total* stimulus to aggregate demand. The top economic policy-makers of the Administration continue to insist on *exclusive* reliance on tax-cutting when there is a clear-cut choice of this kind.

This unbalanced approach has repeatedly fallen short of predicted effects on the unemployment problem in the last three years. The current value of the tax cuts of these three years is about $22 billion per year; yet the advocates of this approach continue to prescribe more and bigger tax cuts. I believe that the nature of the unemployment which remains and the large unmet needs in the public sector both show that greater emphasis on the expenditure side of fiscal policy is overdue.

NOTES

1. For the reference to this monograph see footnote 2 in the chapter by Edward Kalachek.

2. See *Economic Report of the President*, January 1964, p. 172.

3. In his discussion (which follows this one) Lester Thurow undertakes to explain away this unquestioned fact. His comments deserve more attention than they can be given in this footnote. Two points are especially noteworthy. First he states that "the poorly educated . . . are concentrated in the older age-sex groups . . . ." The average age of poorly-educated workers is higher than for the whole labor force, but I believe that Mr. Thurow greatly overstates the point. In 1964, about half (more than eight million) of the labor force with eight or fewer years of education were less than 50 years old; only 9.3 per cent were age 65 and over. If the suggestion is that we can safely ignore the employment problems of this group because that are dying off and retiring so "very rapidly," it should be noted it will be an awfully long wait for many millions of them.

Second Mr. Thurow presents some discussion of *average* participation rates for selected parts of certain segments of the labor force. His average participation rates are a good example of unreasonable aggregation and illogical exclusion which obscure the patterns that should receive serious attention. To cite only one example: Participation rates at ages 18 to 24 among the higher educational attainment groups (but *not* among the least-educated) have been greatly reduced over the years by increased rates of school attendance; nevertheless, Mr. Thurow includes these ages in his calculation of "average" participation rates for "the normal working years." On the other hand, he finds that participation rates for the least-educated have dropped very sharply in the 65 and over age group, although the rate was above 50 per cent for male college graduates 65 and over in 1964 and 3,000,000 of the employed workers of the country were in that age bracket; so he defines "the normal working years" to exclude all years after the 64th. Thus, by careful inclusions and exclusions of strategic age groups, Mr. Thurow achieves averages which purport to show that there are only a negligible number of labor-force dropouts among the poorly educated. Furthermore, his discussion implicitly assumes that there have been no labor-force dropouts since 1957 among workers with *more* than eight years of education; an assumption clearly unwarranted with regard to the large classification of high school dropouts. Exclusion of this classification from his comparison group would compel drastic modification of his conclusions.

My discussion was keyed to the group with eight or fewer years of education because of Miss Bancroft's statement that technological change had not eliminated employment opportunities for this group in recent years.

4. As stated in the preceding footnote, the 18-to-24 age group among the higher educational attainment groups is an exception to this generalization.

5. The patterns of participation rates among women appear to be more strongly affected by noneconomic factors than is the case with men. However, the first generalization in the text is broadly applicable to women as well as men. The long-term trend is more sharply upward for the best-educated women, less sharply upward at the middle levels of education, and almost flat among the least-educated. (This generalization is based on changes by specific age group, not changes in the average for all ages at a given level of education.)

6. It should be emphasized that these calculations do not utilize *average* participation rates. They are based on the most detailed figures published for specific age and educational attainment classifications. For example, the reported 1964 participation rate for males 25 to 34 with eight years of school was 95.4 per cent; the 1957 rate for this group was 98.7 per cent; application of the latter rate to the 1964 civilian noninstitutional population reported for this group yields the 1964 hypothetical labor force. The figures in the text are the sum of the differences between hypothetical and actual labor force in each age and education classification.

Discussion

BY LESTER C. THUROW

Both papers (Chapters 5 and 6) at this session seem to be moving toward the position that the structure of unemployment is changing over time but that this is due to alterations in supply and not demand. The papers' investigations of occupational and industrial employment and unemployment reveal that the dispersion of unemployment rates is much less now than it has been in the recent past and that employment opportunities for the least skilled have been growing at rapid rates. On the supply side, however, the influx of women and especially younger workers has altered the supplies of labor that need to be absorbed. Both women and teenagers have been obtaining more than a proportionate share of the economy's employment gains, but these gains have not been large enough to make a big impact on their unemployment rates. Thus the economy has been adjusting to changes in the supplies of labor but not fast enough to eliminate a deterioration in the unemployment rates of women and young workers.

Teenage Unemployment

I am inclined to be less pessimistic about teenage unemployment than Gertrude Bancroft. Teenage unemployment rates are certainly too high but they need to be put in the proper context and this context is not a comparison with the married men's unemployment rate of 2.5 per cent. In 1956 the national unemployment rate was 4.2 per cent and the teenage labor force had not entered a period of rapid growth, yet the unemployment rate for teenagers was 11.7 per cent. (This rate would be even higher if it were adjusted to the post-1957 definition of unemployment.) In the whole postwar period the lowest teenage unemployment rate was 7.1 per cent in 1953. The teenage unemployment rate is currently slightly less than three percentage points higher than in 1956 despite a higher national unemployment rate and a very rapidly growing labor force. This does not deny that three percentage points represents 200,000 teenage workers and that Negro teenagers account for a disproportionate part of this increase.

Teenagers are not unemployable. During the four years from May 1961 to May 1965 the American economy generated over one million new teenage jobs. (In the 13 years from 1948 to 1961 the economy only generated 324,000 new teenage jobs while the teenage labor force grew by 823,000.) An ability to generate one million teenage jobs indicates that the pattern of demand for teenagers has not changed unfavorably and that most teenagers are eminently employable, but it also indicates the size of the problem. Over the same period the unemployment rate for teenagers only dropped from 14.8 to 14.5 per cent.

During the postwar period teenagers have improved their position in the job market vis-a-vis adult workers. Using the Knowles-Kalachek definition of structural change, the percentage gain in teenage employment can be made a function of the percentage gain in total employment plus a trend term. If the trend term is positive, teenagers have improved their employment position. If the trend term is negative, the teenage employment picture is deteriorating relative to the adult population. When a regression is actually run for the years 1949–1964 a very strong positive trend term appears:

$$E_t^{14-19} = -4.16 \quad + \quad 1.95 \, E_t \quad + \quad .34 \, T_t$$
$$(1.11) \qquad\qquad (.34) \qquad\qquad (.11)$$
$$\bar{R}^2 = .73 \qquad \text{D.W.} = 1.73$$

where E^{14-19} = percentage increase in teenage employment
  E = percentage increase in total employment
  T = trend term

Over time teenagers have been increasing their employment position relative to the rest of the labor force. The other coefficients of the regression confirm our knowledge of the teenage labor market. Teenagers suffer very severely from recessions and benefit greatly from growth. If total employment were constant teenage employment would fall by 4 per cent, but at the same time the elasticity of teenage employment with respect to total employment is almost 2 per cent. Thus on the margin a 1 per cent increase in total employment leads to a 2 per cent increase in teenage employment.

We are in the midst of a sharp but short-run increase in the teenage labor force. In 1965 and 1966 the teenage labor force is expected to grow by about 500,000 per year, but in the four years from 1966 to 1970 it is expected to grow, on the average, by only about 60,000 per year.[1] Thus the big supply shifts of 1965 and 1966 are not expected to continue into the future. If the economy continues to generate good employment gains, the chance of reducing teenage unemployment in the near future is excellent.

Miss Bancroft points out the deterioration of the unemployment position of young women aged 14 to 24 relative to young men. This is a product of three factors. First, with large increases in the female labor force among older women there is more competition for jobs traditionally held by women. Even if young women win out in this competition in most cases, it is certain to have a marginal impact. Second, young women are concentrated in occupations not very responsive to marginal increases in aggregate rate of growth, such as clerical work. Young men are more concentrated in occupations which expand rapidly with higher growth rates. Third, the population in the 25 to 34 age group is currently falling. Both young women and men benefit by being able to fill jobs that would customarily be held by people in this age group, but women in the 25 to 34 age group have low participation rates since most are at home with their families. Thus there are fewer extra female jobs available due to low population levels in the 25 to 34 age group.

Why should teenage unemployment rates be so much higher than those for the rest of the labor force? Using the Special Labor Force Reports mentioned by Miss Bancroft,[2] it is possible to estimate roughly the quantitative impact of the causes of higher teenage unemployment.

Three factors explain high teenage unemployment rates. (1) Many teenagers are looking for their first jobs. (2) Many shift jobs voluntarily to improve their present status and future prospects. (3) Teenagers are more likely to lose jobs. Both finding the first job and shifting jobs, voluntarily or involuntarily, take time.

Because a major fraction of the teenage labor force is looking for its first job during any one year, the process of finding this job makes a major addition to the unemployment rates of teenagers even if they do not have to search for a long time. In April 1965 half of teenage unemployment was attributable to individuals looking for first jobs.

ANALYSIS OF UNEMPLOYMENT, APRIL 1965
(Not seasonally adjusted)

Causes of Unemployment	All Ages	Teenagers
	(percentage points)	
Looking for first job	0.8	7.7
Voluntarily and involuntarily left job	4.0	7.5
Rate of unemployment from all causes	4.8	15.2

Even after this adjustment unemployment among individuals who have found their first jobs is almost twice as high as the national percentage (7.5 percentage points versus 4.0 percentage points).

Part of the higher unemployment rate for experienced teenagers can be explained by their occupational distribution. They are slightly more concentrated in occupations with high unemployment rates, but the difference is not great; most of the difference is attributable to higher mobility.

The BLS study reveals that the percentage of the work force changing jobs was twice as high for younger workers as for the entire labor force in 1961 (10 per cent for all workers versus 21.5 per cent for those 18 to 24 years of age). This information for 1961 and similar information for 1955 revealed that younger workers were twice as likely as all workers to lose jobs and twice as apt to change jobs voluntarily to improve status. Since the time lost between jobs for young people was not very different from the time lost for the population generally, job mobility was the major factor leading to high unemployment among young workers who had succeeded in obtaining their first jobs.

In 1961 the percentage who lost jobs involuntarily and the

percentage who changed jobs voluntarily were approximately equal for young workers. (For males 18 to 24, 14 workers per 100 changed jobs to improve status and 13 workers per 100 lost jobs.) In a more prosperous year such as 1955 the proportion who lost jobs was smaller, but the percentage who left jobs voluntarily was considerably higher, so the over-all proportion of job changers was higher than in 1961. (In 1955 19 males per 100 left jobs voluntarily and 11 males per 100 lost jobs.) Thus in both recessions and prosperity, job mobility adds substantially to teenage unemployment. In prosperity the drive to obtain better jobs accounts for much unemployment, but in recessions many teenagers are laid off against their wishes. The character of unemployment changes even if the level does not fall dramatically to the same rate as for married men.

Increasing teenage employment opportunities would reduce the time necessary to find first jobs and the time necessary to change jobs. However, a major fraction of teenage unemployment represents the efforts of individuals to improve status by changing jobs and also represents a major fraction of the mobility of our entire labor force.

Edward Kalachek has correctly pointed out that the path as well as the level of unemployment is relevant to the structure of labor supplies. In addition to its effect on the demographic composition of labor supplies, the path of unemployment affects the supplies of labor by industry and occupation. This can be seen most clearly in durable goods employment and unemployment. During recessions workers laid off in durable goods manufacturing sometimes find jobs in other industries. During expansions some of these workers return, since durable goods is a high wage sector, but the proportion who return has in recent years been much smaller than the proportion who left. From the first quarter of 1957 to the third quarter of 1958 (just six quarters), the durable goods labor force fell by almost 900,000 workers. Unemployment of durable goods workers actually rose from 3.9 to 11.6 per cent but it would have reached 18.9 per cent if the labor force attached to the industry had not fallen. After the 1958 recession the durable goods labor force rose slightly, lost these gains in the 1960–1961 recession, and did not recover to the level of the first quarter of 1957 until 1963. In the interim the total labor force had risen by five and one-quarter million. When durable goods employment started to grow rapidly in late 1963, unemployment dropped very rapidly. Many workers had left the industry and the industry had not needed to train any new workers in the intervening six years. At the present time, durable goods unemployment is 3.5 per cent, below the 4.0 per cent rate of 1956. In part this low rate of unemployment is explained by the path of the economy in the intervening period. Rectification of this change will depend partly on the willingness of companies and unions to institute training programs which will expand the durable goods labor force.

The Poorly Educated

Finally I would like to comment on Charles Killingsworth's view that employment opportunities for poorly educated workers are disappearing and that these workers are being squeezed out of the labor force.[3] Although falling unemployment rates for older workers create a certain presumption that this is not true, the number of employed workers with eight or less years of education did fall by 4.1 million from March 1957 to March 1964 and the participation rate for this group did fall from 54.0 to 48.9 per cent.

Most of the decline in employment and participation rates can be traced to the age structure of the poorly educated. They are concentrated in the older age-sex groups and their numbers are falling very rapidly. From 1957 to 1964 the population with eight or less years of education fell by 4.1 million but the decline among individuals in the normal working years, 18 to 64, was an even sharper 5.5 million.

While the average participation rate for this poorly educated group declined, the rate for those between 18 and 64 years of age was essentially constant, falling from 64.7 to 64.5 per cent. The male participation rate fell by 3.1 percentage points, but the female rate rose by 3.2 percentage points.

In 1964, the average participation rate for men with eight or less years of education was 18.8 percentage points lower than for men with more than eight years of schooling (69.9 versus 88.7 per cent), but most of this difference is attributable to the number of poorly educated workers who have reached retirement age. The participation rate for male workers aged 18 to 64 with eight or less years of education was only 2.9 percentage points lower than the participation rate of the same age group with more than eight years of education (89.3 versus 92.2 per cent). Thus in the normal working years there is very little difference in the participation rates of male workers by education. Between 1957 and 1964 the gap between the participation rates for these two groups widened slightly by 1.1 percentage points. Even if all of this decline represented involuntary changes, only 137,000 males would be involved.

Over the same time period the female participation rate for those aged 18 to 64 with eight or less years of education rose by 3.2 percentage points. This is not as large an increase as the 4.6 percentage-point rise for females with more than eight years of education, but the increase certainly indicates that poorly educated women have not been squeezed out of the labor force.

The population of individuals 65 and over with eight or less years of education rose by 1.3 million from 1959 to 1964. The participation rate for this group has fallen faster than for the aged with more than eight years of education. To the extent this reflects voluntary retirement, it does not represent an employment problem. To the extent it reflects involuntary retirement, the economy is not generating enough jobs for those who are both old and poorly educated. I confess to not knowing how to estimate the magnitude of these two elements.

NOTES

1. Editors' note: this pronounced drop in the expected *increase* in the teenage labor force is largely explained by the leveling off in the size of the population of this age group which will occur when it is composed entirely of cohorts born from about 1948 to 1953, when the birth rate was fluctuating somewhat below the peak reached in 1947.

2. Special Labor Force Reports, Nos. 35 and 46 (Washington, D. C.: U. S. Bureau of Labor Statistics, 1963 and 1964.)

3. All of the data in this section come from Special Labor Force Reports, Nos. 1 and 53 (Washington, D. C.: U. S. Bureau of Labor Statistics, 1960 and 1965.)

PART **V**

UNEMPLOYMENT AND THE

STRUCTURE OF WAGES

CHAPTER 7

Wage Levels and Differentials

BY GEORGE H. HILDEBRAND

AND GEORGE E. DELEHANTY

Introduction

The purpose of this chapter is to examine the relationship between the structure of wages and the structure of unemployment in the United States in recent years. It should be viewed as a first report of a larger investigation.

The theoretical underpinnings for the inquiry are these. The labor force is composed of different types of labor as regards skill, general vocational preparation (literacy and primary mathematics), work experience, and personal capacity (physical strength and level of intelligence). We are dealing with a continuum of several dimensions, all of which affect worker productivity. Suppose for convenience we partition these groups into three admittedly oversimplified classes: skilled, semiskilled, and unskilled. To some extent they are substitutes for one another, especially at the lower end of the spectrum. In addition, those at the lower end in general are more vulnerable to replacement by machinery.

It seems appropriate to test the classical hypothesis that if competition is fully effective the relative prices (wages) for the services of these groups and changes in these prices should reflect their comparative scarcities, in particular longer-run changes in conditions of relative supply. This question has particular importance for the present day, when the unemployment problems of youngsters and the unskilled generally are a central issue for public policy.

In relation to more recent studies, this investigation is an extension of the Phillips-Lipsey empirical approach to over-all wage behavior. If aggregate movements of the wage level are functionally associated with aggregate unemployment rates, should not unemployment rates for occupational segments of the labor force reflect themselves in diversity of wage movements? If this expectation is not borne out by the evidence, perhaps alternative explanations of the wage-making process, particularly as it affects relative wages, are in order.

An additional rationale for this study is that relatively little work has been done on movements in the occupational wage structure in recent years.[1] More than this, most of the work in this field has concentrated upon high-wage, highly unionized industries, principally in manufacturing. This is partly because the data are more readily available here. These sectors should be examined, for they are relevant to the larger problem of wage structure, but it is equally important that some effort be made to assemble data for other industries and occupations as well.

Wages and Unemployment Among the Unskilled

In the debate over the reasons for high rates of general unemployment since 1957, little attention has been paid to wages. Some exponents of the demand deficiency explanation have cited the danger of a general wage push as a factor restraining an all-out policy of demand expansion, but their reasoning is conducted in highly aggregative terms and this seems to have foreclosed interest in the microeconomic problems of relative wages.[2]

As for those who make primary appeal to structural factors, it is rare to find any recognition of the role of wages at all, either as a wage level or as a set of relative prices.[3]

We are in accord with the general view that the over-all problem of unemployment is mainly one of deficient aggregate demand. However, if one looks at the composition of unemployment over the past fifteen years it at once becomes apparent that certain groups have been much more vulnerable than others. These are the teenagers, the unskilled and inexperienced, the poorly educated, and the non-whites, and to some extent these strata are interpenetrating. Let us grant that even for these categories cyclical movements have much importance, and to this extent part of their unemployment is demand-induced and susceptible to reduction by demand expansion. However, these segments of the labor force have been far more exposed to unemployment than others since 1950. Relative to the over-all rate their segmental rates have been much higher while their shares of total unemployment have been large.[4]

Since detailed evidence about the structural characteristics of unemployment has been presented in other chapters in this volume and elsewhere, our comments will be brief. In the postwar years, in good times and bad, workers without previous job experience, much vocational preparation, or much skill have been much more exposed to unemployment than other groups, and have accounted for a significant part of total unemployment. During 1963–1964, the position of the teenagers sharply deteriorated, although their previous experience was already poor. Granting that the figures for this group are inflated at all times by much voluntary turnover does not explain away its prominent place in the structural problem. Attention should be called to another facet of that problem—the experience of the occupational group known as laborers (except farm and mine). Like the teenagers, this category has consistently experienced unemployment rates of more than double the over-all rate while contributing more than 10 per cent of the total unemployed throughout the postwar period. However, during 1963–1964 its relative rate and relative share declined perceptibly, although they still remained unfavorably high.

The teenagers and laborers illustrate a problem that shows

up when the same measures are applied to nonwhites or the poorly educated. Over the postwar years there has been a persistent lack of "vestibule jobs" (Reder); that is, enough points of entry from the external market into the internal job structures of the firms in the economy. As a result the relative rates and shares of unemployment borne by these exposed groups have stayed too high, even during cyclical advances. We take this to be evidence that inexperienced and unskilled workers consistently have been in relatively greater excess supply.[5] It becomes pertinent to ask whether relative occupational rates have responded appropriately. Have they widened to bring about equilibrium, or not?

Abstracting from the business cycle, the theory of the matter is a relatively simple problem in microeconomics. We start from the assumption that the elasticity of demand for the services of unskilled labor, as with any type, is greater than zero and less than infinity with respect to the wage, and its sign is negative. We assume further that the order of magnitude for this elasticity is greater for the long period than the short, for the usual reasons.

Looking at the demand side, if employers try to maximize profits, then given relative wage rates, and for the short period, their production functions, they will select a combination of labor inputs that will yield the following relationship:

$$\frac{W_u}{MP_u} = \frac{W_{ss}}{MP_{ss}} = \frac{W_s}{MP_s},$$

where W is wage rate, MP is marginal product, u is unskilled, ss is semiskilled, and s is skilled labor. If unskilled labor becomes excessive in supply at existing wage rates, say for demographic reasons or because of an influx of immigrants, competition would reduce its price. This involves an inequality of the ratios to which the appropriate short-run response is to use more unskilled labor until its marginal product falls sufficiently to restore equality. However, it is the long-run process that matters most. Suppose supply conditions are such that employers have good reason to expect unskilled wages to remain depressed for some time. This would give them incentive to adapt their production functions fully, substituting unskilled labor in the semiskilled ranks and perhaps even higher, and also for certain kinds of equipment. At the same time, competition would enforce some substitution at the goods level, in favor of products requiring high proportions of unskilled labor.

What is this process likely to mean for relative occupational differentials over the long run, when unskilled wages are depressed absolutely for the period? On the factor and goods sides the initial consequence is to create excess supplies of labor, at given wage rates, for workers in the semiskilled and skilled ranks. But here a certain asymmetry enters between the unskilled and the rest. First, the technical elasticity of substitution is higher between common labor and machines than between more skilled labor and machines. At the highly skilled levels, for example maintenance workers, the relationship may be complementary. In consequence, a relative decline of unskilled wages may be diverted to some extent in its effects to substitution against capital instead of against the services of the groups above that level, thus checking somewhat the creation of excess labor supplies at these levels.[6] Second, these excess supplies, likely to be greatest in the lower skill brackets, can be absorbed by nonprice adjustments, even in an otherwise fully competitive economy. If surpluses develop within the internal market of the plant or firm and involve jobs above starting levels, the employer can move workers across job families and down occupational ladders, adjusting the distribution of workers by skill level and reducing labor cost per hour worked without actually cutting job rates. Here too the effect is to curtail the downward pressure against skill rates.

For the conditions stated, then, we would expect competition to widen relative occupational differentials, and in so doing clear the markets for all grades of labor if over-all demand conditions remained steady. If, instead, unskilled labor was to decrease in relative supply over a long period, say because of rising levels of education or closure of immigration, the whole process would operate in reverse and we would expect relative differentials to narrow.[7]

However, it is our view that unskilled labor has been in relative surplus for some years, notwithstanding the general finding of numerous studies that it has been in secular decline for several decades. The reason for this apparent conflict in interpretation is that we are concerned with the postwar period, not with half a century, and in this period some powerful forces have emerged to create this surplus, although they may eventually reverse themselves.

One of them is the baby boom, which for reasons that in part are still obscure has been conjoined to a drop-out problem of grave importance to our civilization. Another is the poor adaptation of our system of formal education to the changing vocational requirements of our economy. For twenty years we have escaped the full consequences of this deficiency by dependence upon the massive contribution of the armed forces to vocational preparation during World War II. Now we have to turn to new sources, and have failed to develop them in time to deal adequately with the large flow of youngsters into the labor market in recent years and in the years immediately to come.

There is another factor of great significance for the over-all problem: the flight from agriculture, which has involved large families whose members enter the metropolitan labor force badly deficient in basic education and vocational skills. In 1940, agriculture accounted for 20 per cent of the civilian labor force. In 1950 its share dropped to 12 per cent, while today it is less than 7 per cent. This rapid exodus from farming has embraced many poor Negroes from the rural South, probably the most badly educated group in the whole population.

Finally, there is a longer-run influence central to the poverty problem today: the malign effects of imperfections in the section of the capital market that supplies investment in human beings. If we assume that skill potential is normally distributed over the population, some members of the labor force will have subnormal earnings simply because of meager native endowments. But imperfections in the distribution of investment outlays also enter to inflate the low end of the distribution with people who possess intrinsically higher skill potential. One of these barriers is discrimination against the Negro, which appears in formal education of much lower quality and in exclusion from opportunities for apprenticeship. Also, workers in poor families usually cannot afford formal vocational education, and opportunities for on-the-job training and participation in formal company classes have been restricted for some years by soft labor markets.

We conclude that unskilled labor has been in persistent excess supply. Now suppose that relative occupational wage rates are not freely determined by full competition, but instead largely by intervention of non-economic forces. To depict the situation, consider that the manual labor force is distributed among three tiers in the economy, each of which uses some unskilled, some moderately skilled, and some highly skilled workers, although not necessarily in equal proportions. At the top are the highly unionized, high-wage industries—durable-goods manufacturing, mining, construction, and transportation. Below this deck is a second group of industries that are less extensively unionized and generally pay lower average and entry wages, with the latter close to the federal minimum wage or set at a comparable height by state law. At the bottom is a nebulous group of activities mostly exempt from effective unionism or minimum wage statutes. This layer will not only consist of manual employees but will include many small entrepreneurs working on their own accounts. Its ranks will be made up of farm laborers, petty service workers, family labor, small farmers and share-croppers, proprietors of news and bootblack stands, retail store owners, side-of-the-hill coal miners, and so on. In general, the incomes earned in this tier will be very low. Traditionally these activities have served as sponges for absorbing excess labor of all types, particularly the poorly trained or poorly endowed. But this absorptive function may well have atrophied in recent times, with the rapid decline of the agricultural labor force and the small proprietor and with extensions of the federal minimum wage.[8]

In this three-decker structure, entry rates at the top layer will move mainly with union settlements, which tie the unskilled to the rest despite any relative competitive disadvantage and overall conditions of excess supply in their ranks.[9] It is quite normal for the union to settle for flat general increases, although at times craft restiveness may make it necessary to redress differentials. In the middle layer, entry rates will also reflect union influence to some extent, but some of them will be thrust upward by periodic revisions in the federal minimum and by a rather widespread employer acceptance of comparable standards of "fairness." By contrast, the bottom group will embrace those left largely exposed to the harsh winds of competition. These lack organized intervention in their behalf, and their number may be augmented or at least checked from more rapid decline by the advance of entry and skill rates in the upper tiers of the structure, since the advance may lead to expulsions from above, at the same time making it even more difficult for unskilled beginners to force the gates of the high-wage citadel.[10]

Since entry rates in the middle and upper decks of the structure are largely set by union and statutory intervention for purposes divorced from the aim of increasing the employment of unskilled workers, there is no reason to expect them to be adjusted over time in a fashion likely to eliminate the excess supply of unskilled.[11] Indeed, there is every reason to expect that they will preserve or even increase the surplus of these workers. Entry rates accordingly are likely to rise rapidly enough to maintain or narrow relative skill spreads. In turn, employers in the upper decks will find it profitable to decrease their relative use of these workers and to raise their hiring standards to take advantage of persistently soft markets for this group.

The next step is to examine the evidence on relative spreads, first on a sector and industry basis, and then by standard metropolitan statistical areas.

The Behavior of Relative Occupational Wage Spreads

In total manufacturing. A first approximation of the behavior of relative wage spreads can be gained at an aggregative level by examining distributions of straight-time hourly earnings for production workers in manufacturing as a whole, nationally and by regions. This can be done from sample estimates prepared by the BLS for 1954, 1958, and 1964. Summary results appear in Table 1.

On the basis of the measure of dispersion used here, it appears that relative spreads in hourly earnings have widened consistently for the country as a whole and for three of the four regions; whether they have widened enough is another matter. Bear in mind that these figures are derived from global distributions that lump together high-and-low-wage industries and hence embrace

TABLE 1. RELATIVE DISPERSION IN AVERAGE STRAIGHT-TIME
HOURLY EARNINGS OF PRODUCTION WORKERS IN MANUFACTURING[a]

Year	United States	Northeast	South	Midwest	Far West
1954	0.419	0.401	0.584	0.294	0.271
1958	0.485	0.426	0.650	0.350	0.299
1964	0.509	0.480	0.575	0.382	0.367[b]

Source: U. S. Department of Labor, Bureau of Labor Statistics, *Factory Workers' Earnings: Distributions by Straight-Time Hourly Earnings, April 1954*, Bulletin No. 1179 (March 1955), p. 14; *Factory Workers' Earnings, May 1958*, Bulletin No. 1252 (June 1959), p. 20; Wage and Hour and Public Contracts Division, Report Submitted to the Congress in Accordance with the Requirements of Section 4(d) of the Fair Labor Standards Act, January 1965, *Manufacturing Industries*, p. A-129; and (Far West only) *Employee Earnings and Hours in Manufacturing, March 1964*, Preliminary Release (March 1965), p. 4.
[a] The measure of relative dispersion is the ratio of the interquartile range ($Q_3 - Q_1$) to the median.
[b] This figure is for non-supervisory workers. The 1964 distribution for production workers is incomplete. In the United States as a whole and in the other regions, the differences under this measure of dispersion as between production and non-supervisory workers in 1964 were 0.01 or less.

workers in both the upper and middle tiers of the structure. They reflect the influence of two recession years, the entry of new firms and the exit of old ones, redistribution of the labor force southward and westward, and changes in skill-mix and sex-ratios. Note that the South shows the highest dispersion values on all three dates, with a peak in 1958 and a significant narrowing thereafter. It may be conjectured that southern spreads initially were made large by the postwar invasion of high-wage national firms into territory hitherto dominated by small low-wage enterprises and that the continuing industrial development of the region subsequently tightened labor markets there, aided by the rise of the federal minimum wage in manufacturing from $1.00 to $1.15 in 1961 and to $1.25 in 1963. Perhaps there have been intervening extensions of unionism as well.

The High-Wage Sector

Consider, next, relative spreads in the high-wage sector. How have their "port-of-entry" rates moved relative to the federal minimum for manufacturing since 1950? Table 2 supplies a partial answer. If we compare 1950 and 1961, each a year when the federal

TABLE 2. ENTRY RATES IN HIGH-WAGE INDUSTRIES RELATIVE
TO THE FEDERAL MINIMUM WAGE, 1950–1964
(Minimum wage = 100)

Industry	1950	1954	1956	1957	1961	1962	1964
Basic steel[a]	168	209	182	189	183	203	—
Automobiles[b]	181	224	187	199	203	210	204
Bituminous coal[c]	229	299	265	275	260	260	250
Railroad shops[d]	165	204	177	184	186	195	—
Building construction[e]	207	261	220	237	259	—	263
Local transit[f]	160	193	—	155	161	165	160
Motor trucking[f]	107	147	120	140	152	152	148
Printing[f]	120	173	130	140	157	—	—
Minimum wage ($)	0.75	0.75	1.00	1.00	1.15	1.15	1.25

Source: U. S. Department of Labor, Bureau of Labor Statistics: (basic steel), Report No. 186; (automobiles), Report No. 198; (bituminous coal), *Bituminous Coal Mines, 1933–*, *Monthly Labor Review*, various issues, and Bureau of National Affairs, Collective Bargaining Negotiations and Contracts (March 27, 1964); (railroad shops), *Monthly Labor Review*, LXXXIV (September 1961), 977–978, and LXXXVI (April 1963), 410; (building construction), Bulletin Nos. 1011, 1051, 1124, 1175, 1192, 1205, 1227, 1245, 1269, 1290, 1316, 1397, 1432; (local transit), Bulletin Nos. 1019, 1177, 1229, 1313, 1354, 1431; (motor trucking), Bulletin Nos. 1012, 1178, 1206, 1230, 1314, 1356, 1433; (printing), Bulletin Nos. 1018, 1176, 1207, 1228, 1315, 1399.

[a] Minimum plant rate, northern district, U.S. Steel Corp.
[b] Hiring rate, Chrysler Corp.
[c] Inside helper rate, Appalachian region.
[d] Regular apprentice, first period.
[e] Average national base rate, building laborers.
[f] Lowest ½ per cent of national frequency distribution, all trades.

minimum for manufacturing was increased, it turns out that in all industries, except local transit, starting rates increased their relative advantage over the statutory minimum, in some cases sharply. In 1950 these rates ranged from 7 per cent (helpers in motor trucking) to 129 per cent (helpers in bituminous coal) over the minimum. If we construct a simple average of the eight entry rates for 1950 and 1961, we can compare the over-all movement of the high-wage group relative to the minimum. For 1950, the average stood at $1.26 per hour, as against $2.24 in 1961, an increase of $0.98 or 77.7 per cent. In the same period, the federal minimum rose from $0.75 to $1.15, or by $0.40 and 53.3 per cent. On the base date, the average high-wage entry rate had a 68 per cent advantage over the minimum. By 1961 this had grown to 95 per cent.

On the evidence from this initial sample of high-wage industries, employers in this sector were paying a substantial premium in their starting rates in 1950, and this margin has been growing both absolutely and relatively, although excess supplies of unskilled labor have been prominent throughout the period.[12] But one may ask: what is the relevance of the federal minimum as a benchmark for comparison with these entry rates? The answer cannot be that the minimum wage is a competitive market-clearing wage, because throughout the period surplus labor has been available consistently and there are uncovered occupations paying even less. The real reason is that the federal minimum has been designated by an act of legislative judgment to be the standard of "fairness" that fixes the lowest "just price" at which unskilled labor should be hired. To the extent that this grade of labor is homogeneous in efficiency, that disutilities are similar for jobs filled by these workers, and that such labor is mobile, we would expect competition to establish an approximate uniformity of rates around this minimum, regardless of whether in the sense of an over-all weighted average the industry pays high or low wages.[13]

The comparison shows that entry rates in this high-wage group started with a 68 per cent average spread in 1950 which by 1961 had widened to 95 per cent.[14] One possible explanation for the large size and subsequent widening of this margin is that both were needed to overcome greater disutilities for starting jobs in the high-wage industries, to obtain an adequate intake of new labor. However, this seems implausible: disutilities are likely to be greater in low-wage firms and probably have been declining all around because of increasing emphasis upon outlays for this purpose. Another possibility, suggested by Melvin Reder, is that the high-wage group cited here hires white males primarily, which would make its entrants somewhat noncompetitive with the rest of the unskilled workers. Perhaps some weight should be accorded this factor, but not much. White males have always constituted the biggest portion of the unskilled group, and their number could hardly have become relatively scarcer while the group as a whole was growing in surplus.

A more plausible explanation, also proposed by Reder, is that this widening spread represents the premium high-wage employers willingly pay to gain greater selectivity among candidates for jobs.[15] What they seek is not possession of skills as such but the capacity to acquire skills after entry and the ability to provide steady work habits. They prefer high school graduates for these reasons. This is a consideration of some importance, but it is unconvincing as a full explanation. Traditionally, many of these industries did not require high-school certificates from entering labor, and it is doubtful that their job specifications even today have risen this much. More than this, it hardly seems likely that high school graduates have been becoming relatively scarcer for high-wage firms, particularly in the last few years. Finally, and most important, the actual order of causation may be the reverse: because employers must pay a high premium for entering labor, they have a surplus of candidates at all times, all the more so because total blue-collar employment in the group has been virtually stagnant until very recently. Given the premium, it pays to impose higher requirements as a rationing device and as a means of combatting high labor costs by upgrading the efficiency of entering workers.

If this widening spread is to be fully explained, we must recognize effective unionism as a force of substantial independent importance. This is not to say unionism is the primary reason why this sample of industries pays high wages. Factors such as high capital investment per man, product-market concentration, rapid technical advance, favorable demand shift, and quality of management must all be considered, and in some cases may be sufficient. But granting all this, unionism still contributes something of its own, functioning in a setting where wages are already high for diverse reasons. It probably requires less power for unions to bend the wage structure of a high-wage firm in favor of the lower job brackets than it does to force all job rates higher, although their ability in the latter domain is not to be entirely discounted. If the union is of the industrial type, it has a natural interest in wage relationships across the board and an orientation toward the less skilled majority. This will tie starting rates more closely to the rest of the internal rate structure regardless of external conditions of supply, whether the union seeks flat-rate or flat-percentage general increases or even mixed increases.[16] If the firm has multiple craft unionism instead, this is likely to lead to patterns of general increases that link unskilled rates to movements in those for journeymen.

From the organizational standpoint four of the high-wage industries in Table 2 bargain for national contracts, three on an industrial-union basis, and one (railroad shops) by multiple crafts. In all of them starting rates have long been tied to the rest of the job structure by a policy of general increases, frequently in the form of flat-rate advances (coal, automobiles, railroads). In the remaining four, two usually involve a single craft group (motor trucking and local transit) where the job structure itself is highly compressed for technical reasons and entry rates are tied closely to advances for the rest.[17] In effect, then, entry ing, multiple craft unionism prevails. Patterns of increases are the rule in construction, and this pulls up the laborers along with the journeymen. In printing, too, increases for low-wage occupations such as bindery women, mailers, and apprentices are tied closely to advances for the rest.[17] In effect, then, entry rates are linked through unionism to the over-all movements internal to these industries and have been consistently quite insensitive to external conditions of excess supply. If this turns out to be the general case in the high-wage sector, the influence of collective bargaining in pushing up starting rates may turn out to be a much more important factor than the federal minimum wage in generating unemployment among the unskilled and in making low wages even lower.

The next step is to examine the behavior of internal relative wage spreads in the high-wage industries. In Table 3 this is done along lines originally suggested by Clarence Long which involve comparison of the effective minimum to the average rate in the segment. In some cases *faute de mieux*, average straight-time

TABLE 3. MOVEMENTS IN RATIO OF AVERAGE WAGE TO EFFECTIVE
MINIMUM RATE, HIGH-WAGE GROUPS, 1950–1964
(Effective minimum = 100)

Category	1950	1957	1961	1963–1964	Direction[a] 1950–1961	1957–1964
Manufacturing						
Durable goods[b]	195	212	210	209	W	N
Basic steel[c]	135	143	150	142	W	C
Automobiles[c]	131	124	122	126	N	C
Printing[d]	252	209	185	185	N	N
Nonmanufacturing						
Bituminous coal[e]	109	105	105	105	N	C
Railroad shops[f]	138	125	122	121	N	N
Building construction[g]	158	143	135	136	N	N
Local transit[h]	125	134	133	138	W	W
Motor trucking[h]	200	166	159	170	N	W

Source: For durable goods, *Economic Report of the President*, (January 1965), p. 225; all others are from sources cited for Table 2.

[a] W denotes widening, N, narrowing, C, constant relative spread.

[b] Average straight-time hourly earnings, relative to federal minimum.

[c] Average gross hourly earnings; straight-time earnings not available.

[d] Weighted average rate, all trades, relative to lowest ½ per cent of distribution.

[e] Simple average of base rates, all occupations except pumpers and helpers.

[f] Simple average of craft rates including helpers, relative to apprentice, first period.

[g] Weighted average for journeymen, relative to that for building laborers.

[h] Average national rate (drivers, motor trucking; union rates, printing crafts) relative to national rate for lowest ½ per cent of distribution.

or gross hourly earnings had to be used, whereas in others averages of base rates excluding the bottom occupation could be computed.

Taking the more inclusive durable-goods group first, in which weight-shifts complicate matters somewhat, we note that some widening of relative spread did occur between 1950 and 1961, but in the later period of 1957–1964 moderate narrowing prevailed. For 1950 and 1961 only two segments experienced any widening—basic steel and local transit—while all of the others experienced narrowing spreads. For 1957 versus 1963–1964, local transit and motor trucking had small amounts of widening, and all the others either had narrowing or constant relative spreads.[18] If excess supplies of unskilled labor grew worse after 1957, it follows that pressure for widening increased in this period. In all but two cases widening did not occur, whereas in the two exceptions it amounted to no more than 1.8 per cent of the base year relative spread in local transit and 2.9 per cent in trucking. On this set of measures, Long's expectations about the behavior of relative spreads generally stand up.

Since several of these comparisons turn upon pure basic hourly rates, it may be asked if inclusion of fringe benefits would make any difference to the observed behavior of relative spreads. Adequate evidence is lacking to permit a test of this question in the present context, but a study for certain plants of General Motors by Robert M. Macdonald shows that inclusion of fringe benefits leads to additional narrowing of about 0.9 per cent.[19] A priori, it seems that fringe costs will probably preserve relative spreads or narrow them slightly. First, supplements based upon a uniform percentage mark-up of the job rate, for example overtime premiums, maintain existing spreads provided overtime is equally distributed among all classifications. Second, benefits that involve a flat-rate mark-up per hour, such as shift premiums, SUB plans, or group insurance based upon a uniform flat charge per man-hour, will compress relative spreads. Third, payroll taxes for OASDI and UC also produce narrowing in high-wage industries, because these forms of social insurance involve a percentage tax up to a comparatively low taxable maximum, making the percentage incidence higher for low-bracket jobs. Fourth, fringes involving flat sums tied to the base rate—paid vacations, holidays, and sick leave—preserve relative spreads. Finally, where seniority controls most promotions, fringe costs will be higher for the higher-wage jobs because vacations are usually tied to length of service, and implicit medical and pension costs are larger in these brackets, and both factors will widen relative spreads. But since the widening components normally are a small part of total supplemental wage costs, it seems safe to conclude that fringe benefits at most leave relative spreads unaltered, and may even narrow them.

We can examine the behavior of relative spreads in greater detail for some segments of the high-wage group. First consider the automobile industry, using the janitor rate as the effective minimum (=100). The main semi-skilled job—assembler, line and bench—has undergone a fall in margin from 117 in 1950 to 110 in 1957 and to 109 in 1963. By comparison, electricians and tool and die makers kept their margins about constant at 135 and 144, respectively, while patternmakers widened theirs.[20] In this industry, narrowing occurred before 1957 and has primarily involved the semi-skilled groups.

Turning to basic steel, we encounter a much broader and far more diverse job structure than in automobiles. Table 4 indicates the changing positions of certain key jobs relative to that of sweeper, which is at the bottom of the CWS evaluation system. Considering the highly rated jobs, sharp narrowing is evident for both classifications of heater and for roller and rougher while marked widening occurred for charging machine operator and first helper. Among the medium rated jobs, narrowing took place for the cut-off machine operator and hydrostatic tester while the machinist, pipefitter, and bander held constant, and the stock unloader widened. Taken as a whole, some relative compression occurred in this industry.

In bituminous coal mining and railroad back shops an interesting parallelism of behavior is manifest despite sharply contrasting forms of unionism—a single industrial union in coal and multiple crafts on the railroads. Yet in both industries relative compression has been continuing without reversal from 1937 through 1962 (railroads) and 1964 (coal). The reason lies in the regular recurrence of flat general increases. In railroading, the main crafts have long had identical basic hourly rates against which

TABLE 4. RELATIVE WAGE SPREADS, SELECTED OCCUPATIONS IN
BASIC STEEL, 1951 AND 1962[a]
(Sweeper = 100)

Occupation	1951	1962
Highly rated jobs:		
Heater, blooming and slabbing mills	216	200
Heater, continuous hot strip mills	249	222
Roller	251	237
Rougher	229	206
Charging machine operator	172	188
First helper	206	226
Medium rated jobs:		
Cut-off machine operator	147	133
Hydrostatic tester	143	135
Bander	136	138
Stock unloader	113	121
Machinist A	154	152
Pipefitter	143	141

Source: U. S. Department of Labor, Bureau of Labor Statistics, *Wage
Structure, Basic Iron and Steel*, series 2, No. 81 (January 1951), pp. 9–12;
Industry Wage Survey, Basic Iron and Steel, Bulletin No. 1358 (January
1963), pp. 10–15.
[a] Figures based upon average straight-time hourly earnings. All jobs
ranked by CWS evaluation system. Prior to August 3, 1956 the bottom
jobs were in class 0-1; since this date, the bottom jobs have been in
class 2, and class 0-1 was dropped. The spreads for the highly rated jobs
may be somewhat affected by variations in incentive earnings in these
two years, which are the only ones available.

the rate for regular apprentices has been steadily moving upward
relative to these jobs. In coal mining, the inside jobs have been
grouped in four classes (five since 1959) with very small absolute spreads among them from the start and with the helper rate
advancing relative to the others; by 1964 the maximum relative
spread above this category had fallen to only 10.9 per cent as
compared to 17 per cent in 1951.[21]

The last high-wage industry for which we have been able to
examine changes in internal relative spreads is building construc-

tion, in which multiple-craft bargaining prevails on a local level. Table 5 presents the over-all national behavior of journeymen-appropriate helper rates for three major crafts. Clearly, considerable relative compression has occurred in all three, although much less so for plumbers.

Because building negotiations are conducted on a local area basis, it is pertinent to look into the behavior of relative spreads for 20 large cities for which aggregate data for manufacturing and nonmanufacturing are presented below. In building, comparison was made between three traditional skilled crafts and building laborers, and between equipment operators (light and heavy) and laborers, all on the basis of union hourly rates for 1950, 1957, and 1964. For bricklayers, relative spreads narrowed consistently in 18 cities, widened after 1957 in one, and held constant after 1957 in the other. For plasterers, relative compression occurred in 19 cities while in one it was followed by constancy after 1957. The plumbers' case differs somewhat: consistent narrowing in 10 cities, narrowing followed by widening in four, initial narrowing followed by constancy in three, and mixed behavior in the remaining three. In the equipment jobs, mostly controlled by the Operating Engineers and largely a postwar development, there is no clear-cut pattern. Thus in the traditional crafts narrowing has predominated after 1950 in all regions and in settings varying in degree of unemployment, whereas in the newer occupations, which mainly displaced un-

TABLE 5. Relative Spreads Between Journeymen and Their
Helpers, National Level, Union Rates in Building
Construction, 1950, 1957, and 1964[a]
(Appropriate helper = 100)

Occupation	1950	1957	1964
Bricklayer	153	144	131
Plasterer	151	134	122
Plumber	149	141	137

Source: See "building construction" in source note to Table 2.
[a] Based upon a weighted average of union rates for country as a whole.

skilled types of work, neither compression nor widening seems to predominate. We suspect that the laborers, most vulnerable to capital substitution, have nonetheless been able to follow a consistent policy of rapid wage advances, made possible by mutual respect for picket lines by the other crafts, by the apparently limited sensitivity of these crafts to relative compression so long as they too can gain large increases, and by the indifference of the laborers to the adverse employment effects of their wage policy.

In Metropolitan Areas

This completes the review of the high-wage industries. We turn now to an examination of some relative skill spreads within metropolitan areas. The Occupational Earnings surveys of the Bureau of Labor Statistics are the principal sources of data. Their use involves some difficulties, but they still provide a good means of comparing wage rate changes in different geographical markets by industry.[22]

The first question to explore is whether the skill differential measured by area has tended to change over the period, including the years unemployment rates remained high. Table 6 presents the data on relative increases in average straight-time hourly earnings for skilled maintenance trades, unskilled plant workers, and office workers for 22 metropolitan areas for various intervals in 1952–1964. The ratio of the index of skilled rates to unskilled rates is then presented as the measure of narrowing or widening of the differential over the period.

Examination of Column 3 in the table shows that the differential between the skilled and unskilled group appears to have widened in five areas: Boston, Chicago, Cleveland, Los Angeles-Long Beach, and Kansas City. The spread has not been great; the index values for Boston and Chicago are highest—106 and 104, respectively.

In all other areas the differential appears to have declined or remained constant as measured by the index. The index fell to 91 in Newark-Jersey City and Baltimore and to 93 in Houston. In the remaining areas the value was within four points of 100; for five areas the level stood at 99.

TABLE 6. INDEXES OF AVERAGE STRAIGHT-TIME HOURLY EARNINGS
IN MANUFACTURING FOR SKILLED MAINTENANCE TRADES, UNSKILLED
PLANT WORKERS, AND OFFICE WORKERS, VARIOUS METROPOLITAN
AREAS AND PERIODS, 1952-1964[a]
(Beginning year of period = 100)

Period and Area	Index of Skilled Earnings	Index of Unskilled Earnings	Index of Differential[b] (1) ÷ (2)	Index of Office Earnings	Index of Office Differential[b] (4) ÷ (2)
	(1)	(2)	(3)	(4)	(5)
1952-1964					
Atlanta	163	169	96	163	96
Boston	160	152	106	159	105
Buffalo	161	167	96	163	97
Chicago	164	157	104	159	101
Cleveland	167	165	101	166	101
Los Angeles-Long Beach	165	162	102	170	104
Milwaukee	169	170	99	166	97
Minneapolis-St. Paul	170	171	99	160	94
Newark-Jersey City	162	177	91	162	92
New York City	165	166	100	164	99
Philadelphia	163	171	96	163	95
St. Louis	164	165	99	168	102
San Francisco-Oakland	168	172	97	161	93
1953-1964					
Baltimore	164	180	91	159	91
Dallas	151	154	98	151	93
Kansas City	161	157	102	154	99
1960-1964					
Cincinnati	114	118	96	112	95
Detroit	113	113.5	99	112	99
Houston	108	117	93	111	96
Paterson-Clifton-Passaic	114	115	99	114	99
Pittsburgh	107	112	96	112	99
Seattle	112	117	96	115	99

Source: Computed directly from Tables 3, 4 and 5 of Bureau of Labor Statistics Bulletin
1427, *Wage Indexes; Long-Term Trend Data for Selected Occupations and Metropolitan Areas,*
Washington, D. C., January 1965.
[a]Figures for office workers are based on straight-time weekly earnings.
[b]Calculated from unrounded indexes.

Conclusions must be guarded, given the nature of the data
and the small ranges involved. Like all such measures these indexes are subject to bias because of conditions in the terminal
years. In the original data it was possible to check the direction
of movements for the periods 1952-1961 and 1961-1964.

Although there are exceptions, it appears no great violence is done by the short-cut methods used here.

Percentage wage increases for skilled and unskilled groups can be compared for 50 areas for the four-year period preceding the latest occupational wage surveys carried out from June 1964 to April 1965. This group includes smaller areas not shown in Table 6. The results are generally consistent. Over the four-year period the skill differential, measured as in Table 6, narrowed in 29 of the areas, widened in 14, and remained about constant in 7.[23] Accepting the measure as reasonably accurate, it seems it would not be correct to characterize the skill differential as relatively stable over this period. Although the theoretical expectation is that differentials should have widened, we see that this generally has not taken place. The narrowing that has occurred is generally slight but the evidence indicates it has occurred in the majority of labor-market areas. It is interesting to observe from Table 6 that comparisons with the earnings indexes for men and women office workers show similar relative gains by the unskilled group.

Earlier studies have not reached the same conclusion. A BLS evaluation by a different method which compared the 1961–1962 skill differential with that for 1953 resulted in the conclusion that the differential had been unchanged during that period.[24] Martin Segal, in a study covering the period 1951–1961, compared average wage rates for six skilled occupations with three unskilled occupations and found a widening of skill differentials in manufacturing in eleven out of sixteen cities. We have not attempted to reconcile the two findings. The differences may be a result of the time period, the measurement technique used, or the inclusiveness of the occupation averages. It is also possible that minimum wage adjustments are responsible for some of the narrowing we find and that they are not reflected in the data used by Segal.

Another method of examining inter-area changes in skill differentials is to compute the ratios of average earnings for a skilled job and an unskilled job by area for different years. We have done this for maintenance electricians and janitors in manufacturing, and the results are summarized in Table 7. There is increased diversity in these results. Ratios of the earnings rates

TABLE 7. RATIOS OF AVERAGE STRAIGHT-TIME EARNINGS OF
ELECTRICIANS AND JANITORS IN MANUFACTURING FOR 20
METROPOLITAN AREAS, 1952–1953 AND 1963–1964

Area	Ratio of Electricians' to Janitors' Earnings		Change in Ratio
	1952–1953	1963–1964	
Dallas	191.1	170.9	Narrowing
Memphis	187.2	183.4	Narrowing
Philadelphia	175.0	146.9	Narrowing
Atlanta	174.4	174.5	Constant
New York	168.2	161.4	Narrowing
St. Louis	158.5	150.2	Narrowing
Boston	154.2	154.5	Constant
Newark-Jersey City	149.3	147.8	Narrowing
Chicago	149.0	159.9	Widening
Denver	148.8	149.1	Constant
Minneapolis-St. Paul	148.2	152.2	Widening
Providence-Pawtucket	147.0	156.0	Widening
Baltimore	146.9	145.6	Narrowing
Los Angeles-Long Beach	146.0	150.4	Widening
Kansas City	145.3	151.8	Widening
Milwaukee	142.4	144.5	Widening
Portland, Oregon	142.2	153.4	Widening
Cleveland	140.0	140.7	Constant
San Francisco-Oakland	139.0	141.1	Widening
Buffalo	138.1	136.7	Narrowing

Source: Computed from data taken from the area bulletins of the Bureau
of Labor Statistics, *Occupational Wage Surveys*, for 1952–1953 and
1963–1964.

for these jobs, interpreted as differentials, have narrowed in some
areas, widened in some, and remained relatively constant in
others. In some cases the changes have been marked; in others
they have probably been insignificant. One general interpretation
is possible. The areas in Table 7 have been ranked from highest
to lowest according to the ratio of the two earnings rates. It
is clear that areas with the highest ratios in 1952–1953 have

tended to show a decline in the ratio. Similarly the ratios tended to increase for those with the lowest values for 1952–1953. The evidence is too shaky to make much of this, but at least one can observe that the tendency was for the inter-city variation in differentials to narrow. While this may have been the result of competitive forces, it could also have been affected by minimum wage increases, especially in narrowing the differential for southern cities.

We have tested our predictions about the behavior of wages in high-wage industries relative to those in a low-wage sector using the same data and technique as above. We compared the ratio of the earnings of janitors in manufacturing to those in retail trade for thirteen cities. The initial hypothesis was that the spread between these unskilled rates should have widened over the period on the ground that retail trade was less likely to have been subject to federal wage minima than manufacturing. Federal minima were pushing up the floor in manufacturing, and the high-wage occupations might be thought of as pulling up the average in manufacturing. The results, shown in Table 8, are not clear-cut. In seven areas, the industry differential appears to have widened when the over-all experience is evaluated. In some of these, as well as in those where the evidence is mixed, there seems to have been a greater widening between 1952–1953 and 1957–1958, followed by some narrowing from 1957–1958 to 1963–1964. In three cases, Baltimore, Boston, and Chicago, the ratio in the final period was lower than in 1952–1953.

Generally, with the caution the crude techniques and difficult data require, we are inclined to accept these results as somewhat weak support for our hypothesis on the progress of earnings in the high-wage group. The behavior classified as "mixed" here may be related to the greater sensitivity of wage rates to market conditions in the low-wage retail trade sector.

As a test for the impact of unemployment on the movement of wage differentials, we began with the hypothesis that the differential between skilled and unskilled rates should have widened most for areas with highest unemployment. On the assumption that 1960 Census of Population area unemployment rates are a good representation of the differential unemployment experience for these areas over the period 1952–1964, we com-

TABLE 8. Ratios of Average Straight-Time Hourly Earnings,
Janitors in Manufacturing Relative to Janitors in Retail
Trade, 13 Areas, 1952–1953, 1957–1958, and 1963–1964

Area	Ratio of Earnings of Men Janitors in Manufacturing to Those of Men Janitors in Retail Trade			Change in Differential
	1952–1953	1957–1958	1963–1964	
Baltimore	162.0	164.8	159.7	Mixed
Atlanta	139.2	159.1	150.8	Widening
Philadelphia	128.8	124.8	137.4	Widening
Denver	128.3	155.0	139.6	Widening
Minneapolis-St. Paul	127.0	130.9	128.0	Widening
Dallas	124.7	150.0	136.5	Mixed
Portland, Oregon	123.1	117.9	122.5	Mixed
Boston	119.1	125.2	115.1	Mixed
Chicago	118.5	126.6	117.1	Mixed
Providence-Pawtucket	117.0	n.a.	118.3	Widening
New York	116.8	120.6	128.6	Widening
Newark-Jersey City	115.2	120.6	146.4	Widening
San Francisco-Oakland	111.6	115.8	112.2	Mixed

Source: Computed from area bulletins of the Bureau of Labor Statistics,
Occupational Wage Survey, for the indicated periods.

pared the rates with the level and apparent trends in the wage
differentials. There was no evidence of any relationship. Use of
1964 insured unemployment rates for the areas resulted in the
same conclusion. A more specific approach to the problem, now
underway, involves looking at the year-to-year behavior of unemployment rates and differentials in particular areas. The results
of the preliminary efforts in this direction are interesting but
inconclusive. Scranton, Pennsylvania, for example, had an
insured unemployment rate of 12 per cent or over each year
during 1960–1963, and in 1964 the rate fell to 8.9 per cent. The
ratio of electricians' to janitors' earnings shows a sharp decline
from 1951 (the only year surveyed before 1960) to 1960, and
a slower decline thereafter. Lawrence, Massachusetts, had a similar unemployment record; the ratio for the two occupations declined from 1956 to 1959 and widened thereafter. The variation

is interesting although the contrast between the directions of the trend are puzzling. In contrast, Denver, a city with consistently low insured unemployment rates from 1952 through 1964, shows a remarkable stability in the ratios of earnings for the two jobs over that period.[25] Another method which we are now exploring involves the comparison of wage differential changes with employment changes, area by area.

Low-Wage and High-Wage Sectors

The multiple-sector labor-market reasoning introduced above leads us to expect that excess supplies of labor in the unskilled grades should have been shifted toward the lower-wage sector. Or, perhaps more directly, equilibrating shifts of labor from low-wage sectors to high-wage sectors were precluded because of inflexible wage rates or institutional control of labor supply. The supply of labor to the low-wage sectors at existing rates would have been greater than it would be at equilibrium. On the other hand, employment declines in some high-wage industries may have produced a direct shift in labor supply toward the low-wage sector. This should have led to a reduction in wage rates in the low-wage sector relative to the high-wage sector.

Testing this proposition with area and industry variables controlled turns out to be a very difficult task. Ideally the task requires area and industry averages of wage, employment, and unemployment rates for skilled and unskilled workers. Unfortunately, the various employment measures are neither detailed nor frequent enough. Even more of a problem are the changes which have occurred in federal and state minimum wage laws. Coverages are expanded and amounts increased during periods when one might wish wage rates could be regarded as determined by market forces. We think a reasonable compromise is to use a benchmark unskilled occupation in a low-wage "uncovered" sector and to construct, if possible, good time series of employment, wage rates, and earnings by area for that job. These could be compared with the same data for the high-wage sector. So far we have not been successful in doing this. The results of approximations to this technique, shown below, may be interesting, though still puzzling.

Table 9 presents some average hourly earnings data for industry aggregates, where possible covering the period 1952–1964. It shows that on the average the differential between average earnings in manufacturing and in retail trade has narrowed during this period. The movements in the indexes indicate, however, that the advances in retail trade were made during intervals that contained the effects of the 1961 amendments to the Fair Labor Standards Act. Another complicating factor is that the earnings data for retail trade pertain to all nonsupervisory employees while those for manufacturing cover only production workers. Various white-collar, non-sales occupations would thus be included in the retail trade series but excluded from manufacturing. Retail trade earnings include commissions for some sales employees. No earnings by occupation are available, and distributions of hourly rates can be secured for only 1956, 1961, and 1962. Using these distributions and comparing 1956 and 1962 we find: (a) average hourly earnings increased 19 per cent; (b) median hourly earnings increased 17 per cent; (c) relative dispersion (measured by the ratio of the interquartile range to median) increased from 56 per cent to 60 per cent; and (d) the difference in cents per hour between the mean and the median increased from 17 cents in 1956 to 23 cents in 1962.[26] There appear to be at least two sets of forces at work. The lowest earnings are being pushed up by the minimum-wage changes, and the distribution is becoming more skewed to the right as those in higher earnings categories increase in number or get a greater relative increase in earnings.[27] On balance we believe no verdict is justified; one cannot say that the "low-wage" retail trade sector has gained or lost in *wage rates* relative to the manufacturing sector.

Two other low-wage industries, hotels and motels and laundry and dry cleaning establishments, have data available for only part of the period. The increase in average hourly earnings for hotels and motels was 18.4 per cent from 1958 to 1963 and that for manufacturing was 15.6 per cent. In laundries, dry cleaning and dyeing plants the 1958–1963 increase was 13.7 per cent, below that for manufacturing. The hotel earnings series is somewhat suspect, due to the inclusion of occupations in which tipping is prevalent and for which wage data have uncertain mean-

TABLE 9. AVERAGE HOURLY EARNINGS FOR VARIOUS INDUSTRY GROUPS AND PERIODS, 1952–1964[a]

Year	Manufacturing		Retail Trade		Hotels and Motels	Laundries, Cleaning and Dyeing Plants	Men Washers in Power Laundries		Agriculture	
	Hourly Earnings	Index 1952 = 100	Hourly Earnings	Index 1952 = 100	Hourly Earnings	Hourly Earnings	Hourly Earnings	Index 1952 = 100	Hourly Earnings	Index 1952 = 100
1952	$1.59	100.0	$1.18	100.0			$1.31	100.0	$0.661	100.0
1953	1.68	105.7	1.25	105.9			1.35	103.1	0.672	101.7
1954	1.73	108.8	1.29	109.3					0.661	100.0
1955	1.79	112.6	1.34	113.6					0.675	102.1
1956	1.89	118.9	1.40	118.6					0.705	106.7
1957	1.99	125.2	1.47	124.6					0.728	110.1
1958	2.05	128.9	1.52	128.8	$1.03	$1.17			0.757	114.5
1959	2.12	133.3	1.57	133.1	1.06	1.19			0.798	120.7
1960	2.20	138.4	1.62	137.3	1.09	1.24			0.818	123.8
1961	2.25	141.5	1.68	142.4	1.14	1.27	1.64	125.2	0.834	126.2
1962	2.31	145.3	1.74	147.5	1.18	1.30	1.70	129.2	0.856	129.5
1963	2.37	149.1	1.80	152.5	1.22	1.33			0.880	133.1
1964	2.44	153.5	1.87	158.5			1.74	132.4	0.904	136.8

Source: Data for manufacturing, retail trade, and agriculture are from *Economic Report of the President*, January 1965. Hotels and motels and laundries, cleaning and dyeing plants are from Bureau of Labor Statistics, *Employment and Earnings Statistics for the United States 1909–1964*, Bulletin 1312–2. The series on men washers in power laundries is constructed as the unweighted mean of the averages for the nine areas (Baltimore, Boston, Chicago, Detroit, Los Angeles-Long Beach, New York City, Newark-Jersey City, Philadelphia and San Francisco-Oakland) for which data were available for all years in Bureau of Labor Statistics *Industry Wage Surveys*.

[a] Earnings for manufacturing and power laundries exclude overtime.

ing. A longer series was constructed for men washers in power laundries. The earnings figures are unweighted means of the average earnings for the nine areas for which data were available.[28] The movement of manufacturing earnings away from this series appears to be steady.[29] The laundry and dry cleaning industry is fairly highly unionized, especially in the large cities for which the averages are calculated,[30] but is not (except in "border" situations) subject to the federal minimum wage. Except for the degree of unionization, this would be a good "benchmark" industry, but the occupation reported here is one of the better-paid jobs. With these qualifications, it is still reasonable to accept this evidence as supporting the hypothesis of downward pressure on rates in the low-wage sector. It is perhaps coincidental but rather striking that the laundry series and agricultural hourly earnings seem to have moved at about the same rate over the period.

Extending the comparison of manufacturing as a high-wage sector with other low-wage industries, we have summarized data from various sources in Table 10. The objective is to compare, area by area, the changes in earnings for manufacturing with unskilled workers in laundries, hotels, and hospitals. Occupations were chosen with a view to minimizing distortions created by meals, lodging, and tips, although some influence may still be present. Comparisons were possible on the full range of earnings for only a few cities, and the record is diverse.

In Baltimore, gross hourly earnings increased much more in durable manufacturing than in non-durables—about 10 per cent more—in the period 1953–1963. Unskilled plant workers' straight-time earnings increased about 73 per cent during the same period compared to an increase of about 61 per cent for skilled maintenance trades. Male washers in laundries earned only about 30 per cent more in 1963 than in 1953 while women shirt pressers improved earnings by 44 per cent. Data are available for nongovernmental hospital earnings for the period 1956–1963; increases were striking—ranging from 47 per cent for porters to 73 per cent for maids, and this occurred despite the fact that Maryland had no state minima applicable to hospitals. Thus, of the two low-wage comparisons with manufacturing, in one case the spread widens and in the other narrows sharply.

TABLE 10. PERCENTAGE INCREASES IN EARNINGS, LOW-WAGE INDUSTRIES
COMPARED TO MANUFACTURING, 1952–1963 AND SUB-PERIODS

Industry and Occupation	Period	Balti- more	Boston	Chicago	Los Angeles- Long Beach	New York	Newark- Jersey City	Phila- delphia	San Fran- cisco- Oakland
Gross average hourly earnings									
Manufacturing	1952–1963	60.1	n.a.	n.a.	53.8	n.a.	n.a.	49.4	59.0
	1956–1963	27.9	n.a.	n.a.	28.6	n.a.	n.a.	24.8	33.6
Durable goods	1952–1963	64.7	n.a.	n.a.	55.6	n.a.	n.a.	n.a.	58.8
	1956–1963	30.7	n.a.	n.a.	30.5	n.a.	n.a.	26.7	34.5
Nondurable goods	1952–1963	54.5	n.a.	n.a.	48.9	n.a.	n.a.	n.a.	59.2
	1956–1963	25.8	n.a.	n.a.	26.2	n.a.	n.a.	23.6	32.8
Straight-time average hourly earnings									
Unskilled plant workers— manufacturing	1952–1963	73.0[a]	48.5	55.1	58.3	61.1	71.3	64.1	64.9
	1956–1963	47.9[b]	31.9[b]	28.9	30.2	35.4	31.9	32.0	38.7
Skilled maintenance trades— manufacturing	1952–1963	60.8[a]	55.7	58.7	61.2	60.3	55.9	58.2	61.7
	1956–1963	37.8[b]	38.2[b]	29.8	31.1	34.1	30.2	30.2	38.1
Laundry: Washers, men	1952–1963	29.8	36.7	28.8	47.4	12.9	39.2	30.8	57.3
Shirt-pressers, women	1952–1963	44.0	52.5	42.9	52.8	43.4	37.6	61.6	48.7
Hotels: Housemen	1955–1963	n.a.	27.8	28.0	28.6	45.5	n.a.	n.a.	36.1
Hospitals: Men dishwashers	1956–1963	63.6	36.0	53.6	18.5	53.8	n.a.	43.7	25.2
Men porters	1956–1963	47.2	30.8	47.9	28.5	76.7	n.a.	58.8	22.9
Maids	1956–1963	72.9	41.8	39.6	29.1	78.8	n.a.	70.5	32.1

Source: Gross earnings in manufacturing from U. S. Department of Labor, Bureau of Labor Statistics, *Employment and Earnings Statistics for States and Areas 1939–1963*, Bulletin No. 1370–1. Skilled and unskilled rate increases computed from Bureau of Labor Statistics, *Wage Indexes: Long-Term Trend Data for Selected Occupations and Metropolitan Areas*, Bulletin No. 1427. Laundry data are from Bureau of Labor Statistics, *Industry Wage Survey: Laundries and Dry Cleaning Establishments* for various years as reported in: Bulletin No. 1401 for 1963, and a BLS Special Release for 1952. Hotel data are from BLS, *Industry Wage Survey: Hotels and Motels, June 1963*, Bulletin No. 1406, and *Earnings of Hotel Employees, Summer 1955*, BLS Summary Release, November 1955. Hospital data are from *Industry Wage Survey: Hospitals, 1963*, Bulletin No. 1409 and, for 1955, Bulletin Nos. 1210–1 to 1210–16.

[a] 1953–1963.
[b] 1955–1963.

In Boston the spread between unskilled workers in manufacturing and men washers in laundries widened during 1952–1963, but the increase for women shirt pressers exceeded that for manufacturing. Housemen in hotels increased earnings by 28 per cent during 1955–1963 compared to 32 per cent for unskilled manufacturing workers. Increases for hospital occupations tended to equal that for manufacturing. The state minimum in Massachusetts applicable to hospitals was $1.25 as of November 1964, and the average earnings in 1963 for the reported occupations were generally within 10 cents of that figure.

In Chicago the pattern is similar, with laundries and hotels falling behind while hospital occupations—without the aid of state minima—outran manufacturing by a good margin from 1956 to 1963.

Los Angeles-Long Beach and San Francisco-Oakland show hospital workers falling further behind unskilled manufacturing workers during 1952–1963. The California minimum for hospital workers is $1.30, and these two large cities, despite an average earnings differential for these reported occupations of 20–30 per cent, showed a similar pattern of increases in earnings. In these two cities the laundry workers' earnings, while not keeping pace with unskilled workers in manufacturing, were greater than in any of the other areas.

New York City, with hospital earnings far ahead of its 1964 minimum of $1.25, showed striking increases during 1956–1963. Laundry workers seemed to do least well there, but housemen in hotels appeared to make gains on manufacturing.

Although the rates of increases in earnings in hotels and laundries relative to those of unskilled workers in manufacturing appear to be consistent with the hypothesis for the supply of unskilled workers, the increases in hospital earnings do not. Few hospital employees in the occupations reported here are represented by unions.[31] They are exempt from the Fair Labor Standards Act, but in some cases subject to state minimum wage laws. Because of the interesting behavior of unskilled hospital wage rates, we compared 1956–1963 wage increases for male porters and female maids for six areas subject to state minima with those in eight areas not covered by such regulation. The unweighted averages of the increases for these occupations were 53 per cent and 52 per cent for maids and 39 per cent and 41 per cent for porters. Although this test is not very discriminating, it does not suggest any significant differences in behavior between areas covered by state minima and those not covered.[32]

There are a number of possible explanations for the behavior of hospital wages. Increases in state minima may have had some effects. Trends toward providing cash wages in place of meals and other perquisites may have been an influence. The most important cause, however, is likely to have been the strength of demand for hospital services. Increases in employment appear to have been substantial, although precise numbers are not available. The latest estimate seems to place the increase in full-time employment in nongovernmental hospitals between 1948 and 1963 in the neighborhood of half a million.[33] It seems quite reasonable to expect that the need to increase both professional and nonprofessional staff this rapidly would have created upward pressure on wage rates. This is not to say that wages for nonprofessional hospital employees are high. For the U. S., 29 per cent of all employees received less than $1.25 in hourly cash earnings in mid-1963.[34]

Some Tentative Conclusions

For this large and diverse body of evidence, the behavior of relative occupational and industrial differentials since 1950 has, as one might expect, been mixed in nature. For the most part it indicates that relative spreads have held constant or narrowed within the industries and areas studied, and widened between entry rates in the high wage industries and the federal minimum wage. Perhaps a better way to formulate the over-all verdict is to say that relative spreads between high- and low-wage occupations and high- and low-wage industries have not been widening to the extent one might expect, given the persistence of excess supplies of unskilled and inexperienced labor in this period.

This finding poses the following major questions for public policy if the purpose of such policy is to relieve low-quality workers of their disproportionate burden of inadequate job opportunities in recent years.

1. Should the higher wage industries in particular undertake much greater resort to juvenile progression rates in order to in-

troduce greater relative spreads into existing insensitive wage structures?

2. Would it be desirable to embark upon fundamental reforms in vocational education, linking together high school education with part-time on-the-job training more effectively for a large range of industries and jobs?

3. Should a general income-supplementation such as a negative income tax or a family allowance, of a type that divorces the supplement from higher employment costs, be developed for low-wage workers so that their economic welfare can be improved without damaging their opportunities for employment?

4. Has the time come to extend the principle of a multiple federal minimum wage, which disappeared after 1945 and was briefly reintroduced in 1961, to go along with proposed extensions of coverage so that employment opportunities for those directly affected will not be injured?

These questions almost suggest themselves. It will require practical answers and hard choices if federal employment policy is to deal more effectively with the already formidable problems of low-productivity workers.

Much work remains to be done on the general problem and the hypotheses posed in this paper. The results of the limited efforts reported above are mixed, but we think provocative. In order to carry the work forward, we plan to:

1. Examine more of the high-wage industries for which data are available, extending their scope to several areas and relating wage movements to local labor market conditions by periods.

2. Study in more detail the shapes of the frequency distributions of hourly earnings by occupations, industries, and areas.

3. Try to develop better data for earnings and wage rates for the diverse occupations that make up the bottom deck in the occupational hierarchy cited earlier.

4. Introduce if possible the changing industrial composition of employment as a variable in the study of shifts in area wage differentials.

5. Gather and analyze data from the Census of Population and other sources on the characteristics, mobility, and work experience of workers in low-wage occupations and industries.

NOTES

1. Among the earlier studies are Harry Ober, "Occupational Wage Differentials, 1907–1947," *Monthly Labor Review*, LXVII (August 1948), 127–134; Philip W. Bell, "Cyclical Variations and Trends in Occupational Wage Differentials in American Industry since 1914," *Review of Economics and Statistics*, XXXIII (November 1951), 329–337; W. S. Woytinsky and Associates, *Employment and Wages in the United States* (New York: The Twentieth Century Fund, 1953), pp. 466–474; Lloyd G. Reynolds and Cynthia Taft, *The Evolution of Wage Structure*, with a section by Robert M. Macdonald (New Haven: Yale University Press, 1956), pp. 17–166 and 184–192; and M. W. Reder, "The Theory of Occupational Wage Differentials," *American Economic Review*, XLV (December 1955), 833–852. The empirical data in these studies end with the early fifties.

More recent work includes Martin Segal, "Occupational Wage Differentials in Major Cities during the 1950's," in Mark Perlman, editor, *Human Resources in the Urban Economy* (Baltimore: Resources for the Future, Inc., and Johns Hopkins Press, 1963), pp. 195–207: M. W. Reder, "Wage Differentials: Theory and Measurement," in H. G. Lewis, editor, *Aspects of Labor Economics* (Princeton: National Bureau of Economic Research and Princeton University Press, 1962), pp. 257–311; and M. W. Reder, "Wage Structure and Structural Unemployment," *Review of Economic Studies*, XXXI (October 1964), 309–322.

Mention should also be made of special studies by the Bureau of Labor Statistics at irregular times of occupational earnings in industries such as basic steel and motor vehicles. These are cited at later points in this paper.

2. An exception is L. E. Gallaway, "Labor Mobility and Structural Unemployment," *American Economic Review*, LIII (September 1963), 694–716.

3. There are two notable exceptions. One is Clarence Long, who sought to account for high over-all rates by the hypothesis that there has been a gradual upward creep in unemployment of low-quality labor, which he attributed to constancy or narrowing of the relative spread between what he called the "social minimum wage" and average wages, as against a supposed widening in what he termed the "relative productivity spread" between average and low-quality labor. See Clarence D. Long, "A Theory of Creeping Uemployment and Labor Force Replacement," unpublished, a paper delivered to the Catholic Economic Association, December 27, 1960.

The other exception is Harold Demsetz, who gave demand deficiency some weight as a factor in high rates of over-all unemployment, but also found through some ingenious tests that the hypothesis that there exists a hard-core of unemployables that grows secularly and is a significant percentage of over-all unemployment was not refuted. He also suggested that the phenomenon derives from minimum wage statutes and union wage rates. See Harold Demsetz, "Structural Unemployment: A Reconsideration of the Evidence and the Theory," *Journal of Law and Economics*, IV (October 1961), 80–92.

4. R. A. Gordon has used two simple measures of the comparative vulnerability of groups composing the various strata of the labor force to unemployment: the relative group rate, $U_i/L_i/U/L$, and the relative group share, U_i/U, where U is unemployment, L is labor force, and i is any group. See R. A. Gordon, "Has Structural Unemployment Worsened?" *Industrial Relations*, III (May 1964), 53–77.

5. There is no doubt that their supply has been in absolute excess, but there is room for argument about whether it has been relatively greater. We think that it has. Thus, while operatives and kindred workers have roughly accounted for between 25 and 30 per cent of the total unemployed during the period, their relative rates of unemployment have run well below 2.0.

6. Another way of putting the matter is that it involves a problem in the cross-elasticities of demand for semiskilled and highly skilled labor when the wage for common labor undergoes relative decline. Our argument is that the cross-elasticities are greatest for workers just above the common labor grade and that they fall as one ascends the skill ladder.

7. It can be objected that occupational differentials are a means of equalizing net advantages, in response to differing job disutilities, and hence do not turn solely upon relative skill. But some of the main disutilities—heat, dirt, danger, and noise—have been greatly reduced in recent times by outlays that yield largely indivisible benefits to all workers alike, at uniform cost per dollar of earnings. Two effects follow: disutilities have declining importance for job differentials, while expenditures on their removal are akin to a flat general wage increase, hence narrow relative spreads.

8. The federal minimum embraces about 60 per cent of all private wage and salary employees. In 1961 its coverage was extended from manufacturing into parts of construction, wholesale trade, retail trade, and services. Pending proposals of the Johnson Administration would bring in an additional 4.5 million workers, mostly in hotels, restaurants, and additional segments of retail trade.

9. The reason for the competitive disadvantage is an asymmetry between the positions of the skilled and the unskilled. The former can compete with the latter for the same jobs, but the latter cannot compete with the former for the better jobs.

10. It does not follow that full extension of the minimum wage would solve the problem of low earnings for those in the bottom deck, for even if this could somehow be done for those in own-account labor it would force some members of this stratum into unemployment or withdrawal from the labor force. To prevent this expulsion would require a higher rate of demand expansion, with probable inflation and concomitant deterioration of the real wages of those whom the minimum wage is supposed to help.

11. This is not at all to deny the influence of factors other than unionism or to assert that unionism is the principal reason why wages are high

in some given industry. However, unionism is a factor of appreciable importance in shaping the wage structure of such industries and in partially isolating entry rates from market forces.

12. If the costs of fringe benefits and initial hiring expenses were included, the margin would probably have risen even more. Fringe benefit provisions are likely to be more liberal in high-wage industries, and because such benefits are largely geared to the basic rate, they are larger where entry rates are higher. There is also reason to expect hiring expenses to be larger: high-wage employers spend more on costs of search in order to gain greater selectivity. They are also induced to spend more on training, because their production processes involve more capital per man and are probably more intricate, while losses from spoiled work by beginners are likely to be costly.

13. In truth, unskilled workers are not a homogeneous class. They vary in educational preparation, learning capacity, physical strength, and aptitude for industrial discipline. However, they probably are more mobile then other groups. In consequence, if competition were fully effective, persistent spreads in starting rates over the minimum must be explained by differences in efficiency and in job disutilities.

14. The years shown in Table 2 were chosen to include those in which the federal minimum was increased and to reflect good and bad times, subject to availability of data.

15. When FLSA was enacted in 1938, it set a target minimum of $0.35, allowing for lower rates in weak industries. At that time U. S. Steel Corporation had a minimum plant rate of $0.625 in the north and $0.45 in the south while Chrysler Corporation (1939) paid $0.68. The spreads over the minimum were 79 and 29 per cent in U. S. Steel and 94 per cent at Chrysler. Since unionism was weak in both industries, it could be surmised that the northern premiums were voluntarily paid by these corporations.

16. Industrial unions in basic steel, automobiles, and bituminous coal succeeded in knocking out traditional southern differentials. This is important evidence of their effectiveness in shaping wage structures.

17. The data for local transit, motor trucking, and printing rest upon national frequency distributions but are available for several cities as well. The figures for building construction involve national weighted averages for the laborer group and are also available on a local basis. All of these statistics are for union-scale rates.

18. As of 1962 roughly 4.8 million workers were employed in the eight segments, excluding durable goods.

19. Robert M. Macdonald, *Collective Bargaining in the Automobile Industry: A Study of Wage Structure and Competitive Relations* (New Haven and London: Yale University Press, 1963), pp. 45–49 and 144–145.

20. U. S. Department of Labor, Bureau of Labor Statistics, *Wage Structure: Motor Vehicles and Parts, 1950*, Bulletin No. 1015 (1951), pp. 6–7; *Wage Structure: Part 1, Motor Vehicles*, Report No. 128 (July 1957), pp. 12–13; *Industry Wage. Survey: Part 1, Motor Vehicles,* Bulletin No.

1393 (January 1964), pp. 8–9. The data rest on average straight-time hourly earnings.

21. The data for coal were taken from *Monthly Labor Review*, various issues, and for 1964 from Bureau of National Affairs, *Collective Bargaining Negotiations and Contracts*, No. 491 (March 27, 1964); for railroads, *Monthly Labor Review*, LXXXIV (September 1961), 977–978, and LXXXVI (April 1963), 410.

22. The principal problems as we see them are: (a) differences in the dates the surveys are taken in different areas, (b) the discrete nature of wage increases can make year-to-year changes vary considerably, (c) variation in industry composition within aggregates from city to city, (d) difficulties in achieving complete comparability of job descriptions in different industries and areas, and (e) the substantial dispersion of occupational wage rates within given areas.

23. These most recent data appear in U. S. Department of Labor, Bureau of Labor Statistics, *Occupational Earnings and Wage Trends in Metropolitan Areas, 1964–1965*, Summary Release, No. 1 of 3 (27 areas) (February 1965); and Bureau of National Affairs, Inc., *Daily Labor Report*, No. 112 (June 11, 1965), pp. B1–B9.

24. Donald J. Blackmore, "Occupational Wage Relationships in Metropolitan Areas, 1961–1962," *Monthly Labor Review*, LXXXVI (December 1963), 1426–1431. The method used there measures the skill differential as "the median in an array of city-wide average differentials between 12 skilled jobs and janitors in manufacturing" (p. 1431, footnote 7).

25. The data are not reported here because of space limitations. Sources are the individual area bulletins for these cities for the years indicated.

26. These are calculated from the distribution in U. S. Department of Labor, Bureau of Labor Statistics, *Employee Earnings in Retail Trade, June 1962*, Bulletin No. 1380, Table 2, and *Employee Earnings in Retail Trade in October 1956*, Bulletin No. 1220, Table 3. The increase in average earnings calculated from the Bulletin data does not agree with that given in Table 9.

27. Because the lowest-wage employees tend to be those who work part-time, the extension of overtime pay has tended to increase the skewness of the distribution.

28. This series is for power laundries only; dry cleaning establishments are not included. Averages which include earnings from both types of establishments tend to be higher because earnings are somewhat higher in dry cleaning plants due to greater skill requirements and because more men are employed than in laundries.

29. The same trend over a longer period, with somewhat different data, was noted by Melvin Reder in his "Wage Differentials: Theory and Measurement," *op. cit.*, p. 261.

30. All of the cities included in the average had 50 or more per cent of employees in establishments with union contracts. See Bureau of Labor Statistics, *Industry Wage Survey: Laundries and Dry Cleaning Services*, Bulletin No. 1401, p. 2.

31. By one estimate, less than 5 per cent. See U. S. Department of Labor, *Nongovernment Hospitals: A Study to Evaluate the Feasibility of Extending the Minimum Wage Under the Fair Labor Standards Act* (Washington, D. C.: January 1965), p. 13.

32. Data used for these calculations were taken from Bureau of Labor Statistics, *Industry Wage Survey: Hospitals*, Bulletins No. 1210-1 to 1210-16 for 1956, and Bulletin No. 1409 for 1963.

33. See U. S. Department of Labor, *Nongovernment Hospitals, op. cit.*, p. 25, Table 8.

34. *Ibid.*, p. 58.

Discussion

BY H. M. DOUTY

I am glad to have an opportunity to make a few rather unsystematic comments on this challenging analysis of the relation of wage structure to unemployment in the United States in the postwar period.

In view of our preoccupation in recent years with the level and composition of unemployment, it is indeed extraordinary that so little attention has been devoted to employment barriers in the structure of wages. In her excellent review article on the postwar literature concerned with United States manpower and employment policy, Mrs. Gordon made only one reference to wages. She wrote that we need, among other things, to take a look at "the whole question of barriers to entry of young people into employment, including problems of wage structure, employer personnel policy, and union rules."[1]

I am not certain precisely why the exploration of wages as a factor in current unemployment has been neglected. It is a difficult area of research, and it involves examination of wage behavior resulting from public wage policy and the operation of powerful institutional forces in the private economy. This is all the more reason to be grateful to Professors Hildebrand and Delehanty for a paper that analytically adds to our knowledge of wage behavior and poses a basic question for employment policy.

The Major Findings

The central conclusion of the chapter with respect to wage structure is that from 1950 (after the war and the immediate postwar inflation) the wage differential between skilled and unskilled workers continued, on the whole, to narrow. Since this conclusion is derived largely from an analysis of BLS occupational wage-survey data, I find it difficult to disagree with. Our impression, in fact, has been that the marked decline in the skill differential during and immediately after the war, which Professor Reder's theory of wage structure[2] helps greatly to explain, was arrested but certainly not reversed in subsequent years. I would like to add only one piece of evidence. Since 1960 we have been able to estimate average wages and wage distributions for selected occupations for all metropolitan areas combined for an exceedingly broad industry coverage. Between 1960 and 1964, the wages of workers in the skilled maintenance trades for all industries[3] increased by 12.7 per cent; the increase for unskilled male manual workers was 13.8 per cent. The corresponding percentages for manufacturing were 12.1 and 14.2 per cent.[4]

It is stated that entrance rates in the top (high-wage) tier of a three-tier industry model are generally determined through collective bargaining on the basis of "flat general increases, although at times craft restiveness may make it necessary to redress differentials." If "flat general increases" mean uniform money increases this statement is somewhat too sweeping. We have a record of the nature of wage changes in all major collective bargaining settlements for the five years 1959–1963.[5] These settlements were made predominantly in the top tier industries. During this period, the proportion of workers receiving uniform money increases ranged from about 31 per cent in 1959 to almost 45 per cent in 1962. The proportion of workers receiving uniform percentage increases varied from 41 per cent in 1961 to 31 per cent in 1962. Nonuniform increases of various types were negotiated for the remaining workers.[6] In each year, 70 per cent or more of the workers received uniform money or uniform percentage increases. Since the latter serve to preserve skill margins and the former to reduce them, it seems clear that these data on the character of wage adjustments lend support to the finding that in this industry tier relative wages have tended to contract rather than widen in recent years.

Effect of the Minimum Wage

The middle tier of industries in the Hildebrand-Delehanty model consists of those whose entrance rates are subject to collective bargaining to some extent, revisions in the federal statutory minimum-wage rate, and voluntary maintenance by some employers of entrance-rate standards established through public policy or bargaining. The chapter contains no analysis of the course of relative wages in this industry segment. Numerous BLS studies have revealed the sharp initial impact of an increase in the federal minimum on skill differentials in relatively low-wage industries. In many such industries, of which southern lumber is a classic example, differentials tend to be gradually re-established only to decline again with the next increase in the minimum.[7] My impression is that in low-wage, predominantly unorganized industries the minimum wage has largely had a short-run effect on skill margins; that is, increases in the minimum have been spread sufficiently far apart so that between one increase and the next the market catches up with the statutory wage requirement. This impression, however, deserves more intensive investigation.

Perhaps I should make one additional comment relating to the minimum wage. The chapter states that "the official view invariably has been" that the federal minimum has not created substantial unemployment, and this is true. The view is also correct if by "substantial" is meant large-scale disemployment. But it should not be interpreted to mean than the appropriate federal authorities have been unaware of or indifferent to the employment effects of minimum-wage actions. For example, in commenting upon a group of studies of the effects of the $1.00 minimum the Secretary of Labor's 1958 report to the Congress on the Fair Labor Standards Act stated that "the surveys present evidence of disemployment apparently related to the increase in the $1.00 minimum, despite the fact that the economy was rising at that time and there were increases in the general level of prices which facilitated adjustment to the $1.00 minimum."[8] The report recommended against a further increase in the minimum at that time. In his recent message to the Congress on the Fair Labor Standards Act, President Johnson recommended extension of coverage but made no recommendation on the nature or timing of a rate increase. He stated that "The Congress should consider carefully the effects of higher minimum-wage rates on the incomes of those employed, and also on costs and prices, and on job opportunities—particularly for the flood of teenagers now entering our labor force."[9]

With respect to the empirical portions of the chapter, the least satisfactory part, it seems to me, is the effort to measure the movement of wages of unskilled labor in the low-wage sector (exempt from minimum wage-legislation and largely nonunion) relative to wages in the high-wage sector. The purpose is to detect in wage behavior the assumed absence of equilibrating shifts of unskilled labor from low- to high-wage sectors. This is an important and difficult area of investigation, undoubtedly complicated by problems of the availability of data, and one which I hope the authors will pursue.

There has been a long-run tendency for reduction in the relative supply of unskilled labor in the United States and for contraction of occupational wage differentials. However, several forces operating in the postwar labor market appear to have produced relative surplus, perhaps quite temporary, in the unskilled labor supply in the nonagricultural sector.[10] The Hildebrand-Delehanty chapter attempts to measure the behavior of wage differentials under these circumstances, and the authors raise the important question of whether our wage-fixing institutions have been at least partly responsible for the disproportionate share of the burden of postwar unemployment borne by the inexperienced and the unskilled.

While the evidence is not entirely unambiguous, it does suggest that, broadly speaking, skill margins have not been responsive to the labor-supply situation. The evidence presented in the paper lends support to Clarence Long's formulation of a relationship between the persistence of relatively high unemployment at the unskilled level, a "social minimum wage" increasing as fast or faster than the average wage, and a widening of the productivity gap between average workers and those at the lower (unskilled) end of the productivity ladder.[11]

Manpower Policy and Wage Determination

Clearly there is, or should be, a close relationship between policy for employment and manpower utilization on one hand and wages on the other. The term "wages" in this connection refers to level and structure and to such matters as the form of wages (e.g., the question of fringe-benefit practices and expenditures) and methods of wage payment. Thus far wages in relation to employment policy have largely been considered in terms of the appropriate rate of wage increase. This is clearly important, but the structure and form of wages may also have great significance for employment decisions at the level of the firm where most employment decisions are made. It is perfectly plain that we are not going to abandon collective bargaining and legal minimum-wage determination, nor should we do so. But a part of labor-market policy should be to attempt to influence wage decisions that will facilitate the adjustment of demand for labor to the character of the labor supply. This difficult task should be consistent, of course, with vigorous efforts through education and training to shape the skill characteristics of the labor supply to conform as closely as possible with anticipated job requirements.

NOTES

1. Margaret S. Gordon, "U. S. Manpower and Employment Policy," *Monthly Labor Review*, LXXXVII (November 1964), 1314–1321.

2. M. W. Reder, "The Theory of Occupational Wage Differentials," *American Economic Review*, XLV (December 1955), 833–852; and "Wage Structure and Structural Unemployment," *Review of Economic Studies*, XXXVII (October 1964), 309–322.

3. Manufacturing, transportation, communication, and other public utilities, wholesale trade, retail trade, finance, insurance, and real estate, and selected services.

4. Computed from BLS Summary Release, "Wage Trends for Occupational Groups in Metropolitan Areas, 1963–1964" Table 1.

5. Based on the BLS monthly report, *Current Wage Developments.*

6. These included uniform increases supplemented by special increases for skilled workers or by "inequity" adjustments for diverse groups of workers, differential increases for time and incentive workers, selective increases applicable to a substantial proportion but not all of the workers, etc.

7. H. M. Douty, "Some Effects of the $1.00 Minimum Wage in the United States," *Economica*, XXVII (May 1960), 137–147.

8. U. S. Department of Labor, *Report Submitted to the Congress in Accordance with the Requirements of Section 4(d) of the Fair Labor Standards Act, 1958* (January 1959), p. 3.

9. Message of the President to the Congress, May 18, 1965.

10. One possibly important qualification should be noted. We are dealing with very general concepts and categories. The jobs we classify as unskilled are not uniform in their characteristics and requirements. Most jobs require some training in addition to the acceptance of reasonable industrial discipline. Similarly, workers classified as unskilled or inexperienced are by no means homogeneous, and some portion of those thus classified may not constitute an effective part of the labor supply. When account is taken of mobility factors, the supply of unskilled or inexperienced workers to occupations classified as unskilled may not be as great as it appears.

11. Long's concept of a "social minimum wage" appears to be a sort of composite of legal, union, and employer minima, together with standards of social insurance and welfare payments. See Clarence D. Long, "A Theory of Creeping Unemployment and Labor Force Displacement," Catholic Economic Association, 1960; and "An Overview of Postwar Labor Market Developments," *Proceedings,* Fourth Annual Social Security Conference, Upjohn Institute, 1962.

Discussion

BY M. W. REDER

As I interpret it, the role of discussant is primarily that of critic. It is his function to "accentuate the negative." And whenever possible, in making these comments, I play this part. So far as they go, my criticisms are intended seriously, but they do not reflect my view of the paper as a whole. Iceberg like, the very large measure of agreement I share with the authors and my admiration for the quality of their work must remain unexpressed save for this brief prefatory remark.

The points of difference with the authors which I shall discuss can be conveniently placed under three separate headings.

The Impact of Unionism upon Wage Structure

The authors note in Table 2 and in the attendant discussion that there is a persistent differential between entry rates in high wage industries and the federal minimum wage. They also point out that this differential increased during the 1950's. The explanation offered for the "high and widening spread between these entry rates and the minimum wage" is mainly "effective unionism." For several reasons, I find this explanation hard to accept.

1. Although the wage differentials to which the authors wish to draw our attention are real, I doubt the appropriateness of the measures used in Table 2. Industries at or near the federal minimum wage are disproportionately located in the South or New England and are more frequently found in smaller centers of population than are the high wage industries. As a result inter-industry (skill constant) differentials are confounded with those due to city size and region, and this makes the figures in Table 2 exaggerate the differentials they purport to indicate.

2. The high wage industries (in Table 2) employ disproportionate numbers of males and (probably) of whites, as compared with those near the federal minimum. Consequently, the

differentials presented are to some extent due to race and sex rather than to unionism *per se*. The differentials may also reflect the effect of different levels of education.

3. After we correct for the effect of these non-union forces, would the remaining differentials be so large as to be incapable of being explained as premia paid by employers for greater selectivity in hiring? It is not clear to me that the answer is obviously in the affirmative. As the authors point out, hiring selectivity may result from union imposed wage rates as well as from cost minimization under non-union conditions. However, in order to reach their conclusion, it is necessary to distinguish the union-induced effect from the remainder.

Making this distinction is no small job. There has been one serious attempt at estimating the effect of unionism on relative wages, by H. G. Lewis.[1] Lewis estimated that for the period 1945–1949 the "average relative wage effect" of unionism was from zero to 5 per cent.[2] Assuming 1950 not very different in this respect from the years immediately preceding it, I submit that the impression conveyed by Table 2 and the related argument is that the effect was much larger than Lewis found it to be. While I am not entirely convinced of the accuracy of Lewis' estimates, I do believe that they are of a kind that warrant careful consideration.[3] Therefore I ask the authors to explain why they arrive at an (apparently) higher estimate of unionism's relative wage effect than Lewis does.

4. The above remarks refer to the *level* of the differentials in Table 2. Let us now consider their increase during the 1950's. To attribute this increase to unionism requires some explanation of why unions have had greater relative impact on wages in the later than in the earlier 1950's. The authors do not attempt this. Lewis (who also estimates that the wage effect of unionism increased in the 1950's) does offer an explanation. In essence the explanation is that unionism causes wage rates to become more sluggish so that changes in union wage rates tend to lag those in non-union rates when there are marked changes in the price-level or in unemployment. On this interpretation, 1950 would have been a year of disequilibrium in union-nonunion wage differentials, and at least part of the subsequent movement would have represented a corrective adjustment. It is not clear,

however, whether the behavior of the industrial wage structure in the 1950's reflected movements of a union-nonunion differential or of some other differential that indirectly affected the relation between the wages of unionized workers and those of others.

Wage Spreads Within High-Wage Industries

The authors find that within the individual high-wage industries they studied the predominant tendency was for the wage spread between skilled and unskilled jobs to remain constant or to narrow during the interval 1950–1964, especially during 1957–1964. They found that this occurred despite a presumed increase in the relative supply of the less skilled workers, an increase which has been especially important since 1957. The reason offered for the failure of the increase in relative supply of the unskilled to widen skill margins is that unions have been able effectively to shore up the relative rates of the unskilled despite market forces.[4]

The validity of this contention varies from one industry to the next, though it is at least plausible in most cases, but, there is another possible explanation of the facts, though the authors do not discuss it. Consider: two of the most important characteristics that employers seek among job applicants are (a) steady work habits and (b) the capacity to learn new tasks without too much difficulty. One would suppose that both of these characteristics become increasingly prevalent in a population as its minimum educational level rises, but the opportunity for further education and training has also become more widespread, especially in the postwar period, and this further training may remove workers from the field of manual employment altogether. As a result it may have happened that young workers with the aforementioned desirable characteristics who were seeking *manual* employment during the 1950's declined relative to the demand for them. This could have happened even though there was an abundance of applicants (for manual jobs) who did not possess these characteristics.

In other words, the spreading of educational opportunity might create a relative scarcity of reliable and intelligent applicants for manual jobs. This would push up starting wages relative to average earnings among high wage and (presumably) highly selective employers and also relative to community minima. That something of this sort occurred during the 1950's is suggested by the fact that during 1949–1958 the income advantage of male high-school graduates 25–34 years of age increased substantially relative to males of the same cohorts who had merely completed elementary school.[5] This argument is not incompatible with the hypothesis that unionism had the effect alleged; but it does not require the hypothesis.

Skill Differentials and Low-End Jobs

The attention paid to the wage spread between skilled jobs and the low-end occupations in the trade and service industries is especially praiseworthy. I agree that wage behavior in these latter occupations is likely to show the effects of changes in federal, state, and local minimum-wage regulations. I think, however, that a factor of equal or even greater importance in explaining the wage behavior of low-end jobs is the degree of employer tolerance of quality deterioration among employees.

For example, in the fields of personal service, domestic employment, and the like, great variations are possible in the kind and amount of work performed. If the labor market for this type of personnel becomes tight, there is a stronger tendency to tolerate poorer work, more absenteeism, more idling on the job, and so on than if the market were looser. It is always possible for employers to trade off higher wages for better performance. To what extent this is done depends upon employer rates of substitution between cash outlay and worker performance, upon the willingness of the workers involved to give more effort in exchange for higher rates of remuneration, and upon whether the supervisory situation is such as to make it reasonable to suppose that an improved wages-effort trade will get the results employers seek.

Low-end service jobs very often appear to be of such a character that employers do not feel they could obtain enough extra service by offering higher wages to justify the extra cost of obtaining it. Or, as in the case of hospitals, they may believe that customers prefer to extend more efforts of their own or of their families than pay higher prices to obtain better (paid) services. Hence hourly wages stick at a legal or conventional minimum, with market forces determining the characteristics of the workers who can be obtained and/or their degree of effort. I suspect that in many of the cases where there was an increasing spread (between starting rates in manufacturing and earnings in low-end service jobs) there was also a relative deterioration of worker quality in the low-end jobs. Some observable indicators of relative quality deterioration of workers in a particular occupation would be a relative reduction in average years of schooling, a relative increase in turnover, a substitution of females for males, an increase in the proportion of nonwhites, a rise in the fraction of part-time workers, and a relative decline in the fraction of workers in the prime years 25–44.

The extent to which employers can reduce worker quality in order to avoid raising wages reflects not only their own tastes or those of their customers but also legal regulations concerning the employment of minors, pensioners, etc. These regulations and those governing income maintenance for the unemployed, such as the levels of relief payments and unemployment compensation, will set floors to the minimum-labor quality and the wage it can be paid in any given community. These minima vary from one place to another and may be quite independent of current local unemployment rates. The effect of these locationally variable minima may be part of the reason for the uncertain relation between levels of unemployment and changes in skill margins (among localities) found by the authors. In short, wages on low-end jobs tend to respond to the level of unemployment, but the response is mediated by changes in the trade-off between worker quality and wage rates and limited by law and custom concerning minimum rates of compensation (social minimum wage rates) and by other restrictions on the terms of employment contracts.

High-wage employers may vary hiring standards and work loads as well as those operating at the low end of the wage spectrum, but I doubt they are nearly so flexible in this respect as the employers of low-wage service workers. This is hardly the occasion to argue this point in detail; hence I shall not attempt to go beyond assertion save to mention that differential unionism may be one of the factors involved. That is, effective unions in low-end occupations might compel employers to pay higher wages than they do and to seek better workers as a consequence.

NOTES

1. H. G. Lewis, *Unionism and Relative Wages in the United States* (Chicago: University of Chicago Press, 1963).

2. Lewis, op. cit., pp. 193–194.

3. My own views on Lewis' work may be found in a review article in the *Journal of Political Economy*, LXXIII (April 1965), 188–196.

4. The authors' finding of no increase in skill margins prior to 1957 runs counter to the claims of some other investigators, e.g., M. Segal (cited in their first footnote), and R. Perlman, "Forces Widening Occupational Wage Differentials," *Review of Economics and Statistics*, XL (May 1958), 107–115. It would be helpful if the authors would comment upon the divergence between their data and those presented by other students.

5. H. P. Miller, "Annual and Lifetime Income in Relation to Education: 1939–1959," *American Economic Review*, L (December 1960), 962–986, especially Table 8, p. 975.

Discussion

BY LLOYD ULMAN

It is a most pleasant assignment to comment on a paper which should be taken literally rather than euphemistically as a progress report. Although incomplete, the research reported by Hildebrand and Delehanty is not inconclusive; and some of the results even at this stage, I believe, can be taken as solid progress in four related areas.

1. With the aid of empirical evidence drawn from the field of unemployment, they have constructed a hypothesis concerning the expected behavior of relative wages, thereby attempting to provide an independent ordering of "comparative scarcities." As a result they have greatly helped to inject consideration of the role played by wage structure into the controversy concerning structural unemployment—a controversy which might not too unfairly be caricatured as characterized by the implicit assumptions of zero elasticities of supply and demand on one side and of infinite elasticities on the other.

2. They have collated occupational wage data from a wide variety of sources; this in itself is a valuable contribution in an area in which satisfactory data are very scarce.

3. They have offered a broad descriptive framework, in the form of a three-tier industrial distribution of the labor force, as a device for explaining apparently contracompetitive movements of relative occupational wage rates with reference to the influence of "effective unionism" and legislated minimum wages.

4. They have raised several interesting and challenging questions in the areas of both private and public minimum-wage policy.

I have some questions to raise in some of the areas explored in the paper, but I should like to state explicitly at the outset that I regard the major arguments made by Hildebrand and

Delehanty as generally persuasive and generally supported by the evidence they have presented thus far.

Surplus of Unskilled Labor

Let us consider the authors' conclusion that "unskilled labor has been in relative surplus for some years." This conclusion rests on the findings that the unemployment rates of laborers and inexperienced workers have exceeded twice the values of the over-all unemployment rates since the beginning of the 1950's and that the share of the entire unskilled group in total unemployment has been more than double their share of total employment and has even been rising. These findings certainly support the conclusion that the groups in question have been in excess supply, and they are persuasive as to the existence of a *relative* surplus, but they do not preclude the possible existence of excess supply in better educated or better trained groups.

In the first place, even groups with unemployment rates close to the over-all average can be said to have harbored sectors of excess supply during a period in which the over-all rate exceeded 5 per cent. During the years selected by Hildebrand and Delehanty, the craftsmen, foremen, and kindred workers group experienced unemployment rates of 5.6 per cent (in 1950), 4.9 per cent (in 1954), 3.8 per cent (in 1957), 5.3 per cent (in 1960), and 4.2 per cent (in 1964); the corresponding rates for operatives were between 1.2 and 2.7 points higher. In the second place, unemployment levels fail to measure completely the extent of excess or at least highly elastic supply among some groups fairly high up on the occupational (or at least wage) ladder. Underemployment of skilled labor "within the internal market of the plant or firm" is explicitly recognized in the paper as a component of excess supply. Another is the reserve of employed labor capable of being upgraded within relatively short time periods, for moderate incremental training cost. According to Livernash, "Within any such group of related jobs, the number of employees able, willing, and desirous of being promoted far exceeds the number promoted. The better paying jobs appear at any time to be rationed."[1]

Nevertheless, it is plausible to maintain that the unskilled groups are in *relative* surplus. Moreover one can argue, as our authors do, that excess supplies in the ranks above the unskilled are sterilized, as it were, both because employers can downgrade skilled workers in redundant supply and because "of an asymmetry between the positions of the skilled and the unskilled. The former can compete with the latter for the same jobs, but the latter cannot compete with the former for the better jobs."[2] Even if important pockets of excess supply should develop within the ranks of skilled workers as the eventual result of an initial increment to the supply of the unskilled and inexperienced, the quasi-competitive hypothesis advanced by Hildebrand and Delehanty would predict a widening of (intraindustrial) occupational wage differentials. And, if an autonomous increase in demand for skilled labor (due to technological change or shifts in product demand, notably in the defense sector) should be added to the postulated autonomous increase in the supply of the unskilled, the widening would follow *a fortiori* under the assumption of differential supply elasticities.

If, however, a large segment of the supply of skilled labor were highly elastic in response to such an increase in demand (the condition described by Livernash), a vigorous increase in the demand for skilled labor would not necessarily result in a widening of occupational wage differences. It could even result in narrowing, as Reder maintains was the case during and after the war. During the period under consideration, however, the increments to the supply of the urban unskilled (from sources including those itemized in the paper) were probably sufficiently great relative to the strength of demand for skilled labor, and the supply elasticity of most of the highly skilled (technical and professional) groups in greatest demand was probably sufficiently low, to warrant a prediction of widening or at most constancy. Even under the modified conditions I have introduced, there is little reason on competitive grounds to predict narrowing.

Evidence Regarding Wage Differentials

Contrary to the most plausible predictions, the authors report many instances of narrowing (and constancy). (The finding that

entry rates in high-wage industries widened relative to the federal minimum wage also runs counter to the quasi-competitive
hypothesis which would have predicted narrowing in this case.)
However, the bag is mixed, the returns are not all in yet, and
the authors' scrupulous caution may be complemented with reference to some mixed results of other studies.

There is, first, Segal's finding of a widening of percentage skill
differentials in manufacturing plants in 11 out of 16 cities between 1951 and 1961.[3] However, as he points out with reference
to a BLS survey which revealed narrowing during the period
1953–1962, such comparisons may be powerfully influenced by
the (enforced) selection of base and terminal years. In addition,
two other studies may be cited as lending some support to the
hypothesis that wage and salary structures respond to the influence of relatively large market changes, although such response
has been rather sluggish and concentrated mainly in a period
marked by relatively high unemployment and apparently
reduced union bargaining power over wages. A forthcoming
OECD study finds that in a sample of 11 firms and local industries, whereas appreciable narrowing of skill differentials
occurred in eight cases over the period from 1946–1947 to 1953,
it occurred in only three cases between 1957 and 1962. The later
developments, however, were able to affect the direction of
change for the entire period in only one situation; moreover, in
none of these cases did appreciable widening occur. Thus, while
the prevailing direction of change after 1957 appears different
from that in Table 3 in the paper (for 1957–1964), the two
samples do not yield greatly different results.

Another study, covering the period 1948–1960, found evidence
of a lagged relationship between changes in employment and
in compensation among broad (one-digit) industrial classifications and between wages and salaries in manufacturing, with
most of the catching-up process concentrated in the subperiod
1957–1960.[4]

Hildebrand and Delehanty themselves characterize their findings as "mixed, but we think provocative." Since the latter adjec-
tive is defined as "serving or tending to provoke, excite, or stimulate," it appears reasonable that this claim would be substantiated if the sympathetic reviewer were moved to allude to evi-

dence from contiguous areas of research consistent with what he regards as an interesting hypothesis. One piece of supporting evidence might be found in Sara Behman's analysis of the strong positive relationship between changes in money-wage rates and quit-rate levels in the United States during the postwar period.[5] According to this analysis, mobile workers in sectors experiencing increasing product demand trigger off wage increases which are then generalized to other sectors by a set of diffusion mechanisms including pattern-making union settlements, employer fear of organization, strikes, or slowdowns, and the anticipation of possible future stringency in labor markets. Mrs. Behman's trigger and response mechanisms are consistent with the operation of the first two "tiers" described by Hildebrand and Delehanty, especially since it appears that early cyclical upswings in quit rates are concentrated in certain skilled trades (who thus furnish a contrast to the more easily trained and promotable classes of skilled workers discussed above).

Examples of the interrelatedness of wage movements among different occupational groups within the same industry are common knowledge, but two recent examples merit explicit acknowledgment. The first concerns the seafaring crafts, all of which appear to be in abundantly excess supply with the exception of the marine engineers, who in consequence of their shortage (under traditional crew complements) have been extremely aggressive in prosecuting demands but have nevertheless been unable to improve their relative wage standing in the industry. The second concerns the 1965 newspaper settlement in New York City in which the publishers, having granted a more generous package to the printers and photoengravers than to other lower-paid crafts, were obliged to renegotiate with the latter, despite the fact that a history of equal absolute increases had led to the higher-paid crafts' demand for higher settlements in the first place.

Their very interesting data on movements in entry-rates in high-wage industries relative to the federal minimum wage have helped to persuade Hildebrand and Delehanty "to consider the high-wage industries as a non-competing group, largely insulated by wage rates from the general supply of unskilled workers, which in themselves are thus made another non-competing group." This suggests that the industrial wage structure might have widened in the postwar period, and this has been found to have been the case.[6] Similarly, the existence of a strong and increasing negative relationship between industrial wage levels and quit rates is consistent with the hypothesis quoted above. Finally, the "absorption function" attributed to the bottom tier of the unskilled and institutionally unprotected might have played a role in contributing to the great increase in supply and employment in the services sector and to that sector's inability (until the late 1950's) to register advances in compensation as large as those secured in higher-paid and more slowly growing manufacturing sectors. This, incidentally, suggests that part of the excess supply of unskilled labor to which Hildebrand and Delehanty refer may have been induced by adverse demand movements or wage pushes in the upper tier.

Some Policy Issues

Their wage-structural view of unemployment has led Hildebrand and Delehanty to emphasize policy questions different from those usually stressed by "traditional structuralists" on the one hand and "aggregate demanders" on the other. While they estimate that a high—and indeed rising—share of unemployment has been accounted for by their "unskilled labor" categories, they do not assume that this excess supply is offset by an approximately equal volume of excess demand in the high-wage sectors. (On the contrary, the role assigned to unionism and employer wage policies in these sectors should preclude appreciable excess demand.) Thus—to caricature the situation broadly—while the structuralist zealously advocates improved and expanded vocational education and training in order to equip the unemployed unskilled to fill vacant skilled jobs, Hildebrand and Delehanty speculate courageously about multiple minima, juvenile progression rates, and negative income taxes in order to expand (or at least preserve) the low-wage job area. They raise a thoughtful question about vocational educational reform, but one senses here a tempered zeal which lends credence to their status as members in good standing in the aggregate-demand club. On the other hand, they differentiate their policy approach from that of the conventional advocates of fiscal-monetary policy by insisting on the importance of policies designed to alter existing wage structures.

At this point, I should like to enter a brief demurrer and then to meet the writers' challenging questions on income supplements and multiple minima with a suggestion of my own. The desirability of a multiple-minimum wage is suggested in the context of proposed extensions of coverage, which suggest that the writers are not opposed to extension but they are concerned about adverse effects on employment. This concern is developed more fully in an earlier note wherein is written that "To prevent this expulsion [from employment] would then require a higher rate of demand expansion, with probable inflation and concomitant deterioration of the real wages of those whom the minimum wage is supposed to help." Inflation: there's the rub. Now if extension of the minimum raised the wages of the newly covered groups relative to the general wage level, resultant inflation would be a tax device for redistributing real income in favor of the low-wage groups in question. Or, to cite Hyman Minsky's alternative formulation (in a forthcoming study), changing the wage structure would lead to removal of a subsidy in the form of low product prices due to depressed wages hitherto paid to the affluent majority by the underpaid poor. To the extent that the chapter's analysis is correct, the implied case for extension is a good one. Moreover, to the extent that the existing wage structure is distorted by rigidities, reduction of such distortion by the imposition of a further rigidity can claim support as a second-best solution.

Nonetheless, there are few souls left who would commend the erecting or raising of minimum wages as a device for reducing unemployment, including the large pockets of the unskilled or inexperienced unemployed. When Keynes approached the official door, the Blue Eagle flew out the window. The current case for the establishment of multiple minimum wages as a device for increasing over-all employment supported by conventional partial equilibrium analysis should be considered in the light of more efficient policy alternatives. However, it is well to recall at this juncture that the Keynesian system casts the expansion of aggregate demand in the role of a more feasible and efficient alternative to policies aimed directly at the elimination of rigidities or other imperfections in labor markets. Hence emphasis on expansionary fiscal-monetary policy entailed de-emphasizing reduction as well as enhancement of legal minimum wages. Given existing constraints on the employment of expansionary demand policies (due principally to balance-of-payments problems and the importance of domestic price stability as an objective in its own right), renewed emphasis on reducing wage rigidities might imply a policy trade-off in the reverse direction.

A policy mix resulting from such a trade-off, involving some combination of greater flexibility in minimum wage-setting and less emphasis on aggregate demand, would probably be less efficient in reducing unemployment than a policy to be guided, in spirit rather than literally, by Jimmy Durante's injunction not to raise the bridges but to lower the river. Assuming the initial response of employment to reductions in relative wages would be similar but of opposite sign to responses observed in studies of the impact of increases in minima, it would probably be possible to lower the river. However, the labor demands involved might well be inelastic, so that adverse secondary offsets would occur even under fiscal-monetary policies of given over-all intensity. In addition, any differentiation of the wage structures along the lines referred to by Hildebrand and Delehanty must be presumed to entail some substitution in favor of younger and against older workers under conditions well short of full employment.

In this connection, it is pertinent to consider two findings reported by Eckstein and Thurow, respectively: that as teenagers' (and other rapidly increasing groups') share of the labor force grew, their share of (1) unemployment and (2) employment also rose. The finding regarding unemployment indicates that the wage structure is slow in responding to such changes in relative supply, and thus confirms the findings of the chapter under discussion. The finding as to the teenagers' share of employment, however, suggests that the pattern of employment responds to changes in he composition of the labor force, without the mediation of legislated changes in the wage structure, under conditions of vigorously expanding aggregate demand.

So far the tax-cut policy has contributed impressively to the increase in aggregate demand and has enjoyed the added advantage of being the most politically acceptable among the economically feasible alternatives. It is not well designed, however, to perform with maximum efficiency the job which Hildebrand and Delehanty have cut out for us. For that purpose it should be supplemented with a policy of public spending in which projects can be tailored to the capabilities of those unemployed. Such a policy has the added advantage of providing the only type of economic environment in which manpower-training policies stand a reasonable chance of success. It has the further advantage of tickling the Galbraithian social welfare function—tickling it pink, some would say, for this policy cannot yet command the Great Consensus presently gathered about the tax cut.

A policy of Structural Spending for the Structurally Unemployed can claim some merit in that it would help to neutralize the public's contribution to the relative decrease in the demand for the less skilled which has resulted from the evolution of the defense sector. While the ratio of nonproduction workers to total employment in manufacturing rose from 16.4 per cent in 1947 to 26 per cent in 1964, in ordnance and accessories it increased from 18.5 per cent to 58.6 per cent. From a tie for ninth place in a ranking of 21 industries (by proportion of nonproduction workers) in 1947, ordnance climbed to first place by 1956.[7]

And finally, while income supplementation schemes divorced from employment are preferrable to those which force up employment costs, the former would be rated as inferior to wage income from socially productive employment—especially under a preference system which has in the past rated social insurance above the dole. Improvement of our system of transfer payments is necessary to afford adequate protection to the disabled poor and their young dependents, but for the able-bodied poor there is no substitute for the opportunity to work.

Thus Professors Hildebrand and Delehanty should be able to enjoy membership in both clubs, the Structuralists and the Demanders—but only if they insist on a somewhat exclusive type of membership in each.

NOTES

1. E. Robert Livernash, "The Internal Wage Structure," in George W. Taylor and Frank C. Pierson, editors, *New Concepts in Wage Determination* (New York: McGraw-Hill, 1957), p. 142.

2. These two conditions imply a supply curve kinked about an intersecting demand curve, with a highly inelastic segment above the point of intersection and a completely elastic segment to the left. This has also been used to describe the supply conditions prevailing in sub-markets for the services of skilled and versatile craftsmen.

3. Martin Segal, "Occupational Wage Differentials in Major Cities During the 1950's," in Mark Perlman, editor, *Human Resources in the Urban Economy* (Washington, D. C.: Resources for the Future, Inc., 1963), pp. 195–207.

4. Lloyd Ulman, "Labor Mobility and the Industrial Wage Structure in the Postwar United States," *Quarterly Journal of Economics,* LXXIX (February 1965), 73–97.

5. Sara Behman, "Labor Mobility, Increasing Labor Demand, and Money Wage-Rate Increases in United States Manufacturing," *Review of Economic Studies,* XXXI (October 1964), 253–266.

6. Cf. L. E. Gallaway, "Labor Mobility, Resource Allocation, and Structural Unemployment," *American Economic Review,* LIII (September 1963), 694–716; also Ulman, *op. cit.*

7. *Manpower Report of the President,* March 1965.

PART **VI**

AN OVERVIEW

CHAPTER **8**

Economic Expansion and Persisting

Unemployment: An Overview

BY ALBERT REES

The conjuncture of sustained economic expansion with persistently high levels of unemployment is an unusual and perplex-
ing one, but as we all know, each cyclical phase has unique
features and the business cycle is not perfectly regular, like a
sine curve. It is more like a path through the hills, moving up
and down across constantly changing terrain. Though we have
never before been where we are now, various aspects of the land-
scape nevertheless recall portions of the path behind and though
with less certainty, suggest what may lie ahead.

The lowest level of unemployment reached during a business
expansion depends not only on the vigor and duration of the
expansion but on the conditions from which it started. As R. A.
Gordon has emphasized, an important aspect of the present
expansion is that it started from three years of high unemployment and slow growth; this helps to explain the disappointing

performance of unemployment during the last four years. But if this period has been disappointing, the present situation is far less so, for we stand again on the threshold of full employment. The seasonally adjusted unemployment rate for May 1965 of 4.6 per cent is only three-tenths of a percentage point above that for 1957, the last year of reasonably full employment. Of this difference, two-tenths of a point is explained by changes in the age-sex composition of the labor force, in that 1964 unemployment rates by age and sex applied to the 1957 labor force composition would produce rates lower by this amount.

Although the employment picture at the moment is brighter than it has been in eight years, we still must ask why it has taken us so long to come this far. The answer may lie in the structure of the demand for labor, in the strength of aggregate demand, in the size and structure of the labor supply, or in some combination of these and still other factors.

The Structure of Demand

The explanation of the high unemployment of the last four years with the largest following among noneconomists focuses on the structure of demand. It holds that new technological forces called "automation" or "cybernation" have eliminated many jobs, especially for the unskilled. From their sunlit mansion high above the Pacific, the learned oracles of Santa Barbara issue grim warnings of technological unemployment that seem to come from some colder, grayer clime. In milder form, the same theories are advanced by a few labor economists, one of whom has written of "the great reduction in the number of simple, repetitive jobs where all you need is your five senses and an untrained mind."[1] Labor-saving innovation has eliminated unskilled jobs in this expansion as in previous ones—that is not in dispute—but the issue is whether technological change in recent years has had employment effects markedly different in size or kind from those of earlier periods.

The view that it has had such effects has been received by most economists with great politeness and greater skepticism. The skepticism seems so well founded that one feels apologetic in raising the issue again; yet a review of recent experience is incomplete without it.

The chapters in this book add support to the finding that there has been no major change in the composition of demand in the last five years beyond the continuation of some old trends. Margaret Gordon points out that the need for agricultural workers has continued to decline and the employment of professional and clerical workers has continued to rise. But the decline in blue-collar employment as a share of the total, which should have been accelerated by automation, has been arrested. Within the blue-collar component there has been a rise in the share of operatives and a fall in the share of laborers, but the latter is a continuation of a long-term trend. The employment of service workers, many of whom are unskilled, has increased as a share of total employment.

The evidence from unemployment statistics is even stronger. Gertrude Bancroft concludes, "Automation and technological change in the past few years have *not* permanently and drastically reduced the number of blue-collar jobs and left stranded . . . increasingly large numbers of American workers without college or high school education" (her emphasis).

Miss Bancroft's case rests first on the occupational composition of the experienced unemployed. The data show a substantial decline in the ratio of the unemployment rate of blue-collar workers to that of all experienced workers from the first quarter of 1957 or 1960 to the first quarter of 1965, and similar declines in the ratios for operatives and nonfarm laborers taken separately. There was a rise over the same period in the relative unemployment rate of service workers. However, this is probably better explained from the supply side than in terms of technological change, which has not been rapid in service occupations. I am aware, of course, of the shortcomings of the system now in use for classifying occupations into major groups; for our purposes it is unfortunate to lump together bootblacks and policemen. However, it would be stretching this point much too far to argue that it invalidates Miss Bancroft's and Mrs. Gordon's findings.

There is some futher support for Miss Bancroft's conclusions in her data on unemployment rates by educational attainment. The preliminary figures for March 1965 show that since March 1957 unemployment rates have actually fallen for men with

fewer than eight years of school completed and for women who
have completed eight years. At the opposite extreme, the unemployment rate of male college graduates has risen much more
rapidly than that of all males. The findings are mixed for inter-
mediate levels of educational attainment; high school graduates
as well as high school dropouts of both sexes have experienced
a rise in relative unemployment. The data do not indicate a falling relative unemployment rate of the most educated. Unlike
some data that have been used to support such a finding, they
are all from one source, and therefore avoid the serious problem
of how best to adjust the 1950 Census data for comparability
with the Current Population Survey.

Let me add evidence of another nature. The National Industrial Conference Board has recently released the first findings
of an exploratory study of job vacancies in the Rochester, New
York, labor market area. This area has had a low unemployment
rate, and a concentration of employment in industries with
highly sophisticated technology, such as photographic equipment, optical goods, and copying equipment. The N.I.C.B.
data were collected from a carefully designed probability sample
of employers. The estimated vacancy rate for February 1965 was
3 per cent of the total of vacancies and employment, and the
estimated number of vacancies was about 8,000. The important
figure for our purposes is that in all occupations combined more
than 36 per cent of the vacancies required fewer than twelve
years of schooling, though most vacancies with low educational
requirements did require previous experience.

The day may still be coming when automated machines
guided by a few highly educated workers will do all the world's
work, and the chief problem of the great mass of people will
be how to use their vast leisure time. Nevertheless, one can say
with confidence that automation and the structure of demand
have not been major forces in the unemployment experience of
the last four years.

Labor Supply

Let us turn now to the structure and size of the labor supply.
When we do so, we find that there *has* been a change in the

structure of unemployment during the present expansion, but it has occurred on the supply side of the market, not the demand side.

One reason for the persistence of high unemployment was the rapid growth of the labor force during the last two years of the expansion. We have had to create 4,925,000 additional jobs between February 1961 and April 1965 in order to reduce unemployment by 1,231,000. Only one-fourth of the increase in employment during this period corresponded to a reduction in unemployment; the other three-fourths took care of labor force growth. This growth, as is well-known, was concentrated among teenagers and women. For adult men, the expansion of employment has resulted in a substantial reduction of unemployment; the May unemployment rate for men 25 and over was 2.8 per cent, below the rate for the first quarter of 1957.

The recent growth in the labor force has had two main sources. The first is demographic: the large number of babies born in 1942 and in the years just after World War II. These cohorts have added substantially to the number of young entrants to the labor force in the last two years; the size of the younger group is, given existing employment practices and wage structures, a major cause of the very high unemployment rate for teenagers. The second source of the growth in the labor force is the economic expansion itself. During the postwar years, labor-force participation rates in every major age-sex category with the possible exception of males aged 25 to 54 responded positively and strongly to changes in economic opportunity. The recent research so ably summarized and evaluated in Jacob Mincer's chapter has substantially changed our thinking about the responsiveness of labor-force participation to cyclical changes in demand—perhaps, he suggests, too substantially. Still, we cannot quarrel with the conclusion that the elasticity of labor supply in response to demand fluctuations is far greater than we suspected a decade ago.

In one sense this responsiveness of labor supply makes it harder to reach full employment because it reduces the share of new jobs going to those unemployed. In another sense, however, it eases the task of aggregative economic policy. It reduces the danger that stimulation of demand when unemployment is slightly above the full employment level will result in over-all labor shortages or substantial wage increases arising from market forces. It does not, of course, reduce the possibility that persistent full employment will bring larger negotiated wage increases in unionized industries insulated from supply pressures.

An additional aspect of teenage unemployment deserves some comment. It has been widely noted that the unemployment rates of high school dropouts are higher than those of high school graduates. The resulting emphasis on reducing the number of dropouts may have given the impression that this number has been increasing. Of course, it has not. The proportion of young people enrolled in school has continued to rise, and paradoxically would have risen faster if we had been less successful in expanding employment. As Mincer's Chart 3 suggests, dropouts (like other sources of labor supply) respond positively to improved employment opportunities.[2]

I would also include largely under the rubric of labor supply the increased supply of nonwhite workers in urban areas. The rise in the ratio of nonwhite to white unemployment rates is not a phenomenon of the last four years. It took place between 1949 and 1955, and since then the ratio has fluctuated without trend. What has not been generally realized is that this rise can be largely explained by the migration of Negroes from the South to the North or West. In a perceptive recent paper, William Bowen has pointed out that the ratio of nonwhite to white unemployment rates in urban places alone actually declined slightly from 1950 to 1960.[3] The rise in the over-all ratio therefore reflects the drastic decline in the proportion of the nonwhite labor force living on farms (from one-sixth to one-fourteenth) and the rise in rural nonwhite unemployment rates. Overt unemployment of nonfarm Negroes has replaced underemployment on farms that is reflected in income statistics but not in the 1950 labor-force statistics. That this exchange nevertheless represents an improvement in well-being is suggested by the large size of net Negro migration from the South between 1950 and 1960.[4] However hard the lot of the Negro arriving in the northern city, that of the Negro in the rural South is harder still. While part of this contrast reflects political and cultural environment, another part reflects the increasing mechanization of Southern agriculture, which would be counted as a shift in demand. From the point of view of labor supply, however, Negroes, like women and teenagers, have been an available source of recruits to non-agricultural employers and have helped to maintain the over-all looseness of many urban labor markets during the expansion.

Wage and Benefit Structures

It is important to consider wage structures and the structure of benefits under income maintenance programs as they bear on unemployment experience. Unfortunately, this is an area where the data are poor and where little research has been done. One obstacle to better research is that data on earnings and employment by detailed occupations within industries are infrequently and irregularly available.

Nevertheless, the chapters by Hildebrand and Delehanty and by Mincer suggest some interesting possible effects of wage structure on employment in the present expansion. Mincer suggests that the dips in the labor-force participation of secondary workers in 1957 and 1962 could have been related to the increases in the minimum wage that took effect March 1, 1956 and September 1, 1961. The reasoning, one may infer, is that the higher minima for low productivity workers induced employers to contract employment or to substitute adult males for secondary workers. This could have led discouraged secondary workers to withdraw from the labor force. Perhaps, therefore, the 1961 increase in the minimum wage contributed to the slow growth of employment relative to Gross National Product during the first two years of the present expansion.

Whatever the merit of this reasoning, the labor-force data are much too gross to afford it substantial support. I have tried to find evidence that would test Mincer's conjecture in the employment data for low-wage industries, and there seems to be some support for his view in both episodes.

The 1956 increase in the minimum wage was large, from 75 cents to $1.00 an hour, and had a visible impact on average hourly earnings in a number of industries. I have constructed two employment series for low-wage industries for this period. The first uses national data on employment by sex for April 1955

AN OVERVIEW

and April 1957 for seven industries whose 1955 average hourly earnings were $1.35 or below; these include wooden containers, cigars, two branches of textiles,[5] and three of apparel.[6] The total employment of this group in April 1955 was 920,000. Average hourly earnings in these industries increased from 11 to 15 cents between 1955 and 1957. Employment dropped 3 per cent in the group as a whole from April 1955 to April 1957 as compared with a rise of 0.7 per cent for all non-durable goods. (Wooden containers, not in nondurable manufacturing, has a very small weight in the series.) However, the precentage of women in total employment in the low-wage industries rose from 70.8 to 71.5 over the period, only slightly less than in all nondurable goods.

The second series uses annual state data on employment and earnings by industry. Since many series are available, this can focus more narrowly on places where the minimum wage has the greatest impact. The series chosen are those for which average hourly earnings were $1.25 or below in 1955.[7] It is possible to find increases in hourly earnings of production workers of twenty cents or more in these industries between 1955 and 1957. For example, in the apparel industry in Mississippi earnings increased from 94 cents to $1.15. The data cover thirty-four series representing fourteen states, with a total 1955 employment of 627,000. Durable goods manufacturing is better represented than in the national data, with several series for lumber and wood products and for furniture and fixtures. Coverage of nondurables is broadened by series for food, agricultural chemicals, and leather goods. Employment in this set of industries and states declined 1.8 per cent from 1955 to 1957 compared with a rise of 1.7 per cent in manufacturing employment nationally and a fall of 0.3 per cent in nondurable manufacturing nationally.

The increase in the minimum wage in the areas covered was much smaller in 1961 than 1956, from $1.00 to $1.15, and not only was it smaller in absolute amount, it was smaller still relative to the wages prevailing before the increase. I have looked at wage and employment series for fifteen national industries for 1960–1962, using a finer industry break than in 1955–1957 because more four-digit employment series were available. The industries included are wooden boxes, poultry dressing and packing, cigars, four branches of textiles,[8] and eight branches of apparel and related products,[9] all of which had 1960 average hourly earnings below $1.55. The total 1960 employment in these industries was 906,000. The impact of the increase in minimum wages on the average earnings series was very slight: only three of the fifteen series increased more than ten cents from 1960 to 1962. It is therefore not too surprising that employment rose more for the low-wage group than for all nondurables, 1.9 compared with 0.5 per cent. There was also a sharper rise in the low-wage group than in all nondurables in the employment of females, 2.5 compared with 1.3 per cent.

The state data on manufacturing employment by industry provide thirty-nine consistent series of employment and earnings in which 1960 average hourly earnings were $1.40 or below. These represent sixteen states and a 1960 employment of 643,000. Again, the impact of the increase in the minimum wage is less than in 1956; in almost half the series, earnings rose by ten cents or less from 1960 to 1962. The rise in employment from 1960 to 1962 is 4.5 per cent, considerably larger than the national rise in manufacturing employment of 0.3 per cent or nondurable goods employment of 0.5 per cent.

I conclude that the 1961 increase in the minimum wage in manufacturing was not large enough to prevent low-wage manufacturing industries from growing more rapidly than manufacturing employment generally. However, this is not the end of the story. The 1961 amendments to the Fair Labor Standards Act extended the coverage of the minimum wage to large establishments in retailing and services and initially set the minimum for newly covered employers at $1.00 an hour. Because of the complexity of the exclusions from coverage, it is not possible to identify earnings and employment series corresponding at all accurately to the area of extended coverage. However, the industry "limited price variety stores" is most likely to be affected, because its wages are low (the 1960 average was $1.09) and because the leading enterprises and many of the individual units are large, qualifying under both the enterprise and establishment provisions of the amendment. The broader industry "general merchandise stores" is a less likely area of impact since it includes department stores whose wages are higher. In the South, however, the amendment may have affected general merchandise stores as a group. The 1960 average hourly earnings of nonsupervisory workers in this industry were $1.08 in North Carolina, the only state for which earnings data are available, and they increased 18 cents from 1960 to 1962. Department stores are often large enough to be covered under the amendments even if they are not parts of chains.

Between 1960 and 1962, employment in limited price variety stores fell from 327,500 to 320,600 or 2.1 per cent nationally, while employment in all retailing rose 1.5 per cent. The drop in employment was sharper for women employees, 3.5 per cent. During the same period, employment of women in all retailing rose 1.8 per cent.

There are eight southern states for which series on employment in general merchandise stores are published. The sum of these series rose from 276,700 in 1960 to 283,400 in 1962, or 2.4 per cent, while the rise for general merchandise stores was 4.1 per cent nationally. During the same period, the rise in all nonagricultural employment in these eight southern states was 4.6 per cent, almost twice the national average.

My tentative conclusion is that the 1961 increase in minimum wages in previously covered areas did not contribute materially to the sluggish rise in employment in the first two years of the expansion. However, the extension of coverage under the 1961 amendments may have contributed to this sluggishness.

Having tarried too long over minimum wages, I now turn to benefit levels under income maintenance programs. These operate from the opposite side of the market. While high minimum wages can restrict the number of workers demanded, high benefits for retirement, unemployment, or relief of general poverty can restrict the number willing to work. Again, to say that a program can have such effects is not the same as saying that it does.

Mincer has noted the sharp drop in the labor-force participation rates of men 65 and over and the smaller drop in participation rates for men 55 to 64. He relates these to improvements in the benefits and coverage under Old Age, Survivors, and Disability Insurance and under private retirement plans, and this certainly seems reasonable. Withdrawals from the labor force may also have contributed to the declining unemployment rates of older men during the present expansion, though the 1964 rates for both groups were still above those for 1957.

There can be little objection to alleviating unemployment by inducing voluntary retirement through adequate pension plans. Those who do uninteresting work are often more than ready to retire by 65, and an affluent society can afford the loss of their output. However, Mincer also reports an increase in the proportion of workers retiring because of compulsory retirement provisions. The forced retirement of people able and anxious to work is not a sound remedy for unemployment. We would like to have enough demand to permit a degree of flexibility in retirement age and to provide some retired workers with less exacting post-retirement jobs.

I find it hard to see the level of unemployment insurance benefits as an important inducement to remain unemployed rather than employed. Average weekly benefits for total unemployment were $35.85 in 1964, 34.7 per cent of average weekly earnings in manufacturing and 51.3 per cent of average weekly earnings in retail trade. Both percentages have fallen slightly since 1960, suggesting that any disincentive effects of unemployment insurance benefits levels have weakened over the period. For secondary workers, the availability of unemployment insurance benefits may lead to reporting periods of voluntary withdrawal from the labor force as unemployment. This is especially so because registration with the Employment Service is an acceptable method of looking for work under the official definition of unemployment and because in the vast majority of cases the Employment Service cannot adequately test availability for work in loose labor markets. The receipt of unemployment insurance benefits by those not actually in the current labor force is encouraged when benefit qualification requirements, stated in fixed dollar amounts, are eroded by rising levels of weekly earnings. Such erosion is prevented by the type of requirements now in force in thirteen states which define eligibility in terms of weeks of covered employment. In short, if unemployment insurance has contributed at all to the persistence of unemployment, it is more likely to have done so through obsolescent qualification requirements than through over-generous benefit levels.

Public assistance seems even less likely to be a barrier to accepting employment. The average monthly payment per recipient under aid to families with dependent children was $33.34 in January 1965, and the average under general assistance was $28.77. To receive these small amounts, families had to tolerate supervision by case workers. We should no doubt be doing more than we are to rehabilitate employable relief recipients, though much progress has been made in recent years, but the basic problem is one of developing adequate techniques for working with the poor, not one of excessive largesse.

A final factor that may be related to the structure of wages and labor costs is the behavior of overtime hours. Average weekly overtime hours of factory production workers reached unusually high levels in late 1964 and early 1965; the average for the first quarter of 1965 was 3.4 overtime hours per week.[10] For 1964 as a whole, the average was 3.1 hours, compared with 2.8 hours in the high employment year 1956. Average weekly overtime was above the 1956 level in fifteen of twenty-one two-digit manufacturing industries, including all but one in nondurable goods. This, of course, raises the question whether employment would not have been higher if less overtime had been worked.

One possible explanation of the high level of overtime hours is that the expansion of demand in 1964 found manufacturers with inadequate capacity in particular products and lines, even though capacity appeared to exceed output on an over-all basis. Manufacturers were unable to meet added demand by hiring new workers because they had not had time to create work stations for them to man.

A second explanation, which could provide at least part of the answer, is that overtime premiums may have fallen relative to hiring costs, making overtime relatively cheaper in 1964 than in 1956. I use the term "hiring costs" as a kind of shorthand for the fixed costs of employment; these costs are not the same as fringe benefits, nor can fringe benefits be used as a proxy for them, a confusion that has seriously weakened some recent analyses of this problem. Some hiring costs, including the costs of recruitment, induction, and training, do not appear in production-worker compensation as wages or as fringes. Some fringe benefits, such as pensions not fully vested from the date of hire or extra vacations for long-service employees, have precisely the opposite effect of hiring costs. By helping to reduce turnover, they permit hiring costs to be amortized over a longer period and thus reduce the barrier to hiring new employees.

The kind of fringe benefit that *is* a hiring cost is best represented by unemployment insurance. In part this is so because hiring new workers and later laying them off increases the employer's tax rate under experience rating plans. In part this is so with respect to both unemployment insurance and OASDI because of the fixed annual dollar amount of the tax base. Overtime hours worked by employees who will in any case earn more than the base amount do not increase the employer's contribution to social insurance; hiring new employees does. At the 1956 level of average straight-time hourly earnings in manufacturing, all unemployment insurance taxes in most states were paid on the first 1587 straight-time hours of annual employment; at 1964 levels of earnings, all such taxes in most states were paid on the first 1230 straight-time hours of annual employment. It is in this sense that overtime costs have been falling relative to hiring costs.

The most common proposal for reducing overtime hours is to raise overtime premium rates. Limited legislative recommendations of this kind are being advanced by the Administration. There are dangers, however, in moving too far toward an alternation of increased hiring costs and offsetting increases in overtime premiums. Each swing of this pendulum raises the cost of labor relative to the cost of capital, and therefore may induce further investment in labor-saving technology. Spreading social insurance contributions over a larger tax base would help to reduce hiring costs without raising the cost of labor in general.

Aggregate Demand

In 1962 and 1963 most economists blamed the disappointing performance of employment and unemployment on the lack of sufficient aggregate demand. They reached this conclusion by a process of elimination; on careful examination none of the other possible causes of high unemployment seemed powerful enough to account for anything like the level of unemployment

actually experienced. The case for the tax reduction of 1964 rested on this reasoning.

Now, sixteen months after the enactment of the tax cut, the case for the primary role of inadequate demand in causing persistent unemployment is much more direct. The tax cut together with the associated monetary expansion has worked as its advocates hoped it would, and its full effects are not necessarily all felt yet. If the primary problem had been the structure of demand, the tax cut would not have led to a substantial reduction in unemployment but would have produced a much more pronounced rise in prices instead, as its opponents feared. There was, of course, no acceleration of the rise in consumer prices during the year following the tax cut, and signs of pressure on prices are only now appearing. In the range of unemployment from 5.5 to 4.5 per cent, the costs of reducing unemployment in terms of the rate of price increase are apparently negligible, at least in the short run.

Some critics of the tax cut, who believe that our problem is primarily the structure of demand, have argued that the tax cut has not succeeded because the unemployment rate is not yet down to 4 per cent. I can recall no one rash enough to promise that it would be. The *Economic Report of the President* for January 1964 predicted an unemployment rate of 5 per cent by the end of 1964, and this is exactly what was achieved. It remarked further that the attainment of the 4 per cent rate lay beyond 1964.[11] A year later the *Economic Report* promised only some further reduction in 1965 of the 5.2 per cent rate that was the average for 1964. That modest promise seems certain to be fulfilled.

In retrospect, it is clear that if the amount of the tax reduction was not correct, it erred on the side of being too small rather than too large—but prudence required that the error be in this direction. Since no one could predict the exact consequences of the reduction, the possibility of too much stimulation and resulting inflation could not be ignored; overstimulation would have been difficult to reverse. On the other hand, substantial if incomplete success could and will be supplemented by additional measures to expand demand.

The substantial success of the tax cut has led R. A. Gordon

to comment that the reduction eventually made in 1964 should have been made in 1958. From a strictly economic point of view, he is undoubtedly right, but the remark does not reckon with the spirit of the times. A glance back at the *Economic Report* for January 1958 reveals, in the midst of a clearly recognized recession, continued concern about the danger of inflation and the need for a balanced budget. The tax reduction was daring even in 1964 and even for a Democratic administration. To win acceptance of a massive tax reduction when the budget was already heavily in deficit and employment and output were rising required a major educational effort in the public, the business community, and the Congress. That this effort succeeded is to the everlasting credit of Walter Heller and his associates.

The success of the tax reduction is also responsible for the present strong support for the reduction of excise taxes in the Administration and even more enthusiastically in the Congress.[12] There has been some grumbling from the left that excise tax reductions are not the most effective possible method of increasing demand. Perhaps not, but they have important collateral benefits. Selective excise taxes distort the structure of resource allocation and are probably regressive even when called luxury taxes. Moreover, reductions in excise taxes have the peculiarly happy property of increasing demand and at the same time reducing the measured price level. In terms of Kalachek's diagram, they move us due southwest toward the bliss point. I recognize, of course, that this involves something of an illusion; the inclusion of indirect but not direct taxes in the price indexes is more a matter of convenience than of principle. But we have suffered too long from the opposite illusion that price level rises when the government raises gasoline taxes to build more free roads. Finally, the economist's desire to maintain aggregate demand sometimes makes it necessary for him to find political allies. It is not immoral to side on occasion with the manufacturers of perfumes, playing cards, or saxophones when their understandable search for tax relief happens also to be in the general interest.

While the political left is concerned that the enthusiasm for tax reduction has led to the neglect of expenditure programs, and speaks of "reactionary Keynesianism," the political right is concerned that this same enthusiasm has led to the abandonment of the balanced budget principle. Perhaps it has, and perhaps it should. When in the thirties and forties we moved away from the idea of an annually balanced federal budget, we moved first toward the notion of a budget balanced over the cycle; surpluses in good years would offset deficits in bad years. It has not worked out that way, but this is not necessarily bad. The case for a budget deficit when unemployment is high is a clear one, and so is the case for a budget surplus in an inflation, but if we reach the fortunate combination of full employment and reasonably stable prices, perhaps the budget should be neutral. This is equivalent to saying that reducing the size of the interest-bearing debt is not in itself an objective of budgetary policy. Much of the concern over debt reduction is misplaced, in view of the steady fall of the federal debt in the postwar period relative to Gross National Product, federal revenues, and private debt. However, if debt reduction is desired it can easily be achieved without budget surpluses. We can substitute noninterest-bearing for interest-bearing debt as part of the necessary process of expanding the money supply to keep pace with the growth of output.

Manpower Policy

Let me turn next to the role of manpower policy during the present expansion. A great deal has been happening in this field, and no brief summary can do it justice. It is not unfair to say that only in the last four years have we had anything that could be called a national manpower policy in peacetime.

Perhaps the most important part of this policy has been the retraining programs conducted under the Area Redevelopment Act and the Manpower Defense and Training Act. It is very difficult to make an estimate of the number of people who have found employment because of these programs. The Secretary of Labor has reported that as of the end of 1964 more than 90,000 people had completed training courses under MDTA and about 73 per cent of them were subsequently employed.[13] This implies that about 63,000 MDTA "graduates" found jobs. An additional 39,000 workers had been enrolled in ARA programs through December 1964, and more than three-fourths of those who completed training found jobs.[14] If we assume the same completion rate as the two-year average for MDTA (73 per cent) and ignore those still in training, this suggests that somewhat more than 21,000 ARA "graduates" found jobs. The true contribution of the programs to employment is obscured by the fact that some trainees find work unrelated to their training, or would have found work in any case, while some dropouts leave to take jobs related to training in progress.

Even if we knew the importance of these factors we could measure only the gross contribution of the training programs to employment, not the net contribution. Some trainees who get jobs because of their training take the place of others without training who would have gotten these jobs, and who now remain among the unemployed. In view of these factors, it seems generous to conclude that MDTA and ARA training programs reduced unemployment by 84,000 to the end of 1964. The modesty of this contribution relative to the contribution of aggregate demand can be appreciated by noting that on more than one occasion in the past year seasonally adjusted unemployment has declined by 200,000 in a single month.

Are we to conclude from this that training programs are not worthwhile? Not at all; training programs may be a fine investment yielding a high rate of return. Should we conclude that the scale of training programs has been too modest? I doubt that this follows. The real limitations on the growth of training programs have been the institutions, the attitudes, the personnel, and the knowledge needed to carry them out. We have made tremendous advances in all these fields in a brief period. Had we attempted to move much faster, there would have been many more mistakes, far more waste, and perhaps a much less general acceptance of federal retraining programs than there is now.

A major accomplishment of the manpower program has been not its contribution to employment in the present expansion but the establishment of machinery that will be valuable over the long run. This role is not so much the elimination of unemployment as the reduction in the severity of potential manpower bottlenecks and local shortages that could accompany the approach to full employment.

Three special accomplishments of manpower policy deserve separate mention. The first is the long overdue reshaping of federal aid to vocational education in 1963, which will permit the correction of grossly exaggerated emphasis on agriculture and home economics and the development of curricula more closely related to employment opportunities. A second is the inclusion of literacy training in the MDTA programs. It seems only sensible to expect that an illiterate adult is more likely to learn to read and write when the learning is directly related to a reasonable vocational goal and if he can be provided with readers that are not about Jane's and Dick's day on the farm with Grandma.

The final accomplishment is the recent expansion of on-the-job training programs within MDTA. Such programs are more likely than institutional training programs to result in the quick placement of successful trainees, and they do not require the purchase of expensive capital equipment to be used only a fraction of the time. Federal aid to on-the-job training is especially useful to small employers who lack the resources to organize training programs of their own. Until recently, such employers have been discouraged from participation by the amount of paperwork involved, but this obstacle is being overcome through the use of intermediary contractors. An example is the contract between the federal government and the Chrysler Corporation for on-the-job training for automobile mechanics in independent Chrysler dealerships.

I do not mean to leave the impression that everything done in the name of manpower policy or the relief of poverty deserves our applause. The major blunder to date seems to me to be the Appalachia program, in which the overwhelming bulk of expenditure is for highways. Some of the ablest and most experienced leaders in the Appalachian community feel that heavier expenditure on education would have done far more to rebuild the economic base of the area. Under the shiny new packaging it seems possible to discern the familiar form of the old pork barrel. However, if the roads do not do all that is promised in luring tourists and industry into the hills, perhaps they will help speed the Appalachian migrant on his way to Cincinnati, Cleveland, or Detroit. The very least that can be hoped is that this program will not be used as a model for other regions whose economic development is lagging.

Probably the most important manpower policy of all is one whose effect on employment lies entirely in the future: the recently enacted federal aid to elementary and secondary education in low-income areas. Perhaps by special efforts to improve the quality of education in urban and rural slums, and by special programs to remedy deficiencies in the home training of children whose parents are uneducated, we can reduce the numbers who leave school without real command of such essential skills as reading, writing, and arithmetic. In this way we can equip tomorrow's teenagers for a society in which these skills are increasingly required of everyone.

Policy for the Future

The organizers of this program have invited me to discuss the policy implications of recent experience, and I have already taken advantage of this privilege at several points. Such views must fall under the heading that one of my favorite newspaper columnists calls "purely personal prejudices," and I need hardly add that anyone is free to disagree with them. To introduce some order into what might otherwise be a miscellaneous collection of wishes, I shall try to stay as closely as possible to policies that will help the growth of employment keep pace with the growth of the potential labor force in the years ahead.

In expenditure policy I have stressed the importance of better education for poor children. Let me add that in my opinion improving the educational system should come *before* any further increases in the age of compulsory school attendance. It is appealing to think we can simultaneously improve the lives of teenagers and reduce unemployment by requiring everyone who does not graduate from high school to stay in school until age eighteen, but we run the risk of turning our high schools into penal institutions. The problems can be brought home by reading *Up the Down Staircase*[15] and recalling that it depicts an average high school in a big city system, not one of the special problem schools. The dropout who leaves school at sixteen may be smart enough to realize that he hasn't been learning anything, even if his teachers are reluctant to admit it. When we can honestly say that we have a good program to offer him, perhaps we will be justified in forcing him to take it, but not until then.

There is no lack of candidates for other federal expenditure programs, from providing pure water to disposing of junk cars, and some of these may be preferable to further tax reductions. The one that seems most directly related to the growth of employment is the improvement of metropolitan mass transportation. Much of the growth of employment has been in the new, light industry of the suburbs and in services for rapidly growing suburban populations. Much of the unused and underused labor supply is in the slums in the heart of the central cities, among people who don't have automobiles. Better and faster public transportation would make employment accessible to many more in this group.

In tax policy, I would give high priority to avoiding increases in the already high levels of payroll taxation on the first $3,000 or first $5,000 of annual earnings. At a minimum, we should raise the tax base for unemployment insurance to the same level as that for OASDI, and hopefully we should raise them both further. We should also give serious consideration to financing more of our income maintenance programs from general tax revenues. If, as may be objected, these measures increase the redistributive effects of social insurance, we can raise the benefit levels for those with higher earnings.

In wage and hour policy, it is worth pointing out that reduction of working time through longer vacations and more holidays does more to expand the demand for goods and services than a shortening of the scheduled hours in each work week. I also agree with the suggestion of Hildebrand and Delehanty that we reconsider the idea of a multiple federal minimum wage. It will not be long before political pressures for an increase in the minimum wage become irresistable again. I suggest that when that time comes we exempt all persons under twenty from the new rates, leaving the minimum applicable to them at the level set by present law. The argument for a higher minimum wage is that $1.25 an hour does not enable a full-time worker to support a family. It makes no sense to apply this argument to a teenager who is living with his parents and usually receives valuable training and experience if he can find an employer who thinks he is worth hiring.

All such specific policy suggestions, however, are secondary to the general policy of maintaining adequate demand. We suffered far too heavily from 1958 through 1963 from unwillingness to act vigorously to expand employment and from excessive concern with creeping inflation and the balance-of-payments. We have learned in the past year that expanding employment need not make these other problems worse, and if in the months ahead the cost of full employment should be some price increases that will not yield to admonition from the White House, I hope this will not be taken as a signal to slam on the monetary and fiscal brakes. Perhaps businessmen and bankers as well as labor leaders and professors have learned that it is not unsound economics to keep 96 per cent of the labor force productively employed.

NOTES

1. Charles C. Killingsworth, testimony before the Subcommittee on Employment and Manpower, Committee on Labor and Public Welfare, U. S. Senate (September 20, 1963).

2. See also Beverly Duncan, "Dropouts and the Unemployed," *Journal of Political Economy*, LXXIII (April 1965), 121–134.

3. Presented at a conference on unemployment Princeton University, May 13, 1965.

4. The estimated migration of Negroes from the South from 1950 to 1960 was 1,200,000. About one-third of this movement took place between 1955 and 1960. See *Historical Statistics of the United States: Continuation to 1962*, p. 10, and the 1960 Census of Population, *Detailed Characteristics*, Table 164.

5. Knitting and yarn and thread. All national data are from BLS Bulletin 1312-2.

6. Men's and boys' furnishings, women's and children's undergarments, and girls' and children's outerwear.

7. All state data are from BLS Bulletin 1370-1.

8. Full-fashioned hosiery, seamless hosiery, knit underwear, and yarn and thread.

9. Men's and boys' shirts, men's and boys' separate trousers, work clothing, women's blouses, women's and misses' outerwear n.e.c., women's and children's underwear, girls' and children's outerwear, and housefurnishings.

10. See *Monthly Report on the Labor Force*, April 1965.

11. An appendix to the 1964 *Economic Report* reproduces the testimony of Walter Heller before the Senate Subcommittee on Employment and Manpower, October 28, 1963. This testimony contains references to the 4 per cent rate that I do not regard as inconsistent with the statements I have made in the text, including: "the road to 4 per cent unemploy-

ment is clearly open to demand-powered measures" and "Had this increase been effective during the past 6 years, it would have . . . allowed our unemployment rate to average 4 per cent." (The reference is to the increase in private expenditures induced by a tax cut of 11.1 billion.) Neither statement argues that a two-stage tax cut would reduce unemployment to 4 per cent within eighteen months of the effective date of the first stage, and six months of the effective date of the second.

12. This reduction was enacted shortly after this paper was given.

13. *Manpower Research and Training,* a Report submitted to the Congress March 31, 1965, p. 4 and pp. 37–40.

14. *Manpower Report of the President,* March, 1965, p. 134.

15. Bel Kaufman, *Up the Down Staircase* (Englewood Cliffs, N. J.: Prentice-Hall, 1964).

Index

Ackley, Gardner, 45n.
Added worker hypothesis, *see* Labor force participation
Aggregate demand, composition of, 19–20, 25–38
  demand deficiency hypothesis, 4, 6, 9, 11, 67, 236, 246, 252–254, 319–322, 340–342, 349
  employment elasticity of, 141–176, 180–183, 194, 224
  industrial composition of, 151–154, 158–159
  relation to wages, 266–267
Agricultural employment, 5, 147–148, 249, 251–252, 270
Altman, Stuart, 76, 107, 108n., 111n., 112n.
Area Development Act, 171, 342–343
Automation, 4, 46n., 191–192, 235–243, 249, 328–329

Backman, Jules, 63n.
Balance-of-payments, 11, 24, 40–41, 68

Bancroft, Gertrude, 3, 4, 5, 146, 191–226, 255n., 329–330
Behman, Sara, 318, 323n.
Bell, Philip W., 297n.
Blackmore, Donald J., 300n.
Blue-collar workers, *see* Employment, by occupation
Bowen, William, 7, 78–81, 85–89, 108, 109n. 121n., 332
Business cycles, 50–51, 180, 327–328
  level of Gross National Product in, 2, 15–22, 29
  level of unemployment in, 19–21, 195–203
  postwar, 15–47, 57–63, 138–176
  see also Consumer expenditures, Fiscal policy, Government expenditures, Investment, Monetary policy

Cain, Glen G., 78–79, 95, 107, 108n., 109n., 111n.
Clague, Ewan, 175n.
Consumer expenditure, 47n., 149, 157
  disposable income and, 29–33

Consumer expenditure, forecasts of, 37–38
savings rate and, 33–38
Cooper, Sophia, 84–89, 108, 110n., 134n., 175n.
Council of Economic Advisers, 1, 22–23, 33–34, 41–42, 54, 248

David, Martin, 243n.
Defense expenditures, 9, 29, 149–151, 174
Delehanty, George E., 8, 138, 265–301, 333, 346
Demsetz, Harold, 297n.
Dernburg, Thomas, 81–84, 85–89, 108, 109n., 112n., 133n., 134n.
Discouraged worker hypothesis, see Labor force participation
Disguised unemployment, 7, 100–105, 118–120, 125, 126, 192
Douty, H. M., 8, 302–307
Duncan, Beverly, 112n., 347n.

Easterlin, Richard A., 7, 126–134
Eckstein, Otto, 3, 5, 48–56, 176n., 251–252, 321
Economic Opportunity Act, 171
Economic Report of the President, 18, 23, 41–42, 45n., 46n., 47n., 259n., 340–341
Education as investment, 270–271
effect on supply of unskilled labor, 310–311
effect on unemployment, 204–206
expenditure on, 9, 10, 296, 344–345
job training and, 10, 171–173, 182–183, 252, 319, 342–344
see also Employment, by educational attainment, Manpower program
Employment, 52–53, 59–60, 137–188
by educational attainment, 215–217, 226n., 249–251, 329–330
by industry, 172–173, 175n., 182, 186, 198–199, 208, 213–214, 260–261

Employment, by occupation, 168–171, 173, 182, 186–187, 210–213, 225n., 329
elasticity with respect to Gross National Product of, 141–176, 174n., 177–179, 180–183, 184–188
forecasts of, 186
goals, see Full employment, definitions of
of nonproduction workers, 167
of part-time workers, 193, 221–223, 226n.
service, 206–207
see also Unemployment
European experience, 56

Fabricant, Solomon, 5, 9, 177–179
Finegan, T. A., 7, 78–81, 85–89, 108, 109n., 113–121, 121n.
Fiscal policy, 31–33, 64–69
income maintenance and, 9, 296, 336–339
job creation and, 9, 182–183, 253–254
recommended, 173–174, 187, 322, 346–347
theory of, 237–243, 245n.
see also Government expenditures, Taxes
Folk, Hugh, 243n.
Franke, Walter, 103–105, 112n., 174n.
Fuchs, Victor R., 175–176n.
Full employment, definitions of, 1, 10–11, 12, 174–175, 187, 248
possibilities of achieving, 3, 24–25, 41–42, 60, 224, 252–254, 328, 340–341, 347–348n.

Gainsbrugh, Martin R., 3, 57–63
Gallaway, L. E., 297n., 323n.
Goldstein, Harold, 5, 10, 180–183
Gordon, Margaret S., 3, 4, 5, 9, 137–176, 302, 306n., 329

Gordon, R. A., 3, 12n., 15–47, 139, 173, 176n., 220–222, 226n., 298n., 327–328, 341–342
Government expenditures, balanced budget, 64–66, 341–342
  effect on employment of, 9, 60–61, 181
  level of, 19–21, 28–33, 149, 157
  see also Defense expenditures, Fiscal policy, Taxes
Greenberg, Leon, 175n.
Gross National Product, forecasts of, 41–42
  growth needed to maintain full employment, 2, 23–24, 42, 49
  potential, see Productivity
  see also Business cycles
Guideposts, wage-price, 41

Hansen, W. Lee, 75–76, 107, 121n.
Heller, Walter, 22, 109n., 248, 341, 347–348n.
Hickman, B. G., 45n., 46n.
Hildebrand, George H., 8, 138, 265–301, 333, 346
Holt, Charles, 243n.
Hours, of work, 156, 338–339, 346

Inflation, 11, 61, 62–63, 68, 137–138, 237–243, 244n., 245n., 320, 332, 340, 347; see also Prices, Wages
Inventories, 39, 149
Investment, 19–21, 25–28, 41, 42–44, 45n., 46n., 61, 64, 149, 157, 165, 173

Johnston, Denis F., 84–89, 108, 110n., 134n., 175n.

Kalachek, Edward D., 4, 6, 227–245, 341
Katz, Arnold, 99
Kaufman, Bel, 348n.
Killingsworth, Charles C., 4, 6, 9, 246–255, 347n.
Korean War, 24, 92, 145
Kuh, Edwin, 164, 175n., 188n.

Labor, organization of market, 207–208
  substitution among skill levels, 268–269, 298n.
Labor demand, as cause of structural unemployment, 4–5, 328–330
  composition of, 147
  for teenagers, 257
  industrial composition of, 161–167
Labor-force participation, 73–112, 113–121, 122–125, 331, 336–337
  by age-sex, 84–88, 95–100, 109n.
  by color-sex, 95–100, 111n.
  by educational attainment, 250–251, 254–255n., 261–262
  cyclical sensitivity of, 6–7, 81–83, 85, 91, 92–100, 110n., 113–115, 121n., 126–134
  effect on measurement of unemployment, 106–107
  historical, 127–131
  in depressed areas, 80, 111–112
  of part-time workers, 124
  of primary workers, 99–100, 106–107, 112n., 192
  seasonal, 73–74, 79, 109n.
  see also Disguised unemployment, Secondary workers
Labor supply, 49–50, 52–53, 146, 194–195, 199–200
  as cause of structural unemployment, 5, 7, 208–209, 224, 256, 321, 330–333
  contribution of population growth to, 128–133, 331
  forecasts of, 132–133
  of skilled, 315
  of unskilled, 269–270, 306, 307n., 315–316
  wage elasticity of, 101–102, 111n.
  see also Labor force participation
Lebergott, Stanley, 5, 184–188
Lewis, H. Gregg, 309–310, 313n.
Lipsey, Richard, 245n.
Livernash, E. Robert, 315–316, 322n.

Long, Clarence, 74, 107, 110–111n., 278–279, 297n., 305, 307n.

Macdonald, Robert M., 279–280, 297n., 299n.
Manpower Development and Training Act, 171, 342–344
Manpower program, 10, 342–345
Manpower Report of the President, 23, 45n., 103, 109n., 110n., 112n., 175n., 323n.
Marital status, effect on unemployment, 202–203
Martin, William, 47n.
Migration, effect on labor force participation, 79–81, 85, 115–117
rural-urban, 5
Miller, H. P., 313n.
Mincer, Jacob, 5, 6–7, 73–112, 133n., 148, 174n., 178, 331–332, 333, 336–337
Minimum wages, effect on labor force participation and employment, 7, 95, 99, 111n., 148, 207, 273, 275, 287, 289, 298n., 304–305, 308, 333–336
multiple, 8–9, 296, 319–320, 346
Minsky, Hyman, 320
Mitchell, W. C., 47n.
Monetary policy, 39–40, 47n., 65
theory of, 237–243, 245n.

National Bureau for Economic Research, 45n.
Newman, Dorothy, K., 225n.
Nonwhites, 95–96, 100, 193, 195–196, 204, 207–208, 332–333, 347n.

Ober, Harry, 297n.
Okun, Arthur, M., 174n.
Older workers, 95–98, 111n., 118, 200, 262, 336–337; see also Secondary workers, Social security

Pearl, Robert B., 108n.
Pechman, Joseph A., 3, 64–69

Perlman, R., 313n.
Pierson, Frank C., 7, 122–125
Prices, 15, 24, 38–39; see also Guideposts, Inflation
Productivity, 22–23, 39, 45n., 48, 148, 154, 156, 158–160, 161–165, 172, 175n., 177, 180–181, 185–186, 191–192
Profits, 31, 39
Public Works and Economic Development Act, 171

Reder, Melvin W., 8, 276, 297n., 300n., 303, 306n., 308–313, 316
Rees, Albert, 4, 5, 9, 10, 111n., 148, 327–348
Reynolds, Lloyd G., 297n.

Schultze, Charles, 188n.
Secondary workers, 48, 85–88, 92, 95–100, 102–104, 107, 109n., 112n., 119–120, 123–125, 192–193, 333
Segal, Martin, 285, 297n., 313n., 317, 323n.
Social security, effect on employment and labor force participation, 7, 31, 97–98, 336–337; see also Taxes
Strand, Kenneth, 81–84, 85–89, 108, 109n., 112n., 133n., 134n.
Structural unemployment, 3–4, 6, 10, 11, 49, 60, 61–62, 170–171, 173–174, 178, 191–192, 193, 217–224, 227–245, 246–255, 298, 314–322, 331
Subcommittee on Employment and Manpower, 45n.

Taft, Cynthia, 297n.
Taxes, effects on savings and consumption, 29–33
excise, 341–342
recommended policies, 346
tax cut, 9, 10, 21–22, 68, 246, 248, 251–254, 321–322, 340–341
see also Fiscal policy

Tella, Alfred, 84–89, 108, 110n., 121n., 134n.
Thurow, Lester, 5, 245n., 254–255n., 256–262, 321

Ulman, Lloyd, 8, 9, 314–323
Unemployment, by occupation, 315, 329
  causes of, 208–209
  composition of, 5–6, 50–54
  duration of, 193–194, 223–224
  elasticity with respect to Gross National Product, 49, 227–235
  insurance, 81–83, 106, 337, 339, 346
  level of, 2–3, 10, 15, 19–21, 42, 45, 50, 53, 59–60, 145–146, 195–203
  of experienced workers, 233
  of primary workers, 198, 233–234, 243n.
  see also Business cycles, Employment, Structural unemployment
Unions, effect on wages and employment of, 8, 271, 276–277, 298–299n., 303, 308–310, 318, 332

Vacancies, job, 51–56, 61, 182–183, 330

Wages, effect on labor-force participation and employment, 8, 76–77, 101–102, 111n., 113–114, 181, 265–324, 333–339
  entry rates, 272, 274, 296, 299n., 303–304, 308–309
  fringe benefits, 279–280, 299n.
  geographical differentials in, 272–273
  internal firm spreads, 278–283, 310–311
  skill differentials in, 8, 265–324 passim
  structure within SMSA, 283–289
  trade-off with quality, 311–313
  see also Guideposts, Inflation, Minimum wages, Unions
Wilcock, Richard, 103–105, 112n., 174n.
Women, 76, 95–96, 110–111n., 112n., 146, 195, 200–201, 225n., 262; see also Secondary workers
Woytinsky, W. S., 297n.

Youth, 5, 98–99, 110–111n., 111–112n., 117–118, 121n., 194, 195–196, 200, 201, 203–208, 256–261, 262n., 331–332; see also Labor-force participation, Minimum wages, Secondary workers